# Specialized classroom management

# Other materials from Boys Town

## Books

The Well-Managed Classroom
Teaching Social Skills to Youth
Basic Social Skills For Youth: A Handbook from Boys Town
Working with Aggressive Youth
Unmasking Sexual Con Games: Helping Teens Identify Good and Bad Relationships
Getting Along With Others
Finding Happiness in Faith, Family & Work: Words of Practical Wisdom from Father Flanagan
Boys Town Prayer Book: Prayers by and for the Boys & Girls of Boys Town
Pathways: Fostering Spiritual Growth Among At-Risk Youth
Effective Skills for Child-Care Workers
Common Sense Parenting®, 2nd Edition
Common Sense Tips on Parenting

## Audio

One to One: Personal Counseling Tapes for Teens
Common Sense Parenting® Audiotapes

## Other

Elementary/Special Ed. Classroom Social Skills Poster Set
Middle/High School Classroom Social Skills Poster Set
Interpersonal Social Skills Poster Set

"When You Help a Child Today, You Write the History of Tomorrow" button, magnet, poster, mug, T-shirt and sweatshirt

For a free Boys Town Press catalog, call **1-800-BT BOOKS.**

# Specialized classroom management

## A Boys Town approach

▶ by Tom Dowd, M.A.,
Lisa Tobias, M.S.,
Theresa Connolly, M.A.,
Andrea Criste, M.Ed.,
Cathy Nelson, M.S.

BOYS TOWN PRESS

BOYS TOWN, NEBRASKA

# Specialized classroom management

Published by The Boys Town Press
Father Flanagan's Boys' Home
Boys Town, Nebraska 68010

ISBN 0-938510-42-8

10  9  8  7  6  5

# Table of contents

# CHAPTER ONE

# Introduction to the Boys Town education model

**T**he concept of classroom management is broader than the notion of student discipline. It includes all the things teachers must do to foster student involvement and cooperation in classroom activities and to establish a productive work environment.

Sanford, Emmer, and Clements, "Improving Classroom Management," **Educational Leadership**, April 1983.

Discussions about classroom management have until very recently placed too much emphasis on controlling unproductive student behavior and not enough on creating a learning environment that encourages productive student behavior.

Thorough reviews of classroom management done by some of the most prominent researchers in the field (Brophy, 1983; Doyle, 1986; Charles, 1989; Duke & Meckel, 1984; Wolfgang & Glickman, 1986; and Jones & Jones, 1990) suggest that five major factors can be correlated with effective classroom management:

1. A sound theoretical foundation and understanding of classroom management and the needs of students.

2. Strong positive teacher-student and peer relationships.

3. Instructional methods that motivate students.

4. Organizational and group management techniques that maximize students "on-task" behavior.

5. Problem-solving and behavior management techniques that empower students to assume responsibility for managing their own behavior.

Effective classroom managers create classroom environments that are positive, supportive, and at the same time, well-structured. Effective classroom managers maintain structure in their classrooms through the effective use of management practices that help students acquire the necessary skills to think and problem-solve, accept responsibility with regard to rules, limits, and the needs of others, and develop a positive self-image.

For more than 75 years, Boys Town's mission has been to improve the way children are treated, regardless of their race, creed, or handicapping conditions. We are proud to expand this mission to include the goal of making the nation's schools a better place for all students.

*There are no bad boys. There are only bad environments, bad examples, bad thinking.*

Father Edward J. Flanagan,
Founder of Boys Town, 1917

When Father Flanagan said these words, love, compassion , and a place a child could call home were sometimes all it took to help a homeless or wayward youth . But as youth problems became more difficult and more complex, Boys Town realized the need to combine compassion with the competence that comes from dedicated professionals working in a healthy learning environment.

Boys Town's programs, as they are known today, have their origins in the efforts of those professionals who designed, developed, and implemented the Teaching-Family Model (Phillips, 1968; Phillips, Phillips,

Fixsen, & Wolf, 1974). From those origins, Boys Town has spent more than 15 years developing its own Boys Town Family Home Program (Coughlin, Maloney, Baron, Dahir, Daly, Daly, Fixsen, Phillips, & Thomas, 1983; Baron, Cunningham, Palma, & Phillips, 1984; Peter, 1986). During those years, Boys Town has devoted time, energy, resources, and personnel to disseminating its technology to programs serving troubled children and youth nationwide.

The Boys Town Education Model is a good example of this technology transfer — taking the basic techniques of its family-based Model and transferring them to a school setting as a powerful and innovative approach to positive and effective interventions for troubled students. A success-oriented program of personalized social skills instruction is the hallmark of the Boys Town Education Model. Initiated in 1977 at a residential school in Montana, the key concepts were brought to Boys Town in 1979 and further developed.

By implementing the Education Model in its classrooms, Boys Town has demonstrated that schools can significantly reduce discipline problems while directly and humanely teaching vital life skills in a positive school climate. Work by professionals at Boys Town and elsewhere (Larson, 1989; Czerwionka, 1987) has shown that difficult-to-teach, behaviorally disordered adolescents can be effectively taught a variety of social skills. Two years after initiating its campus school program, Boys Town became actively involved in the nationwide dissemination of the Model. Today, public and private schools across the country implement the Boys Town Education Model with great success.

Part of the appeal of the Boys Town Education Model is that it is one of the few programs that can be integrated into the entire school day and across the curriculum. This helps to overcome some of the generalization problems associated with programs that occur only in one classroom or outside the school. Research evidence suggests that nonschool programs have little effect on school behavior (Jones & Offord, 1989).

Schools were made for children and learning. This simple premise underlies what we believe should be true about any good school program. It is our contention, therefore, that all students must experience success in school, be it academic, vocational, athletic, or artistic success. Whether the individual becomes a good math student or a poor math student, a good athlete or a poor athlete, is, in all probability, less dependent upon the student's academic and physical characteristics than upon the student's social/emotional skills (Cartledge & Milburn, 1978; Stephens, 1978; Hope & Cobb, 1973; Borich, 1971).

Unfortunately, many youth have not acquired the social behaviors necessary to effectively and appropriately interact with peers and adults in school settings. As a result, they do not achieve academic success. These students are the same youth who have lacked other success experiences as well and have been identified by school personnel as discipline problems, being at risk, behaviorally impaired, or emotionally disturbed. Their problems are compounded by the fact that the very social behaviors they lack are the same ones employers have identified as vital to success in the world of work (Gresham,

1981). There is hope. Researchers have found social skills training to be effective in developing job-related skills in learning-disabled and behavior-disordered adolescents (Montague, 1988).

The last decade has seen rapid growth in the number of youngsters identified as special-needs students and in the programs developed to serve them. Clearly, one of the program needs is social skills instruction. Hansen, Lawrence, and Cristoff (1980) found conduct-disordered youth to have poorer social skills than "normal" youth. Less knowledge of social skills was found highly associated with a wide range of behavioral problems (Venziano & Venziano, 1988).

Present methods of teaching socialization to school-age children rely primarily on nonstructured or informal social experiences encountered in schools, at home, and in the community (Clark, 1980). The importance of school in efforts to teach essential social behaviors comes from the fact that school is the only professionally staffed agency that sees all children. For approximately 180 days each year, the nation's schools provide youth from age 6 to 18 with a sizable portion of their nonstructured informal social experiences. It seems reasonable then to assume that our schools could provide a setting that emphasizes social behavior as a structured part of the school curriculum, thereby beginning a process of assisting students in becoming more socially adept.

Developing a systematic means to routinely teach socialization to school-age children poses quite a challenge. However, shifting the emphasis of instruction from a solely academic curriculum to a combination of academic and social behaviors does not entail lengthening the school day, eliminating required course work, or extending graduation requirements. Rather, it requires the dedication of school personnel in addressing social behavior as an ongoing part of the school curriculum in all classrooms, corridors, playgrounds, and office areas each and every day. Such dedication and vigilance in addressing social behavior obviously requires that teachers and administrators be provided with sound theoretical principles and practical approaches to guide their teaching efforts. Education should not and cannot be for the select few who come from environments that help them become not only academically inclined, but also socially acceptable to peers and adults. Schools have group life, a vast range of possible activities, many caring adults, and a mandate to use these resources for the welfare of all children, including the troubled or troublesome child. Boys Town's goal has been, and continues to be, to develop an effective school program that promotes success through the teaching of social skills and serves as a model for others to use, benefiting youth nationwide. This program is the Boys Town Education Model.

## ▶ Components of the Boys Town Education Model

The Boys Town Education Model is firmly rooted in principles of applied behavior analysis and social learning theory. Its underlying premise is that behavior is learned through feedback on behavior and its environmental consequences (Bandura, 1969). The Model's focus is on teaching because troubled youth have social skills deficiencies and have not yet learned or been effectively instructed how to interact in a socially appropriate way with others (Wolf, Phillips, & Fixsen, 1972; Sarason, 1968; Shah, 1966, 1968).

This behavioral model involves the identification of desirable prosocial behavioral expectations, the effective use of instructional strategies to teach those expectations, the application of an incentive system, and the effective implementation of reinforcement principles. The following elements have been developed and refined for use within a school context:

1. Social Skills Curriculum

2. Teaching Interactions

3. Motivation Systems

4. Administrative Intervention

The combined use of these program components provides educators with the technology to help all students — from those in the regular classroom to those in the most restrictive special education environment — build social skills to maximize their personal effectiveness. A brief review of each of these four program components follows.

## Social Skills Curriculum

The Social Skills Curriculum provides the foundation for a structured educational approach to the socialization of school-age children. The curriculum offers a manageable yet well-defined set of 16 social behaviors (Figure 1) encompassing Adult Relations, Peer Relations, School Rules, and Classroom Behaviors. This set of skills assists teachers to go beyond merely labeling problem behaviors (e.g. compulsive talker, lazy, restless, etc.), which often hinders identifying specific alternative behaviors that should be promoted, reinforced, strengthened, or taught.

## Figure 1

### Boys Town Schools
### Social Skills Curriculum

1. How to follow instructions.
2. How to accept criticism or a consequence.
3. How to accept "No" for an answer.
4. How to greet someone.
5. How to get the teacher's attention.
6. How to make a request.
7. How to disagree appropriately.
8. How to give negative feedback.
9. How to resist peer pressure (say "No").
10. How to apologize.
11. How to engage in a conversation.
12. How to give a compliment.
13. How to accept a compliment.
14. How to volunteer.
15. How to report peer behavior.
16. How to introduce yourself.

## Teaching Interactions

While the social skills identify what to teach, the Teaching Interaction guides **how** to teach, using specialized approaches similar to the direct instructional techniques advocated by Stephens (1978) and the structured role-play activities of Goldstein, Sprafkin, Gershaw, and Klein (1980). The greatest opportunity for skill generalization comes about through the instruction of skills in naturalistic settings, including classrooms, hallways, and offices (Gresham, 1982). Teaching Interactions promote this generalization.

Teaching Interactions differ from other social skill approaches by using a brief interactive instructional sequence with the student when the behavior occurs. This technique uniquely combines efforts to manage student behavior with the care and concern of teaching an alternative appropriate social behavior. Capitalizing on the teachable moment, when the learner is active and the learning is relevant, the Teaching Interaction allows the teacher to deal with behavior problems in an efficient, effective, and humane fashion (Downs, Kutsick, & Black, 1985; Phillips, Phillips, Fixsen, & Wolf, 1974).

Most educators find a smooth flow within the Teaching Interaction sequence. It can be used with any number of social behavior problems and can be applied in regular or special education settings. Teaching Interactions are concrete and provide positive instruction. Anyone who works with students (e.g. counselors, teachers, psychologists, administrators) can use the Teaching Interaction technique. The only stipulation is that educators view the inappropriate behaviors of students as vital learning/teaching opportunities, not as personal insults or challenges of authority.

## Motivation Systems

While the Boys Town Education Model uses Teaching Interactions to establish new behaviors, it is also essential for many troubled youth that this process includes the giving of positive consequences when the student performs desired behaviors so that newly acquired behavior can be strengthened. This systematic application of immediate consequences is part of what is known as the Motivation Systems.

Many students are motivated to learn without extrinsic rewards. For these youth, the combined use of clear behavioral expectations as defined by the Social Skills Curriculum and the instruction offered through a Teaching Interaction serve to develop highly successful student behavior. However, students with significant social skills deficits —students identified as behaviorally disordered, at risk, or emotionally disturbed — often lack motivation to learn and alter behavior. These students must be given help early on through external measures that hopefully will later lead to the development of an internal desire to learn (O'Leary & Drabman, 1971). The Motivation Systems provide a comprehensive framework for consistently applying principles of learning that will maximize behavior change for these students (Downs, Bastien, Brown, & Wells, 1987).

At the root of the Motivation Systems is a token economy. In the context of a Teaching Interaction, student behavior is confronted and results in consequences in the form of points. The immediacy of the consequences (points) helps motivate behavior change. Students accumulate points to gain access to reinforcers, including tangible items, privileges, and activities.

The Boys Town Motivation Systems are incorporated as a comprehensive framework that helps students with moderate to severe behavioral deficits add social skills to their repertoire of behaviors. The three-level token economy reflects stages of skill acquisition and provides the appropriate degree of structure plus support necessary at each developmental level. This multilevel approach meets each student's individual needs while providing a gradual transition from artificial consequences to more naturally occurring forms of feedback and internal controls.

## Administrative Intervention

Historically, schools often have viewed their role in discipline as one of providing punishment for rule-breaking behavior. This punishment frequently has included suspensions, expulsions, shortened school days, administrative transfers, and ignored truancies (Grosenick & Huntze, 1984). These forms of punishment have questionable effectiveness, are potentially harmful, often lead to a punitive school climate, and may, in some cases, violate statutes protecting the rights of handicapped youth.

Administrative Intervention allows school administrators to function as effective change agents in response to more serious or continuing school discipline problems. It extends the teaching focus found in the other components of the Boys Town Education Model to include working with students who are "out of control," and have been removed from the classroom and sent to the office. This approach, which includes Teaching Interactions and behavioral rehearsal (practice) adapted from the Boys Town Family Model, assumes that discipline is a process of training for correction or teaching alternative ways of responding to stressful classroom or school situations.

Deficits in social behavior (e.g. following instructions, accepting criticism, accepting "No" for an answer, resisting peer pressure) often make it difficult for students to remain in the classroom and, eventually, even in the school program (Schumaker, Hazel, Sherman, & Sheldon, 1982). The Boys Town Social Skills Curriculum (Brown, Black, & Downs, 1984) and a set of procedures designed to help administrators remain calm provide the framework for helping students regain self-control, then teaching them vital social skills and school expectations. An established sequence of consequences for office referrals promotes consistency and predictability while allowing for individualization of responses to rule violations. The goal of this teaching procedure, unlike many discipline policies aimed at the student's exclusion from school, is the youth's successful return to the classroom.

The procedures encompassed within the administrative format are used by administrators or designated persons (e.g. guidance counselors, psychologists, behavior interventionists) across the country. While Administrative Intervention is often used independently of other Model components, it provides crucial support when Motivation Systems are used within a school program.

## ▶ Summary

The Boys Town Education Model is a comprehensive, systematic method of teaching prosocial skills to youth. Its four components — the Social Skills Curriculum, Teaching Interactions, Motivation Systems, and Administrative Intervention — help students learn productive ways of managing their own behavior and interacting with others. It combines the best of skill-based teaching with care and concern, resulting in improvements in students' behavior, self-esteem, and relationships with others.

While this manual contains some of the reading material used in training educators and provides an overview of the technical components of the Boys Town Education Model (both of which are vitally important to the proper training of education staff), the reader is cautioned not to view this manual as the sum and substance of the Model. These materials alone do not enable someone to fully understand and operate the Boys Town Education Model. For its own teachers and the staff members of schools that contract with Boys Town, Boys Town provides three to five days of intensive skill-based training on the implementation of the Model's components. The training process includes lectures, videotapes, and behavioral rehearsals which have proven effective in the development of trainees' skills. Furthermore, Boys Town has found that training combined with ongoing consultation from individuals with experience in the Boys Town Education Model and systematic evaluation input form the foundation for a successful education program and effective classroom management.

# Student rights

Historically, children's rights have gone unrecognized. Not until the latter part of this century has this begun to change.

Children are neither an influential lobbying group nor do they have societal power that allows them to advocate for themselves. Because youth spend the majority of their time in school, educators are the advocates responsible for making school a safe and productive environment. Boys Town is committed to this goal and strives to provide a safe haven for each and every child served. This environment not only is free from abuse, but is one where children can grow spiritually, emotionally, intellectually, and physically. It is a place that respects the rights of a child and employs the most positive and least restrictive practices in educating children. Boys Town's mandate is: "As much freedom as possible, as little restriction as necessary."

## ▶ Promoting safe environments

The Boys Town approach to promoting safe environments has multiple components. These are:

1. Policies and procedures

2. Training in positive interaction styles

3. Ongoing program evaluation

4. Regular student interviews

5. Staff Practice Inquiries

6. Training in the rights of children

All of these components are integrated into the education systems with the major emphasis on the provision of safe, humane care. Information from these various components is constantly used to update and modify the school program when necessary.

## Policies and procedures

The commitment of Boys Town Schools to provide safe environments begins (but does not end) here. Each staff member is made aware of written policies and procedures that relate to protecting the rights of children. These not only emphasize the intent of the education program but also contain the procedures followed when potential policy violations occur. Policies and procedures set in motion other specific components.

## Training in positive interaction styles

All staff members are trained in positive techniques for interacting with or helping children change their behavior while respecting their basic dignity, differences, and freedom. (See Chapter 12: "The Teaching Interaction.") Also, all educators are trained to promote positive relationships with each child. (See Chapter 3: "Building and Maintaining Relationships.")

## Ongoing program evaluation

Educators are provided with systematic feedback on teaching effectiveness through regular evaluation reports. These reports give all staff insight into the quality of education provided for children. Routine updates on school attendance, academic progress, and behaviors are a valuable method of monitoring overall program quality. One of the features of a humane school is the extent to which it succeeds in reaching the goals for which it was established. Routine reporting of progress on important goals helps a school achieve its goals.

## Regular student interviews

Interviews are conducted routinely in the teacher evaluation process. During these interviews, each student is asked whether he or she has experienced any mistreatment by Boys Town staff or others. Each child also is requested to express his or her opinion about the pleasantness and supportiveness of teachers and administrators. These questions provide important information regarding the school atmosphere. The emphasis here is on **how** goals are reached and the methods used. Information derived from these questions can be used to improve staff interaction and communication skills if so indicated.

## Staff Practice Inquiries

Any questionable staff practice is followed up by a Staff Practice Inquiry. Staff Practice Inquiries are investigations into situations where the use of inappropriate practices is suspected. These investigations usually result from information contained in a youth report or a consumer report or from observation by staff.

All allegations obtained from any source about less-than-optimal care are investigated thoroughly and promptly. The fact that Boys Town promptly initiates Staff Practice Inquiries makes it clear that Boys Town takes its protective role seriously. The Boys Town practice is to investigate all claims regardless of their perceived validity or their perceived seriousness. Even relatively benign allegations are investigated in order to sensitize all staff members to the importance of maintaining high-quality standards.

It is the collective responsibility of all educators to safeguard the rights of children. Any suspected abuse observed by children, staff, or others should be reported immediately, as mandated by law. When such a report is received, the administration immediately initiates a Staff Practice Inquiry. The child and adult allegedly involved are interviewed along with others who may have relevant information. The facts are established and conclusions reached as quickly as possible. Quick action is important so that any danger or discomfort experienced by a child can be eliminated or so that any harm to a staff member's reputation can be minimized.

Confidentiality is maintained to the greatest degree possible in all Staff Practice Inquiries. Total anonymity can often be maintained. Sometimes anonymity cannot be guaranteed when a child may be at some risk, mainly because relevant persons need some information during the course of the inquiry process. For instance, parents or legal guardians are immediately informed of any allegation. In cases where serious allegations are made, Child Protective Services agencies are informed so that they can decide whether to conduct their own investigation.

Another important phase of Staff Practice Inquiries is the debriefing phase. Verbal and/or written reports are given to persons who have the right to know about any outcomes. It is important that relevant persons are kept informed, not only to protect the interests of the child but also to protect the reputation of any staff members who are involved.

## Training in the rights of children

All Boys Town educators who work with children receive training to increase their sensitivity to the rights of children. Typically, this training occurs before educators work with children. Subsequent to training, educators are updated through materials and meetings provided by their administration. Educators are provided with rules about what to do or not to do in specific situations, as well as guidelines that augment the sound judgment required of any person involved in educating students.

The rules and guidelines used at Boys Town are outlined in this chapter. These are not inclusive but give a good overview of the training content. Legal precedent is noted where appropriate.

## ▶ Boys Town student rights

The goal of a good education program should be to teach children to make good choices and to become self-reliant. Boys Town bases its student rights on this premise; some are further supported by legal precedent. Our student rights are:

## 1. Right to privacy

## 2. Right to one's own possessions

Teachers should not conduct routine secret searches of a student's desk, locker, or person. Searches should be in the interest of a child's well-being and should be conducted by an administrator.

Students' right to privacy was challenged under the 4th Amendment by New Jersey vs. TLO (469 US 325, 1985). The United States Supreme Court determined that schools do not act *in loco parentis* and are governed by search and seizure laws. Schools, however, need only have probable cause, rather than reasonable suspicion which law enforcement authorities must have, in order to conduct a search. Student lockers and desks are possessions of both the school and the student during the school year. Although school administrators have the right to search these, this right should be clearly stated in school policy. Children's school records should be released only with the written permission of his/her parent or legal guardian.

It is important to note that students do not waive the right to privacy when bringing personal possessions on to school grounds. However, teachers should help ensure that no student possesses dangerous items (drugs, weapons, etc.) by notifying administrators if they suspect that a student has such items at school. Administrators have the right to confiscate dangerous possessions and turn them over to law enforcement.

Teachers also should see that each student has the necessary school supplies. If a student does not have supplies, the items should be provided by the school and further replacement items purchased by the student through the Motivation Systems.

Teachers may exercise reasonable control over the personal possessions a student brings to class by instructing that the items be turned over to the teacher. The student also could opt to put the items away and take them home at the end of the school day. If a teacher limits or restricts a student's use of a personal item, the student should be told how to earn back the use of the item.

## 3. Right to freedom of movement

In Boys Town schools, restrictions on break time or recess only occur in response to immediate discipline concerns. These restrictions should not be used routinely or for extended periods of time. Teachers should use time-out very judiciously. Time-out is generally best suited for young children. It involves removing a student from a reinforcing event, not from an aversive event. The key to its appropriate use is to ensure that "time-in" is employed; the classroom must first be a reinforcing environment for the student.

## 4. Right not to be given meaningless work

Homework, additional work, or meaningless assignments are not given as a punishment to students in Boys Town schools. Assigned work is designed to promote academic progress.

## 5. Right to Access File Material (The Family Educational Rights and Privacy Act, 1974)

School records are made available to students with permission from their parents or legal guardians. Students cannot be forced to sign statements agreeing with behavior plans or school reports. They can, however, sign statements indicating they have read the materials. Students have a right to disagree with information in their file and may sign a formalized statement to that effect. Student files should be treated as confidential.

## 6. Right to nourishment

Teachers in Boys Town schools may not make lunch contingent on behavior, or serve a less adequate lunch as a behavioral consequence. Access to water cannot be denied, but teachers can set reasonable periods of time for students to obtain drinks. Snacks may be made available as a privilege through the Motivation Systems.

## 7. Right to communicate with significant others (6th Amendment)

Students have the right to contact their families and to see school support personnel (administrators, counselors, etc.). School personnel may set times when services are available. Although teachers may not deny students the right to communicate, they may exercise reasonable control over the timing and form of the communication.

## 8. Right to treatment

Teachers should assist each student's progress toward educational goals. They should set and maintain both academic and behavioral expectations, adjusting Individual Education Plans IEPs when needed to ensure success. Special education students must have an (IEP) and may not be denied an education (Public Law 94-142).

## 9. Right to interact with others

Extended periods of physical isolation should not be used as a punishment. Separation of the student from the instructional group should be used only for short periods to promote appropriate behavior and academic learning. Teachers should not instruct students to isolate another student as a punishment. Students may, however, be prompted to ignore peer problems.

## 10. Right to respect of body and person

Physical restraint should be used only as a last resort to prevent a student from harming himself or others. Sarcasm, name-calling, labeling, and any other humiliating verbal statements directed toward a student should be avoided. Corporal punishment should be avoided as a disciplinary action. It is not subject to the 8th Amendment; most states have no laws regulating its use. In the case of Baker vs. Owen (423 US 907, 1975), the Supreme Court decided that corporal punishment could be used without prior parental approval under the following guidelines: 1) it not be used as the first line of punishment, and 2) school officials need to be present to serve as witnesses. Boys Town believes strongly that positive methods should be employed in teaching students prosocial behaviors. Suppressing behavior through coercive means has only a temporary effect; aversive discipline methods generate counter-aggression.

## 11. Right to natural elements

Teachers should not routinely restrict a student from outdoor activities, except in response to immediate behavioral concerns. Although they can use loss of recess as a behavioral consequence, teachers should not restrict access to recess for extended periods of time.

## 12. Right to freedom of expression (1st Amendment)

Administrators can regulate freedom of expression associated with curriculum and school activities. They can censor individual expression if it disrupts the educational process or puts the rights or safety of others in jeopardy (Tinker vs. Des Moines, 393 US 503, 1969; Bethel vs. Fraser, 478 US 675, 1986; Hazelwool vs. Kuhlmeier, 484 US 260, 1988).

## ▶ Education for All Handicapped Children Act (EHCA)

In 1977, Public Law 94-142 established rights for all handicapped children. They have a **right** to a free, appropriate education at public expense that meets state educational standards. This education is provided under an Individualized Education Plan (IEP) developed to meet the needs of the student, not the school district (Federal Register, August 23, 1977). The United States Supreme Court decided in the Board of Education vs. Rowley (458 US 176 ) in 1982 that the level of services must maximize the potential of the disabled child equal to the opportunities of nondisabled students. Further, the least restrictive environment must be provided to the maximum extent appropriate. Handicapped students also have a **right** to related supportive services that may be required. These include, but are not limited to, transportation, recreation, health, psychological services or counseling, and speech and hearing services.

Students under EHCA also have a **right** to due process, including the inspection of records and reports, prior notice, independent education evaluations, impartial hearings, and the right to appeal the hearing outcome. Students have a **right** to surrogate parent representation in the educational programming process, which is especially critical for students in residential placement.

Handicapped students have a **right** to not be expelled for behavior related to their exceptionality. In Honig vs. Doe (484 US 305, 1988), the Supreme Court determined that special education students cannot be expelled from school programming for more than 10 days, even if they are considered a threat to themselves or others. Suspensions require prior approval, but students may be suspended for up to 10 days without it being considered a change of placement. If a student's suspension exceeds 10 days, the multidisciplinary team must convene to change the child's IEP. For students in the regular education program, minimal procedures are needed for suspensions under 10 days.

More due process is needed for longer suspensions, with most states requiring students to be represented by counsel (Goss vs. Lopez, 419 US 565, 1975). Currently, U.S. courts are strongly debating the rights of students infected with the AIDS virus to attend school and receive protection under the 14th Amendment and the Rehabilitation Act, Section 504. Though courts have determined that students with AIDS are protected by the Rehabilitation Act, much controversy still surrounds these students attending classes. Individual districts should consult their governing laws.

## ► Convention on Rights of the Child

In order for school to be an environment that fosters self-reliance and self-confidence in our future generations, educators must treat students with the dignity and respect that should be afforded any human being. Successful education programs nurture students and encourage belonging, while recognizing that differences make individuals unique. The empowerment and protection of children as a universal agenda is ever increasing. To that end, the United Nations has become a powerful advocacy group in recognizing the rights of children everywhere.

On November 20, 1989, the general assembly of the United Nations created the *Convention on Rights of the Child*. It con-

tains 54 articles; three specifically pertain to education and many have school impact. Because of its importance, it bears reading by all school personnel. The three articles specifically related to education are summarized here:

**Article 23** states that disabled children have the right to care, education, and training that will help them enjoy a full life and achieve the greatest degree of self-reliance and social integration possible.

**Article 28** provides that children have a right to a free and compulsory education and that school discipline should be consistent with children's rights and dignity.

**Article 29** states that children have a right to an education that develops their personalities, talents, and mental and physical abilities. Education should prepare a child for adult life in a free society. It should foster respect for parents, cultural identity, language, and values, as well as promote respect for others.

## ► Summary

Boys Town is concerned about protecting and assuring the free exercise of all rights and privileges of its children. The guidelines and processes described in this chapter provide evidence of this concern. However, success in assuring children's rights is not guaranteed by procedures alone, but comes from the "sense of quality" that is imbued in each educator. Each person should understand that it is his or her competence in developing and carrying out education plans, and diligence in monitoring personal actions and the actions of others that makes the real difference. Rules, guidelines, and procedures are necessary, but it is the commitment to providing the highest quality care possible that affords all students a safe environment in which to maximize their full potential.

# CHAPTER THREE

# Building and maintaining relationships

Children spend nearly 13,000 hours in school between the ages of 6 and 18 and the majority of those hours are spent with a teacher inside a classroom. The quality of teacher-student relationships significantly affects whether students' needs are met. When students' needs are being met in the classroom, they tend to behave more appropriately and learn more effectively (Jones & Jones, 1990).

The necessity for presenting a chapter on building and maintaining positive teacher-student relationships and creating positive and supportive classroom environments is based on the unfortunate reality that all too often, our classroom environments fail to meet students' basic personal and psychological needs. This is not to say that teachers knowingly or willfully ignore these very critical needs, but rather points out how cliches like, "Be tough," "Be clever," or "Keep them busy and look like you're in charge" — once presented as simple prescriptions for effectively managing a classroom — have impacted our school environments and classroom climates and are still exercised in many educational settings. Teachers' relationships with their students often tend to be directed toward establishing control and fostering compliance rather than focusing on creating a classroom climate that represents an effective blend of warmth, care, and compassion with an appropriate amount of firmness, realistic tolerances, and competent teaching (Shores, Gunter, & Jack, 1993; Steinberg, 1992; Nichols, 1992; Steinberg & Knitzer, 1992).

Too many children enter our schools and classrooms excited, eager, and exhibiting a readiness to learn only to later leave feeling disliked and unsuccessful (Morse, 1964; Cormany, 1975; Mortimore & Sammons, 1987; Purkey & Novak, 1984) and, in many instances, having failed academically as well as socially. This traditional emphasis on content and control as two of the major functions comprising the role of the classroom teacher may make it confusing and difficult to see that relationships are important to education, or more specifically, to agree that relationships do in fact significantly influence a child's educational experience. Current research indicates that teachers can and do make a difference in many students' lives even when facing the many societal factors that make the job of a classroom teacher more challenging and difficult. Teachers increase their effectiveness when they are provided with information about skills associated with effective teaching and when they receive feedback on how their behavior matches criteria for effective teaching. (Jones & Jones, 1990). This chapter discusses the benefits resulting from strong teacher-student relationships and how to facilitate student learning and personal empowerment, and inspire a positive self-concept.

## ▶ Benefits of building strong teacher-student relationships

Teaching is an interactive process. The more positive your interactions are with your students, the more assured you can be that your interactions will be effective and mutually reinforcing. How students perceive themselves as learners and unique individuals, how much responsibility they assume for their behavior, and how well they learn and perform academically are factors that are impacted significantly by what occurs at school and in your classroom. Individuals

learn more effectively in environments that meet their basic personal and psychological needs (Jones & Jones, 1990). As teachers, you control many of the variables affecting your students' needs, which influence their academic achievement as well as their behavior. The nature and quality of the relationships you establish and maintain with your students form the basis of the climate in your classroom. And, a supportive and positive classroom climate creates an instructional environment that not only meets students' basic needs but also motivates them to demonstrate initiative, take risks, and commit themselves to learning. Strong relationships with your students contribute substantially to your ability to help promote growth and change in every student.

In addition to providing strong evidence that academic achievement and student behavior are influenced by the quality of the teacher-student relationship and that positive teacher-student relationships are associated with more positive student responses to school (Aspy & Roebuck, 1977; Norman & Harris, 1981), a significant body of research also indicates that students prefer teachers who display warm and friendly behavior toward them (Rosenshine, 1970; Norman & Harris, 1981). As Robert Bush (1954) noted in *The Teacher-Pupil Relationships*, "Teachers retain their effectiveness as professional persons only so long as they remain warmly human, sensitive to the personal needs of children, and skillful in establishing effective relationships."

The above findings also highlight the importance of modeling theory and its influence on the quality of the teacher-student relationship. Children not only learn by doing, they also learn by watching others. Much of a child's learning occurs by observing and subsequently modeling the behavior of the adults in his or her life. Research by Bandura (1969, 1977) indicates that individuals tend to emulate behavior of significant others — individuals who they perceive as competent, trusting, and who provide a major source of support, direction, and reinforcement. Teachers not only embody these qualities, but also are in an excellent position, second only to that of the child's family, to serve as role models for their students. When students have positive feelings about their school and their teachers, they are more likely to identify with and accept them as important role models. Furthermore, kids tend to model behavior if they think adults benefit by performing these behaviors (Jones & Jones, 1990), and they also are more likely to model behavior exhibited by several adults (Bronfenbrenner, 1970). These variables illustrate how important it is for you, as well as your colleagues throughout the school, to engage in skills and behaviors that create and maintain a positive and supportive environment for the students. Not only do positive relationships increase the effectiveness of your role-modeling, but your students' receptivity to more direct teaching also improves. Students will be more likely to accept your feedback, whether it takes the form of a compliment, praise or recognition for effort, an instruction to redo an assignment, or a Teaching Interaction to correct a socially inappropriate behavior. (See Chapter 12: "The Teaching Interaction.")

While it is true that positive teacher-student relationships will enhance the opportunity for all students to achieve a greater degree of academic and social competence, such relationships become even more critical for those students who enter your classroom with many unmet needs and a variety of behaviors that interfere with their social-emotional development and academic achievement. By improving the quality of your interactions with students, you can significantly increase the amount of productive student behavior (Jones & Jones, 1990). Developing positive relationships with your students, however, will clearly not resolve all classroom problems nor prevent issues from occurring. Again, your concern, caring, and understanding must be delicately balanced with realistic limits, clear and specific expectations, and competent teaching.

## ▶ How relationships develop

Relationships do not develop over the course of a few days, weeks, or even months. Nor can a relationship ever be considered to be "developed." Rather, a relationship can be viewed as continually developing over time and across events and issues that arise as you interact with your students. Two key variables that significantly influence how relationships with your students evolve over time are, 1) the personal or affective quality of the relationship, and 2) how you communicate or relate to your students.

Generally speaking, there is a common set of behaviors and attitudes that are both socially acceptable and generally valued by members of our society. These behaviors and values include such concepts as honesty, sensitivity, concern and respect for others, a sense of humor, reliability, willingness to listen, etc. Many students enter our schools and classrooms not yet having developed such values and behaviors because of poor role models, damaged learning histories, or simply because they have not had the benefit of someone to guide them through a particular phase of development. As with so many other life skills, it becomes the school's responsibility — your responsibility — to teach students the skills needed to develop positive adult and peer relationships. While continuing to focus on the teaching of these critical skills, you also must maintain a high rate of positive interactions with your students, create opportunities during the school day when they can engage in open, personal discussions with you, and demonstrate a genuine interest in their activities.

## ▶ Using quality components

While the components of Teaching Interactions and Effective Praise (Chapter 10) can build relationships, one could use such "procedural" components and still not build relationships. Such teaching procedures must be accompanied by quality components or effective communication skills. Quality components are the positive verbal and nonverbal behaviors that accompany the procedural components. Such quality components include looking at the student, answering his or her questions pleasantly and enthusiastically, having a pleasant facial expression, smiling and using humor when appropriate, expressing concern and empathy, displaying appropriate physical contact such as a hug, an arm on the shoulder, a "high five," etc.

## ▶ Other elements of a positive relationship

As with any relationship, it is important to have shared experiences and "remember when" times to further enhance strong teacher-student relationships. One important way you can show interest and concern for your students is by taking the time to attend activities in which they are involved, both in and out of school. These might include sports, drama activities, dance recitals, scouting events, etc. Evidence indicates that attending students' activities is often associated with dramatic improvement of those students. (Jones & Jones, 1990.)

Eating lunch with students or participating in playground activities also are excellent ways for you to show that you are "human" and that you do like to have fun. This participation not only affords an excellent opportunity to strengthen positive relationships, but also provides a natural setting in which you can model and teach cooperation, sportsmanship, and appropriate playground behavior.

Introducing yourself and welcoming the class through letters or notes sent to students prior to the beginning of the school year or semester, or giving notes at other appropriate times, such as when a student has accomplished a particularly difficult task, shown significant behavioral improvement, or been elected to student council, also helps build and strengthen relationships. Greeting students individually at the door each morning or prior to the beginning of the period and offering some kind of positive statement also lets them know you care and that you're concerned about them. You also can demonstrate your interest in your students, as well as enjoy a good time with them, by participating in school activities such as "hat day," carnivals, and other special events sponsored by student council, various clubs, or other student groups.

Finally, relationship development also is an important part of dealing with problem behavior. As noted earlier in this chapter, the use of effective communication skills and quality components when using Teaching Interactions and Effective Praise contributes significantly to positive relationships. Furthermore, even when addressing ongoing behavior or potentially out-of-control behavior, you should use large amounts of empathy and praise to maintain and continue to develop positive relationships with students during these difficult times.

## ▶ Summary

Building strong relationships with your students is one of the more important aspects of the Boys Town Education Model. This is because strong relationships with your students allow you to accomplish so many other goals. Relationships contribute much to the overall effectiveness of your teaching. Students cannot reach their full potential in school unless you and the other adults in your school encouragingly invite them to do so.

# CHAPTER FOUR

# Problem-solving

During recess, two fifth-graders are chosen to be on the same kickball team; both want to pitch and they begin to argue. On the way to fourth-period PE class, several students approach another student and ask him to skip class with them; the student doesn't want to, but he also doesn't want to lose face with friends. Before school, one student asks a classmate to do a book report for her and offers to pay for it; the classmate would like to have the money but is afraid of getting caught. During lunch, two students observe an older student aggressively attempting to extort money from a new student; one of the observers wants to report the event, the other doesn't.

Problems like the ones described above are not unusual. Students face conflict, confusion, difficult choices, and a wide array of other problematic situations every day.

And, like it or not, as teachers, administrators, counselors, and other school staff, you invest as much time throughout the school day assisting students with problem mediation and social adjustment as you do with advancing their academic progress. Schools provide a unique environment for fostering social adjustment and problem-solving skills in children, since so many of the social interactions and events that occur can be monitored and used as real-life teaching and learning opportunities.

Problem-solving is a lifetime skill, one that students can use in or out of school, now or 10 years from now. There is no question that problem-solving skills are valuable to one's adjustment. It has been said that psychological health is related to a problem-solving sequence consisting of the abilities to recognize and admit a problem, reflect on problem solutions, make a decision, and take action (Kendall & Braswell, 1982). Furthermore, problem-solving ability might be among the factors that contribute to an individual's use of prosocial, rather than anti-social, behavior (Goldstein, 1988). There also is some research that suggests that improved problem-solving skills among students can lead to improved classroom behavior (Spivack & Schure, 1974). Caldwell (cited in Spivack & Schure, 1974) found that as alterna-tive thinking improved, disrespect, defiance, inattentiveness, withdrawal, and overreliance on others all decreased. Inadequate problem-solving skills generally result in a student relying on socially inappropriate and ineffec-tive solutions to real-life problems, particu-larly solutions that are aggressive or coercive in nature. Students with behavior problems have difficulty perceiving as many options, or the same kinds of options or behavioral options, as others, and are more likely to demonstrate rigid thought patterns (Spivack & Schure, 1974).

Why do so many of our students lack the requisite skills needed to effectively solve problems? One of the most obvious rea-sons for this may be modeling. For example, if a student frequently has seen others use with-drawal and submissiveness to solve a problem, he is apt to use this option when bullied by a bigger student who is demanding money. A student who comes from an environment in which individuals settle disagreements and obtain what they want through arguing, fighting, and other aggressive or coercive means — even though she may realize these solutions are unaccept-able — may perceive that her only option is to fight when she finds that another student on

her kickball team also wants to pitch. These examples may help point out why many stu-dents may persist in their inappropriate responses to problems by submitting or retali-ating, or why they may not even be aware that a problem exists. These students need to be taught how to identify and/or solve prob-lems.

If students have an operational process or plan they can use when they face a challenge in school, as well as out of school, they are more likely to successfully recognize and resolve problems. Problem-solving also can be used retrospectively to help students make better decisions in the future.

It also is important to note that there are situations and times when problem-solving may not be appropriate as the first level of intervention. These include situations when you are attempting to teach a new skill to an individual or to the entire class; in such situations, Preventive Teaching, not problem-solving, is the appropriate procedure. You also should not have a student use problem-solving when dealing with inappropriate behaviors such as skill deficiencies (e.g. not accepting criticism, not accepting "No" for an answer, etc.), rule violations, or inattentive ongoing behavior. Such student behaviors require the consistent, concerned use of Teaching Interactions. (See Chapter 12, "The Teaching Interaction.") At times, you may be tempted to help a student problem-solve when he or she is out of control, especially when the student is passive, withdrawn, crying, or complaining about unfairness. (See Chapter 13, "Ongoing Behavior.") In such cases, it is important to stay focused, regain the student's attention and cooperation, and complete the various teaching agendas. Later, when the student is calm and has fully regained control of his or her behavior, you may choose or the student may ask you to initiate a problem-solving session.

There are times when students face serious problems. In such cases, you probably will not, and should not, feel comfortable discussing the problem with the student alone, and should seek the assistance and support of the school counselor, psychologist, or another qualified professional in the community. These problems could include trying to work through the serious illness or death of a friend or family member, parents' separation or divorce, or loss of a boyfriend/girlfriend. A final example is suicide ideation, which in and of itself is so serious that it requires immediate contact for professional help, as outlined in your school district policies and procedures. In fact, anytime you feel uncomfortable with a situation a student has brought to you, contact a qualified school or professional person in the community who can assist the student with the issue.

▶ **What is problem-solving?**

Problem-solving can be defined as a behavioral process that offers a variety of potentially effective options for dealing with a problem, and increases the probability of selecting the most effective solutions from among the various options (D'Zurilla & Goldfried, 1971). Most of the research on problem-solving describes a process which includes the following five stages or competencies: 1) problem identification or general orientation, 2) problem definition, 3) generation of alternatives, 4) evaluation of the solutions, and 5) decision-making (Spivack & Schure, 1974).

The Boys Town Education Model uses the **SODAS** method, a revision of a counseling process developed by J.B. Roosa (1973), to teach students the general skill of problem-solving. **SODAS** is an acronym for the following steps:

**S** — Defining the problem **situation**.

**O** — Examining **options** available to deal with the problem.

**D** — Determining the **disadvantages** of each option.

**A** — Determining the **advantages** of each option.

**S** — Deciding on the **solution/simulation**.

This general framework for problem-solving has a great deal of utility and flexibility. You can use the process to conduct group problem-solving, discussions such as those that occur during a class conference, or peer mediation sessions. Students also can use the skill components to solve **interpersonal** conflicts, such as how to deal with being asked to skip school, or **intrapersonal** problems, such as when a student loses her homework or forgets her PE uniform.

Regardless of whether the problem involves the entire class or an individual student, or is interpersonal or intrapersonal in nature, the primary focus of your teaching should be on using the process and teaching the students how to effectively use the **SODAS** method.

Each component of the **SODAS** method is discussed in more detail in the following section.

## Situation

The problem-solving process begins with you helping the student clearly define the situation or problem, assuming that the student is able to recognize that a problem exists. Not all students possess this skill and this may be where you need to start. A problem can be defined for students as a situation in which they need to do something to get what they want, but they don't know what to do or how to do it (Kaplan, 1991).

Once students can determine whether a problem exists, they are ready to define the problem or situation. This skill component is extremely important; many students who have difficulty problem-solving know a problem exists but don't define it correctly. Oftentimes, students tend to leave themselves out of the problem, or their description of the problem is very vague and emotional (e.g. "I hate math class," "None of the boys in my class like me," "My PE teacher isn't fair and he always picks on me.").

To help a student pinpoint the specific problem, you can use general clarifying questions or statements to help the student more clearly focus on the issues (e.g. "Why don't you explain that further?").

However, it frequently may be necessary to ask more direct, specific questions to help the student talk about his or her issues (e.g. "Why do you hate math class?" or "Why do you think your PE teacher is unfair and picks on you?").

While exploring the situation with the student, it is extremely important that you engage in supportive verbal and nonverbal behaviors that communicate empathy, concern, and encouragement. Without these relationship quality interaction variables, your questions may become more like an interrogation that could cause the student to withdraw.

As the student more clearly defines the situation, you need to summarize what the student is saying. Such a summarization is particularly important before any options are discussed. The summarization helps you assure that all the relevant information has been reviewed and that you accurately perceive the student's situation. If the summarization is inaccurate or incomplete, the student then has the opportunity to correct any misperceptions. This is especially important at this point since the remainder of the process is built around the defined situation. Without an accurate or clearly defined situation, it will be difficult to generate useful options and a viable solution.

## Options

The ability to generate a list of alternatives or options is probably the single most important problem-solving skill because the cognitive skill of knowing what to do in case of failure is one that can prevent or decrease a student's frustration level or the need to engage in withdrawn or impulsive behavior. Spivack and Schure (1974) consider this skill: 1) the most powerful prediction of maladaptive behavior; 2) the skill that is best enhanced through training; and 3) the one that, when fostered, seems to also result in the greatest improvement in student classroom behavior. Knowing how to pursue or select alternative options also may be all the encouragement a student needs to keep on trying and not give up (Kaplan, 1991).

Once the situation is clearly defined, you should help the student generate options in the form of potential solutions to the problem. It is important to have the student generate the option that might solve the problem. You need to remember that the goal is to have the student develop his or her ability to solve problems as well as arrive at a solution.

To help students generate options, you need to specifically ask the student how he or she might solve the problem or deal with the situation (e.g. "Can you think of a way to handle that?" or "What do you think you can do about this?"). After the student suggests an option, you need to continue to solicit options (e.g. "Can you think of any other ideas?").

Initially, students may have difficulty generating options or generating more than one option. Also, the suggestions offered may not be very helpful or realistic. Whenever a student gives an option, it is very important that you remain nonjudgmental.

You can remain nonjudgmental by commenting positively about the student's participation in the process (e.g. "Well good, you've come up with a second option. You're really trying to think this through."). You also can offer a neutral comment and a prompt for more options (e.g. "Okay, that's one option. Can you think of another one?").

Remaining nonjudgmental can be very difficult, especially when the student suggests an option that would only result in more problems for him or her (e.g. "I'll just have to punch him out."). You need to remember that your role at this point is just to get the student to generate options. In that sense, this phase of the process is like "brainstorming." The next phase of examining the advantages and disadvantages will allow you to help the student judge the "wisdom" of his or her suggested options.

During the option phase, you may give your suggestions as well. However, this should be done only after the student has given all of his or her ideas. You may want to phrase the option as a question (e.g. "How about talking to your math teacher after class?") so that the student feels involved in the process. Over time, students will be better able to generate options and will be more comfortable doing so.

Once students can generate three or four different options for every situation or problem, they should be considered competent at this skill. Children as young as four are considered capable of developing this skill (Spivack & Schure, 1974).

## Disadvantages and advantages

Once students are capable of generating several options to a problem, they need to learn how to evaluate or analyze the advantages and disadvantages of each option. Each option should be evaluated according to two basic criteria: 1) efficacy, i.e. "Will this solution help me achieve my goal without causing me any additional problems?", and 2) feasibility, i.e. "Will I be able to take the action outlined in my options?" (Kaplan, 1991).

Your role is to help the student think through the efficacy and feasibility of each option. In a sense, you are attempting to teach the student that there is a cause-and-effect relationship between his or her decisions and what happens to him or her. As in generating options, it is important to have the student think through the advantages and disadvantages, with you skillfully guiding that process. If the student has difficulty thinking through the advantages and disadvantages, you can help by asking more specific questions (e.g. "Well, what do you think would happen if you told your PE teacher off or just didn't go to that class anymore?").

There may be a number of advantages and disadvantages for any given option. Again, since the goal is to help the student learn to think, it also is important in this phase to solicit additional advantages and disadvantages (e.g. "Can you think of any other advantages; any other problems?").

During this process, it is important for you to remain nonjudgmental and not argue with a student about his or her perceptions of the advantages and disadvantages. This can be difficult when the student seems enthusiastic about the unrealistic advantages of an option (e.g. "Yeah, it'd be great to fight it out because then he'd leave me alone and everybody would think I was bad."). Rather than argue about an advantage, you can simply acknowledge the student's view (e.g. "Okay, so you think that an advantage would be..."). Later, you can guide the student's judgment during the discussion of the disadvantages (e.g. "What happens if you don't win?" or "Could you get hurt?" or "What will your boss do if he hears you've fought with another employee?").

If a student clearly does not see or cannot verbalize an important advantage or disadvantage, you should offer your viewpoint and allow the student to react.

After discussing the disadvantages and advantages for the options, you should summarize by reviewing each option and the associated advantages and disadvantages. This summary review further helps the student see the cause-and-effect relationships.

## Solution/simulation

The last step in the **SODAS** process involves having the student select the solution and prepare to successfully implement it by conducting any necessary "simulations" or role-play sessions. As a result of examining advantages and disadvantages, the student typically selects a workable option. It may not always be the best option from your point of view, but it is more important that it is the student's option. The student is more likely to be committed to make an option work if he or she is truly comfortable with it and feels ownership for the choice.

After the student has selected an option, you should encourage and reassure the student that the solution can be successfully implemented. In making the student comfortable with the solution, you can answer any questions the student may have about how to successfully implement it.

Another important aspect of improving the student's chance of success is for you to set up a role-play or practice session. These role-play sessions should be as realistic as possible. Often, you will know the people the student will need to interact with when implementing the solution (e.g. parents, friend, employers, principals, other teachers). Because you know these individuals, you can simulate their behaviors. For example, if an employer is fairly abrupt and somewhat stern, you can best help the student by portraying the employer in that manner. The role-play can be made more realistic by presenting the student with several possible responses so that he or she will be more comfortable and more likely to succeed.

You need to express confidence in the student's ability to implement the solution. However, you should not promise the student that the solution will work. As the practice session ends, you should prompt the student to check back after trying to implement the solution. If the student succeeds in solving the problem, you should praise him or her for doing so and for going through the problem-solving session. If the solution is not workable, you need to be very supportive and empathic. You and the student can then return to the **SODAS** format to find a more successful solution.

Learning to problem-solve is a complex task, but as mentioned earlier in this chapter, it is a lifetime skill and one that is critical to your students' eventual success. Because participating in the problem-solving process is so important, it would be reasonable to have those students who are on a Motivation System (see Chapter 6, "Overview of Motivation Systems") earn significant positive consequences for demonstrating this skill. Since many students have "solved" their problems in inappropriate ways in the past (e.g. running away, becoming aggressive), it is important to positively reinforce a student who indicates he or she would like to discuss a problem (e.g. "I'm having a problem with my PE teacher" or "I'm having a problem at my job. Can you talk with me about it?").

The complete use of the **SODAS** format during a problem-solving session is very important in teaching rational problem-solving skills to your students. When using the **SODAS** process, it is critical that you remember to always engage in supportive verbal and nonverbal behaviors that communicate care, concern, and empathy. In addition, two important distinctions related to how you teach and guide your students in the problem-solving process need to be made at this point. First, students should be encouraged to generate **their own** options to **their own** problems rather than you always telling them what they should do or what you think is the best solution. Students need to take ownership of their behavior. When they begin to generate alternatives, they are more likely to learn that they do have a certain amount of control over what happens to them. They also are learning critical thinking skills. Second, the emphasis again must be on teaching the students the process or skill of how to problem-solve rather than on the rightness or wrongness of their solutions to the problems. Students must be allowed to make mistakes or poor decisions in the process of learning how to make the most effective or reasonably "correct" decision.

Aside from formal problem-solving sessions, there are many other types of formal and informal activities that facilitate modeling and direct teaching of the **SODAS** process. Informally, there will be opportunities for discussion that may be prompted by television programs or current events. As your students express their opinions and points of view, you will be confronted with ideal opportunities to encourage your students to think, to weigh options, and to discuss the possible ramifications of their views and values.

## ▶ Summary

In summary, problem-solving has two important goals — to help students arrive at sound solutions to their problems and to teach them how to solve their problems in a systematic, rational way. The **SODAS** process, coupled with important relationships variables (e.g. active listening, empathy, concern), can help you accomplish these goals. And, because such problem-solving sessions also promote and establish trust between you and the student, critical relationship-building also occurs.

# CHAPTER FIVE

# Principles of behavior

The Boys Town Education Model has its foundation in social learning theory. This chapter will define the major components of this theory in order to give you a perspective on how current behaviors of youth are maintained, how to identify behaviors that may need to be changed, and how to institute a behavior-change process with these youth.

In order to understand and effectively use this theory, one must look at various concepts of the word "learned." A commonly held concept is that if a particular behavior has been taught, then it should have been learned. In the Boys Town approach, a behavior is believed to be learned when it has been successfully demonstrated over time in appropriate settings. When children have problems with a math concept, teachers generally go back and analyze their teaching approach, change it, and reteach the math concept. However, when children have problems engaging in appropriate social skills for the classroom, teachers are generally not as willing to analyze their teaching approach to the problem. They may assume that the skills youth do not know should have already been taught and therefore learned. The Boys Town approach encourages a reteaching process, without the assumptions of learning, until appropriate behaviors are successfully demonstrated over time.

## ▶ Three-term contingency or the ABC pattern

Behavior does not occur in a void. Events that precede a behavior and events that follow a behavior impact on the future occurrence of that behavior. To fully understand the behavior itself, one must know what happens in the environment prior to the behavior as well as what occurs following the behavior. It is helpful for educators to think of the ABC or three-term contingency pattern:

**A = Antecedents** — the events or conditions present in the environment before a behavior occurs

**B = Behavior** — what is done or said by a person

**C = Consequences** — the results, outcomes, or effects following a behavior

Behavior always occurs as a part of a contingency. The universe, according to social learning theorists, is a determined orderly place in which events do not just randomly happen. They happen as a part of a relationship to other events. We call this relationship a contingency. Contingencies are responsible for our learning histories as the probability of the occurrence of behavior is determined by its history of consequences (Cooper, Heron, & Heward, 1987).

## Antecedents

The situation or context in which behavior occurs qualifies as the antecedent to that behavior. These conditions or events can be simple or complex, recent or historical. When analyzing the antecedents of a behavior, pay particular attention to who was present, what activities were occurring, the time of day or season of the year, and the location or physical setting.

Each of these alone or in conjunction with one another can set the occasion for particular behaviors to occur. The more you know about the history of a student, the greater your understanding of the previous learning that has occurred with that student. Learning history can play a role in the antecedents of current behavior.

While all the antecedents for a behavior may be complex, a more simple stimulus (or set of stimuli) often may immediately precede a behavior. A doorbell ringing immediately precedes someone standing to answer the door, a smiling face on a student first thing in the morning sets the occasion for a greeting, a green light at an intersection precedes the continuance of pressure on the gas pedal in the car, a student arguing with a teacher after an instruction is given precedes the teacher's behavior of intervening and teaching how to follow an instruction.

## Behavior

What is behavior? Behavior is anything a person does or says that can be directly or indirectly observed (i.e. seen, heard, felt, touched, or smelled) and measured. For example, a teacher can observe the behavior of writing numbers on a math assignment directly by watching the action as it occurs or indirectly by noting the physical results of the behavior — in this case, by seeing a completed math worksheet.

Similarly, special education teachers can directly observe a child who has been mainstreamed into a regular classroom or can indirectly be aware of his behaviors by asking the regular education teacher to complete a school card each day. Since behavior is observable, it can be measured and progress can be charted over the course of time.

## Consequences

Consequences are environmental changes that occur after a behavior in a relatively immediate, temporal sequence that alters the probability of future occurrence of that behavior (Cooper, Heron, & Heward, 1987). Consequences take one of two forms:

1. A new stimulus is presented or added to the environment, such as a student earning free time on the computer following the completion of a class assignment.

2. An already present stimulus is terminated or removed from the environment, such as a student losing the privilege of going to the water fountain because he did not accept criticism from his teacher about staying on task.

Consequences will either increase or decrease the future rate of a particular behavior. When consequences increase the likelihood of the behavior occurring again, this is called " reinforcement." When a consequence decreases the likelihood of that behavior occurring again, this is termed "punishment."

Consequences can be natural or applied. Natural consequences are the typical outcomes of a behavior without any intentional human intervention. For example, scrapes and bruises are the natural consequences of falling down on a cement sidewalk; falling backwards is a natural consequence of leaning back too far in a chair.

Applied consequences for behavior are outcomes that are purposefully arranged. In the Boys Town Education Model, applied consequences can take the form of points that students earn for appropriate classroom behavior or privileges the students earn for engaging in appropriate academic tasks. They also can take the form of privilege losses for not completing academic tasks to a set criteria, or a loss of points for not engaging in appropriate classroom behavior.

## ▶ Using the ABC or three-term contingency pattern

Understanding the ABC pattern can help educators clarify why a behavior occurs. More importantly, it will aid them in helping their students change their behaviors. Many students engage in classroom behaviors that, if generalized, will isolate them from family, friends, school activities, and their community at large. Due to various circumstances at home, some of these students have no one other than their teachers to help them make the needed changes for success. Using the ABC pattern helps teachers promote change in positive, effective, and efficient ways.

Teachers can help students change their behavior by manipulating antecedents, consequences, or both. Frequently, we think changing the consequence will work, and then are sometimes surprised when we don't get the result we wanted. But there may be times when altering the antecedents is a more effective way to change behavior. An example might be a person who is having trouble getting out of bed in the morning and who keeps hitting the snooze button on the alarm instead of getting up. He could change the antecedent by moving the alarm clock to the other side of the room. This would make it more difficult for him to immediately go back to sleep because he would have to get up and walk across the room to hit the snooze button. Since he is already up, it may encourage him to stay awake. Another example of changing antecedents occurs in particular social situations, such as a school pep rally. Behaviors that should occur during the pep rally can be rehearsed ahead of time and the most relevant behaviors can be pointed out and discussed. Cues and subtle signals that will prompt appropriate behavior at the rally can be explained to the students.

In each behavior, the antecedent conditions have been altered to help achieve the desired behavioral change.

Changing consequences also can be effective. Specific verbal praise can be given when a student appropriately gets your attention. A student can earn positive points for following your instructions to begin an assignment. Likewise, a student may lose points for arguing with you about completing an assignment. By changing the consequences, you can help change a student's behavior.

The Boys Town Education Model has many built-in uses of the ABC pattern. For difficult youth problems, unique problems, or recurring problems, it is up to you, or the administrator or teacher-consultant, to use the ABC pattern to analyze the problem behavior and come up with a solution to help the student change.

# Some principles of behavior

Principles of behavior are the fundamental laws concerning the nature of behavior. They specify the relationships between behavior, the circumstances that surround that behavior, and the resulting outcomes. These principles are critical for educators as they approach the complex task of helping students change their behavior by instituting a behavior-change procedure (Cooper, Heron, & Heward, 1987). See Figure 1 for a chart of behavioral terms. Educators can use the techniques of positive and negative reinforcement to increase behavior, and positive and negative punishment to decrease behavior. They can use the techniques of generalization and discrimination processes to teach appropriate behavior for many different social situations. They also can use extinction, shaping, and fading techniques to help the student learn to respond to naturally occurring environmental reinforcers. Each of these principles of behavior will be discussed on the following pages.

# Positive reinforcement

Positive reinforcement means providing consequences immediately after a behavior to increase the likelihood that the behavior will occur again in the future. If the behavior occurs more often or gets stronger, then it can be assumed that the behavior was "reinforced" by the consequences. Therefore, if a behavior increases, regardless of what the consequence was, it has been reinforced.

## Figure 1

# Matrix of Behavioral Terms

|  | Pleasant/Positive stimulus or event | Unpleasant/Negative stimulus or event |
|---|---|---|
| **Presenting or Applying** | **Term used:** Positive Reinforcement<br><br>**Behavioral result:** Acts to strengthen the response<br><br>**Examples:** Hugs, praise, points, etc. | **Term used:** Punishment<br><br>**Behavioral result:** Weakens or may terminate the response but is highly susceptible to side effects<br><br>**Examples:** Reprimands, threats, corporal punishment, etc. |
| **Withdrawing or Removing** | **Term used:** Response Cost<br><br>**Behavior result:** Weakens or terminates the response<br><br>**Examples:** Loss of points, traffic tickets, time out, etc. | **Term used:** Negative Reinforcement<br><br>**Behavior result:** Acts to strengthen the response<br><br>**Examples:** Turning off a noisy radio; doing something that stops a baby from crying in church, etc. |

Positive reinforcement can occur with natural or applied consequences. An example of a natural consequence for positive reinforcement is the rewarding feeling a high school basketball player gets when he makes a free throw that wins the game. The crowd cheers and his teammates pat him on the back. The results of this public praise will motivate him to continue playing basketball at school. An example of an applied consequence is a teacher's promise to a student that finishing an assignment in 10 minutes will earn her 10 minutes of computer time. When the student finishes her assignment on time, she gets to use the computer. This will help motivate the student to complete other assignments in a timely fashion.

Positive reinforcement can help a student learn a new behavior or maintain appropriate behavior. Figure 1 reviews this concept.

These are some conditions that impact the effectiveness of positive reinforcement:

### 1. Appropriateness of the reinforcer.
Rewards need to be individualized to make sure they are, in fact, reinforcing for the student. Determining appropriate reinforcers can be accomplished by asking the student, observing the student during he or she free time, letting the student try a variety of reinforcers without displaying a certain behavior, having the student pick from a preset menu, and just trying out reinforcers and observing the results from using them.

### 2. Immediacy of the reinforcer. To maximize their effectiveness, reinforcers need to be used immediately after the behavior you want to see increase. The more time that passes between the occurrence of the behavior and the reinforcer, the less effective the reinforcer is in strengthening the behavior. For example, it is the immediate verbal praise following the correct answer that makes a student want to continue to please you by knowing the material being taught. Points are such an effective reinforcer because they can be given immediately after a behavior.

### 3. Amount or size of the reinforcer. The size of the reinforcer should fit the behavior. The longer the behavior takes to perform, the newer the behavior is for a student, or the more difficult it is to perform, the larger the reward should be.

### 4. Reinforcement contingencies. If reinforcement is to be effective, the student must receive the reinforcer only after performing the target behavior. A contingency is an "if...then" statement; if you do the behavior, then you get the consequence. For instance, "If you remain in your seat until I finish the lecture, then you may go to the shelf and get your journal." Be careful to make positive consequences contingent upon positive behavior. You also must analyze negative behavior to determine whether you may be giving rewards that are inadvertently reinforcing or strengthening that negative behavior.

### 5. Reinforcement deprivation and satiation. In order to maximize the effectiveness of a reinforcer, an individual must experience some level of deprivation prior to delivery of the reinforcer. If a child has been playing computer games for the last 20 minutes, adding more computer time as a reinforcer might not be effective because the child may have become "satiated" with computer

time. The concept of satiation also refers to the use of reinforcers when they are most in demand by the students. An example might be use of a compact disc recording as a reinforcer for one week of homework completion. If the CD is Frank Sinatra's greatest hits instead of a popular rock group's latest work, it probably would not be in demand by the teenage student. Thus, the CD would not be considered an effective reinforcer for the homework completion. The effectiveness of positive consequences is maximized by using a variety of reinforcers and by using those that are most in demand by students at the moment.

**6. Use of the Premack Principle**. This is better known as "Grandma's Law" and is another way to fully utilize positive reinforcement. The Premack Principle states that access to high-frequency behavior is contingent upon the occurrence of low-frequency behavior; for example, telling a student, "You may go to recess as soon as you finish questions one through five at the end of the chapter." The concept behind this principle is that a high-frequency behavior (i.e. going to recess) can serve as a reinforcer for a low-frequency behavior (completing assigned schoolwork).

## Schedules of reinforcement

Schedules of reinforcement simply refers to how often reinforcers are given to a student. There are two basic schedules of reinforcement used to deliver reinforcers. One is a "continuous schedule," where a reinforcer is given every time the youth displays the targeted response. A continuous schedule of reinforcement is critical when teaching a new

behavior or skill to the student. You should reinforce the student each time the new behavior is performed to strengthen and encourage the use of the new behavior.

Once the behavior or skill has been established and consistent use is demonstrated, the reinforcement can move to an "intermittent schedule." On an intermittent schedule, targeted behaviors and skills are reinforced only some of the times they occur. For example, reinforcers may be provided every other time or every third time the behavior is performed, the first time the behavior occurs each hour, after two or three days of school attendance, or on any other schedule based on frequency or time. This may seem a bit contradictory, but intermittent schedules of reinforcement actually strengthen a behavior or skill more than continuous schedules. The element of surprise and not knowing when the reinforcer is coming keeps the student's performance of the behavior or skill occurring on a more consistent basis. Intermittent schedules of reinforcement also help fade (a concept that will be discussed later in the chapter) the consequences to a more reality-based schedule where reinforcers are not provided each time a youngster does something well.

## Types of reinforcers

There are two basic types of reinforcers — primary and secondary. Primary reinforcers are unlearned events that, by virtue of their biological importance, serve as consequences that increase the likelihood the behavior that precedes them will occur again. Food, water, oxygen, and warmth are examples of events that do no have to undergo a process to make them reinforcing (Cooper, Heron, & Heward, 1987). In a state of deprivation, they reinforce behavior automatically. With primary reinforcers, it is not necessary for the individual to be aware that these events are reinforcing.

Secondary or "conditioned" reinforcers are neutral events that have acquired reinforcing potential because they have been matched (paired) with primary reinforcers or previously established secondary reinforcers. There are four kinds of secondary reinforcers:

**1. Tangible reinforcers** are objects or activities that increase the probability that the behavior preceding them will occur again. Some examples of tangible reinforcers are trinkets, pins, emblems, marbles, and toys.

**2. Activity oriented reinforcers** are events or privileges such as helping the teacher, playing a game, or having lunch with an administrator. Many activity reinforcers do not have a direct cost so they can be used with programs that may not have the resources to purchase tangible reinforcers.

**3. Social reinforcers** maintain motivation to engage in appropriate behaviors on a daily basis. There are three kinds of social reinforcers. They are physical contacts (handshakes, pats on the back, etc.), proximity (standing or sitting near an individual), and verbal statements ("Good job," "Very good," etc.). Verbal statements can be either informational or affirmative. An example of an informational statement is, "Bobby, you carried your addition from the one's column to the ten's column just as I had

shown you. Good job!" Informational verbal statements describe specific behaviors. An example of an affirmative verbal statement is, "That was the correct answer." Affirmative verbal statements are more general in nature. However, both can be effective social reinforcers.

**4. Generalized reinforcers** are a type of conditioned reinforcer that does not rely on any sort of deprivation to be effective. Tokens, such as points in the Motivation System, and money are two examples of generalized reinforcers. They allow the individual access to a wide array of other primary or secondary reinforcers. They also serve as an interim reinforcer to many others that are available at a later time. Those reinforcers that are available at a later time are called "back-up reinforcers." A benefit of using generalized reinforcers is that they can maintain behavior over extended time periods and are less likely to lead to satiation.

► **Shaping**

Behavioral shaping is defined as the differential reinforcement of successive approximations to a desired behavior (Alberto & Troutmann, 1990). In other words, shaping enhances the gradual development of a new behavior by continually reinforcing small improvements or steps toward the target behavior or goal. Rather than expecting a new behavior to occur exactly the way you taught it, you reinforce any behavior that closely resembles the goal. Now let's look specifically at what is meant by differential reinforcement and successive approximations.

Differential reinforcement means that one behavior is reinforced while another behavior that was previously displayed is not. Both of these behaviors come from the same response class, which means they are similar or related behaviors.

Figure 2 illustrates a shaping process and how differential reinforcement is the key principle in use. The example is a shaping process that a teacher might use with a student who has a problem sitting up straight at his desk. This student frequently slouches down low in his seat. The step-by-step training progression starts with reinforcing the behavior of having the student's behind touching the desk chair. When that behavior is established, having the student move his behind closer to the back of the desk chair is reinforced, and his behind touching the chair is not reinforced. Next, having the student's lower back touching the back of the desk chair is reinforced and the two previous behaviors are not reinforced. The shaping process continues until the student is sitting up straight in the desk and all previous behaviors are not reinforced.

A successive approximation to a desired behavior is any intermediate behavior that is either part of the goal behavior or a combination of successive steps leading to the goal behavior. For example, successive approximations to the desired behavior of a student wearing his glasses all day at school might be first picking up the glasses, putting them on, wearing them for one class period, etc., until the student reaches his goal.

**Some advantages of behavioral shaping include:**

1. It is a positive procedure because reinforcement is delivered consistently upon the occurrence of successive approximations to the goal. The other behaviors that are displayed are not reinforced.

2. Shaping can be used to teach new behaviors. Because shaping is a gradual process, the end goal or desired behavior is always in sight. Shaping can be used with other behavior-building procedures.

**Some disadvantages of shaping include:**

1. Shaping is a time-consuming process. Extended training with the student may be necessary before the final goal is met.

2. Progress in this process is not always an easy movement from one behavior to the next with uninterrupted flow. The student's behavior may become erratic, with considerable time lapses between movement. Certain steps may need to be further dissected into smaller steps so that smaller approximations can be mastered. This requires considerable monitoring to detect subtle indications that the next step in the sequence has been performed.

3. Because monitoring is time-consuming, it sometimes does not occur. This can make the whole shaping procedure ineffective and inefficient.

There are some guidelines that can be useful in making a behavioral shaping program effective and efficient. They are:

1. Select the goal behavior. It is important to define the goal very specifically. The more behaviorally specific you can be, the greater the likelihood of success.

**Figure 2**

# Shaping Process

## Differential reinforcement in action

Sitting upright in the desk

The lower back of the student is touching the back of the desk chair

Behind moves closer to the back of the desk chair

Behind is touching desk chair

The lower back of the student is touching the back of the desk chair

Behind moves closer to the back of the desk chair

Behind is touching desk chair

Behind moves closer to the back of the desk chair

Behind is touching desk chair

Behind is touching desk chair

Steps in differentially reinforcing sitting upright; shaded portion includes behaviors no longer reinforced.

2. Decide the criteria for success. This should be specified so you can tell when the goal has been met. Some common criteria for success may include rate of behavior, frequency of behavior, percentage, magnitude, and duration.

3. Conduct a behavioral analysis of the goal behavior. Analyze each step in sequence that will have the end result of criterion performance of the goal.

4. Identify the first behavior to reinforce. The behavior should already occur at some minimal level. The behavior should be a member of the same response class of the goal behavior. By using these guidelines, you can begin reinforcing immediately and without waiting for a new behavior to occur spontaneously. The first behavior reinforced already has a direct link to the goal behavior, which moves the child closer to goal attainment.

5. Proceed in gradual steps. This is critical for success. The student's approximation of the goal dictates how quickly the goal is attained. Do not move ahead until a step is achieved or learned by the student.

6. Continue reinforcement when a desired behavior is achieved. If reinforcement is not continued, the behavior will be lost and the student's behavior will regress. Reinforce the behavior until the goal criterion is met and a schedule of reinforcement is established.

7. When at all possible, link the behavior to other behaviors that will help the student be more productive at school and in other areas of his or her life.

## ▶ Fading

Fading refers to the gradual removal of antecedent prompts and cues so that naturally occurring events prompt the desired behavior. Fading is an important concept when artificial contingencies such as point systems are used with students in the classroom. One of the first considerations of using the Motivation System should be how the student will be removed from the system (Cooper, Heron, & Heward, 1987). Fading of the Boys Town Education Model Motivation Systems will be discussed in later chapters of this manual.

Here is an example of how fading is used in the classroom: One of your students loses points each time she doesn't pay attention. As a prompt to pay attention, you start using a physical gesture such as looking directly at the student and then putting your finger to your eyes. The next step will be having the youth pay attention without any prompting.

## ▶ Negative reinforcement

Negative reinforcement is another principle used to increase behavior. People often mistakenly think of negative reinforcement as a punishment procedure. This is not accurate because punishment procedures decrease behavior and negative reinforcement increases behavior. The term "negative" is used because the procedure removes or reduces, rather than creates or adds an event. Negative reinforcement is the removal or the reduction of an ongoing event contingent upon a response, thus increasing the likelihood that the behavior will occur again under similar situations. The event that is removed is called the "negative reinforcer." Everyday examples of negative reinforcement include closing a window on a cold day or adjusting the flow of hot water in the shower. Because cold air coming through a window made you shiver in the past, or because water that was too hot in the shower burned you, you remove these events to avoid the negative effect. Refer to Figure 1 for a review of this concept.

As an educator, your behavior is an important factor with regards to negative reinforcement. If you lose your teaching focus with students when they make a mistake, you may add to the potential of them not telling the truth about that situation. Yelling or making judgmental statements to a youth who isn't following instructions and then asking about the situation may be unproductive. The youth may lie in order to avoid or reduce the negative stimulus of the yelling or judgmental terms. In this situation, the student has nothing to lose by lying; if the student tells the truth, he or she will receive a consequence for what happened. On the other hand, if the youth lies and you believe it, the student successfully avoids a consequence. The youth actually is reinforced for lying.

There are two contingencies related to negative reinforcement. They are escape/escape and avoidance/avoidance (Cooper, Heron, & Heward, 1987).

Escape/escape stops an existing event. A teacher might be faced with a situation in which two students in class are loudly calling one another names, and this continues for a few minutes. The teacher might reprimand the students and tell them to stop the bickering. The students stop the bickering momentarily. The teacher now has been negatively reinforced for using reprimands because it stopped the bickering.

Avoidance/avoidance occurs when a person's behavior avoids rather than terminates an event. A student might follow the teacher's instructions to avoid being sent to the office, or a student might sit in the back of the bus to avoid being teased by the other children on the bus. In each case, the student is getting away from a negative stimulus.

## ▶ Positive punishment

To most people, the term punishment refers to the application of physical or psychological pain following the performance of a behavior. Generally, a person would think that a child who was spanked after running into the street had been punished for that behavior. However, the definition of punishment, as a principle of behavior, is the application of an aversive stimulus (following a behavior) that decreases the likelihood that a behavior will occur again. If the child does not run into the street again, then the spanking could be called punishment. However, if the spanking does not decrease the behavior, then it would not be considered punishment. Refer to Figure 1 for a review of the concept.

An aversive stimulus is typically something that is painful, unpleasant, or annoying. However, one must note its effect on behavior. If the stimulus does not decrease the behavior, it is not considered aversive.

There are unconditioned and conditioned aversive stimuli. A stimulus that has not been previously experienced is an unconditioned aversive stimulus. For example: A loud blast or tone is sometimes used as an unconditioned stimulus to reduce the frequency of obscene phone calls. The caller has not been "conditioned," therefore, the unpleasantness of the stimulus may make the caller hang up.

A conditioned aversive stimulus is an event that is initially perceived as neutral, but by repeated pairing with a unconditioned aversive stimulus becomes aversive in nature. An example is the word "No." It is not inherently aversive. However, continually pairing it with a loud, harsh voice tone can make "No" become aversive to students in a classroom.

Three things must happen in order for something to be defined as punishment:

1. A behavior must be displayed.

2. The behavior must be followed by an aversive stimulus.

3. That stimulus alone must decrease the probability that the behavior will occur in the future.

The Boys Town Education Model does not rely on or recommend the use of punishment because it has many negative side effects. These include:

**1. Negative reinforcement of the punisher.** Not only is the person delivering the punishment negatively reinforced because the behavior ceases, but the student-educator relationship that is so necessary to internal izing behavior changes, is damaged. The educator will be more likely to use the same procedure in the future instead of trying something less restrictive.

**2. Emotional or aggressive behavior.** The student may attack, escape, or become physically aggressive toward the punisher in an effort to stop the punishment.

**3. Avoidance and escape.** Avoidance of the punisher can take a literal sense when students avoid the actual punishment or the place they were punished. For example, a student who is punished for being late to class may not go to class. Avoidance and escape behaviors also can occur in a nonliteral sense. For example, a student might escape punishing environments by taking drugs and alcohol, or by "tuning out" (Cooper, Heron, & Heward, 1987).

**4. Negative modeling.** If you punish a child for a behavior, the child will most likely imitate the punishment. Modeling punitive forms of behavior may negate the positive effects of your teaching.

**5. Unpredictability.** Side effects of punishment may be difficult to predict prior to implementing a treatment strategy. Persons utilizing the aversive stimuli should be aware of these effects and have an alternate plan for handling the situation.

## ▶ Response cost/negative punishment

Response cost is a form of punishment in which a specific amount of reinforcement is lost as a result of an inappropriate behavior. This decreases the probability that the behavior will occur again. A student losing part of his free time because he did not follow your instructions or a student losing points because he did not complete his homework are examples of response cost. Refer to Figure 1 for a review of this concept.

There are three desirable aspects of using response cost. They are:

1. Similar to other forms of punishment, response cost usually produces a moderate-to-rapid decrease in behavior. Results of this procedure are apparent after a reasonable trial period, usually three to five days (Cooper, Heron, & Heward, 1987).

2. Response cost is a convenient procedure to use in the classroom. Many studies have shown a decrease in negative classroom behavior by using these procedures.

3. Response cost can be combined with other behavioral procedures in a comprehensive behavior-change program. In the Boys Town approach, the use of response cost is combined with the "fair pair" rule developed by White and Haring (1980). This rule suggests that the teacher reinforces one or more alternatives for every behavior targeted for reduction. It is critical to teach the prosocial alternative to any misbehavior and Boys Town's teaching techniques incorporate this concept. (These techniques are discussed in greater detail later in this book.) The combination of positive reinforcement and response cost helps to motivate the students to change their misbehaviors into more appropriate behaviors.

The same conditions that impact the effectiveness of positive reinforcement also impact response cost: immediacy, choice of the reinforcer to be taken away, and withholding the reinforcer when a negative behavior occurs. Many of these conditions are built into the Boys Town Education Model Motivation Systems. Teachers are responsible for taking these conditions into account as they maximize the effectiveness of consequences they use for each individual student.

## ▶ Extinction

Extinction is a procedure in which the reinforcement of a previously reinforced behavior is discontinued. Used in this way, extinction reduces behaviors that were previously maintained by positive and negative reinforcement and by naturally occurring sensory consequences.

Withholding reinforcers may easily be misused and may be seen as a student rights violation. Therefore, extinction should be used only after extensive consultation and only with administrative approval.

## ▶ Generalization

Generalization means that skills learned in one set of antecedent conditions subsequently are used under different antecedent conditions. For example, skills learned in a classroom can be generalized to other appropriate environments outside the classroom. This principle of behavior means that each skill does not have to be taught in each new environment where it could be used. Generalization can be promoted by having the students thoroughly practice each skill and by conducting the practice under conditions that simulate the student's real environments (e.g. home, other classrooms, sports practices, recreation areas.). You can effectively promote generalization by monitoring how children are behaving in a variety of situations. This feedback, whether it be first- or second-hand observations, can give you opportunities to reinforce your students for generalizing appropriate behavior to new settings.

# ▶ Discrimination

Discrimination means that changes in the antecedent conditions produce changes in behavior. In this sense, discrimination is the opposite of generalization. Discrimination means that a behavior is used only under certain circumstances but not under other, different circumstances. For example, if a youth uses slang with his friends, but uses proper grammar when talking with a teacher, he has appropriately discriminated between those situations. Similarly, aggression that is appropriate in an athletic contest is not appropriate in the classroom.

Much of the teaching done by educators not only helps students learn new skills but also teaches them where and under what conditions certain behaviors are appropriate. Teaching youth behavioral discrimination is crucial. They must learn to notice the environmental cues that call for different sets of behavior.

# ▶ Summary

The principles of behavior discussed in this chapter form the foundation of the Boys Town Education Model and its Motivation Systems.

Learning and applying these principles of behaviors will help reduce problems in your classrooms and help students change some difficult behavior problems. By changing these maladaptive skills into prosocial behaviors, you are giving students a chance for success in their classrooms as well as success in their lives.

# CHAPTER SIX

# Overview of motivation systems

**M**otivating students to do well in school is a challenging task. The difficulty of the task increases considerably when students have a history of school failure, require specialized treatment, or have significant behavior problems.

At Boys Town, we have developed a system which complements an educator's personal skills and abilities. It has its roots in the proven technology of the Boys Town Family Home Program, which utilizes a token economy and contingency management in conjunction with specific teaching to change behavior. The Boys Town Education Model is an adaptation of these methods and it currently is helping educators and students across the nation set and achieve educationally relevant behavioral goals.

As noted earlier, the Boys Town Education Model is divided into four main components: the Social Skills Curriculum, Teaching Interactions, Motivation Systems, and Administrative Intervention. Each component serves to help students change their past inappropriate behaviors and maintain or increase appropriate behaviors.

Although nearly all students can benefit from social skills instruction, most do not need the added structure of the Motivation Systems. Certain students, however, have difficulty changing their behavior without the support of such a system. Most of these students are in self-contained special education classrooms because their past behavior patterns resulted in their removal from a regular classroom setting. Others may still be in the mainstream of regular education to some extent, but may not be responding to the usual contingencies set up for rule infractions or violations. These include losing recess or free time, changes in seat assignment, in-school suspension, and out-of-school suspension. For these students, using the Motivation Systems can provide additional incentive to change their behavior patterns.

The Motivation Systems used in the Boys Town Education model are Daily Points, Progress, and Merit. All students start on Daily Points, the most structured and restrictive system. Through improved behavior, students can move from Daily Points to Progress, then Merit. The ultimate goal is to fade out the systems entirely so the students are responding to the natural consequences and social cues in their environment.

Each level of the Motivation Systems is thoroughly explained to the students — there are no "hidden agendas." Students are aware of the expectations, consequences, and goals for each level. They also are aware of what they need to do to move to the next level. Once prosocial skills are being used consistently, students may look forward to being fully mainstreamed.

## ▶ Benefits of using a multilevel system

A multilevel system allows you to individualize your teaching by varying the amount of attention and instruction given to each student. You can provide different degrees of structure to students depending on their academic and social needs. You can consistently and systematically give each student an appropriate amount of correction and rein-

forcement to obtain desired results. This same flexibility usually is not available when single-level systems are used.

A multilevel system also provides clear goals to students, teachers, and others. Students know what they need to do to improve their skills and can tell at a glance how they are progressing. Expectations for behavior and methods for moving to the less-restrictive levels of the system are consistent and known in advance. A multilevel system has a prescribed method of addressing problems, a plan to teach new skills, and a way to document the amount of teaching done with each student.

Parents, or other caregivers, benefit because they receive daily communication from the school, which tells them how well their child is meeting his or her goals. They also are told how their child is getting along in the classroom and with other students. One major advantage to parents is that they receive positive as well as negative information about the student. This helps create a positive communication link between the school and the home.

Multilevel systems allow teachers to objectively make decisions about each student. The documentation of teaching helps to evaluate program effectiveness while still meeting the goals of Individual Education Plans. Such ongoing assessment helps keep the assistance and support to each student at an optimum level. Many of the decisions related to goals and progress are based on collected data, thereby reducing the need for arbitrary decisions or subjective opinions.

A multilevel system also helps maintain consistent classroom management. Teachers don't need to worry about the overwhelming task of simultaneously managing a variety of motivation plans (e.g. star or sticker charts or tangible reinforcers). Since reinforcers are readily available in the Motivation Systems, teachers can immediately attend to behavior. This helps correct small problems before they escalate and allows reinforcement of desirable behavior so that it can be maintained or further developed.

Having a multilevel system allows students to move at an individual pace toward the goal of reintegration into a regular classroom. It enhances student ownership of progress through the systems toward reintegration because of the objective, data-driven means for moving to less restrictive levels. The student also develops independence by having the artificial consequences and support gradually decreased over time.

# ▶ **W**hy use a token system?

The Motivation Systems use a type of token economy. Although token economies can take many forms, they all have some common elements — tokens are earned or lost depending on the student's behavior and can be exchanged for reinforcers. The Boys Town Motivation Systems' economy uses points as its general means of exchange. Students earn points for appropriate behaviors and lose points for inappropriate behaviors. The number of available points is unlimited; there is no ceiling on the number of points that can be earned or lost.

Students use their points to purchase privileges, tangible items, and bonds. Bonds are the means by which students move from one system level to the next. For a detailed discussion of how and what students may buy with their points, see Chapter 19, "Menus and Purchasing."

There are several advantages to using a point system instead of directly giving and taking away privileges or tangibles. Many of these advantages reflect the basic principles of reinforcement described in Chapter 5, "Principles of Behavior." These advantages, which reflect the basic principles of reinforcement, include:

## Points can be given immediately and as frequently as necessary.

This means students are receiving reinforcement as they engage in a behavior, which makes the reinforcement more powerful. Privileges and tangibles are not always available for immediate use and often are difficult to deliver frequently.

## Point amounts can vary in size to match the behavior.

Subtle or small behaviors may earn or lose only a small number of points while significant behaviors may earn or lose many points. Judgments about how hard or easy a behavior is for a particular student also will determine the number of points involved. Although it is difficult or sometimes impossible to break privileges or tangibles down into smaller parts, assigning a point value that matches the behavior is quite easy.

Assigning small point values to individual steps or components of a skill allow you to shape a student's behavior. That is, you can decide which behaviors or steps to reinforce and then deliver small consequences on a frequent basis to encourage a change in behavior. This same approach is very difficult to achieve when using privileges directly.

## Tokens are easy to use and record.

Students carry cards on which they record positive and negative points. Each type of card has specific areas for recording the number of points earned or lost for the corresponding behavior. The process takes only a few minutes, yet gives you and the student valuable information regarding how well he or she did each day.

## Teachers don't have to come up with "creative consequences."

Many teachers have spent a great deal of time trying to find consequences that will change a youth's negative behavior or motivate the youth to do well in school. Sometimes, a student's rights may be violated in the process. Consequences such as picking up every piece of trash in the school, cleaning every desktop, or kneeling on rice may have been designed to "teach the kid a lesson," but more than likely the short-term gains will be outweighed by the long-term effects of punishment. (See Chapter 5, "Principles of Behavior.")

## Token systems help keep students from becoming "satiated" by privileges or other reinforcers.

Although students need to be conditioned to points (i.e. learn their value), points eventually become more powerful than any single privilege because they, like money, represent all privileges. This is especially true when children are able to choose their own reinforcers from a privilege "menu," since students tend to work harder to obtain something they want and can choose for themselves.

## ▶ Using the Motivation Systems effectively

Points have value for the youth only if they can be exchanged for something the student wants. In a classroom, points are like money. The more points students earn, the more things they can buy. These privileges are the real reinforcers for the youth; points are simply the medium of exchange.

In order for the Motivation Systems to remain strong, privileges must be contingent on earning points. That is, students must earn positive points in order to receive the privileges they desire. When privileges are given outside the Motivation System, the economy is weakened. Again, comparison can be made between points and money. Money is a powerful motivator for most people. But, if people could get what they wanted without money, its worth and the need to earn it would diminish rapidly.

Likewise, the reinforcing power of points hinges on keeping the point system as the source for desired privileges. If students can buy what they want only by earning points, they will work to earn those points.

Points are consequences for behavior, and consequences are important in changing behavior. However, points do not work by themselves. **You do the real work**. Your attention and ability to provide structure through teaching in a caring, consistent environment are the real keys to creating and maintaining an effective point system.

## ▶ The Daily Points System

The first level of the Motivation Systems is Daily Points. All students begin on this level, which is considered the **skill-acquisition** stage. While on Daily Points, students learn basic skills and appropriate alternatives to past behavior problems. At this stage, it is expected that students will make mistakes because their behavioral repertoires are still largely undeveloped. Students and teachers should view "mistakes" as learning opportunities — chances for the student to recognize errors and learn better ways of responding to situations or expressing their needs.

The Daily Points System is highly individualized and interactive. Each student has areas targeted for improvement and the points earned for certain behaviors may vary from student to student. Corrective feedback and positive reinforcement are given frequently. For example, in a self-contained classroom, your goal should be to have 25-30 interactions with each student each day. About 50 to 60 percent of these interactions

should be related to skills you have targeted. Point consequences, both positive and negative, are given immediately. Each student carries a point card, where points are recorded.

Your interactions with students on the Daily Points System should meet or exceed a 4:1 positive-to-negative ratio. In other words, if a student earns negative points for an inappropriate behavior, you should find at least four opportunities to interact positively with that student during the day. This may seem difficult, especially when the student misbehaves frequently, but it certainly is not impossible. You'll need to closely watch the student for small signs of progress, and praise these attempts. The more opportunities you can find to teach a skill, the more likely the student is to learn and use it.

## ▶ The Progress System

The second level of the Motivation Systems is the Progress System. Students on Progress are considered to be in the **fluency-building** stage of skill development. Students on Progress should be demonstrating frequent use of the basic skills they learned while on Daily Points. They no longer should need the immediacy of point exchanges and should manage their behavior more successfully. Although teachers still provide a high level of social skills instruction, students receive pluses or minuses to reflect the nature of the behavior instead of earning or losing points on the spot. The positive and negative marks are divided into major, moderate, and minor categories which indicate the effort required by the student behavior. At the end of each day, the teacher and student negotiate the number of points earned by the student by evaluating the number and degree of positive and negative marks on the card. The target areas for the following day are discussed and entered on the next day's card. Students should be demonstrating many more appropriate behaviors than they did on the Daily Points System.

## ▶ The Merit System

The Merit System, the final level of the Motivation Systems, reflects increased fading of the artificial system and movement toward the **goal of mainstreaming**. The student should appear fluent and "natural" with a broad range of the social skills. Internalization of rationales and anticipation of natural or logical consequences help the youth generalize when to use the skill in other settings. The primary goal of the Merit System is to get the student "off card" and to respond to consequences in the regular classroom. Merit students should enjoy the benefits of increased privileges and independence in school, thereby preparing them for the responsibility of mainstreaming.

The Merit System may be the most difficult level because students have fewer structured interactions with you. Rather, it is based on naturally occurring social reinforcement. Students continue to receive points while they are on the card, but they are awarded noncontingently.

## ▶ Summary

The structure of the Motivation Systems and token economy has been carefully designed to meet each student's changing needs. Through consistent teaching and use of the systems, teachers should find students making continual progress toward their behavioral goals.

# CHAPTER SEVEN

# Teaching the curriculum skills

In order for members of a society to successfully coexist, they behave in certain, agreed upon ways. Those who cannot or do not "fit" within the range of expected behavioral patterns are viewed as deviant, irresponsible, or less intelligent than the "norm." Social skills allow us to pass as normal (Greenspan, 1979) and fit within the mainstream of society.

For many children, school can be the biggest challenge in their lives. Not only do they worry about academic success, but also about how well they make friends and get along with peers and teachers. Their ability to be a part of the school "culture" may overshadow most other aspects of school life.

Children with deficient social skills are more likely to experience difficulties in school and beyond. Children having diffi-culty with certain kinds of social behavior, especially skills related to paying attention, persevering at tasks, volunteering answers, and communicating with teachers, may be at risk for academic failure (Stephens, 1978) and peer acceptance problems (Schneider & Byrne, 1984). The link between poor social skills and many other problems also is clear. Gresham (1981) found that children with social skill deficits experienced a variety of problems, including aggressive and antisocial behavior, juvenile delinquency, learning problems and school failure, mental health disorders, and loneliness and despondency. Since such deficits greatly affect a student's level of success in the regular classroom, these "nonacademic" factors often outweigh academic abilities when determining the appropriateness and overall success of mainstreaming efforts (Downing, Simpson, & Myles, 1990).

There is evidence that social and behavioral deficiencies that are not corrected in childhood frequently carry over into adulthood (Steinberg & Knitzer, 1992), and that without appropriate and sufficient opportunities to learn functional social skills, children will fail to correct the deficiencies on their own (Stephens, 1978).

Meadows, Neel, Parker, and Timo (1991) report that adults who had social skill deficits as children suffered long-term effects ranging from higher rates of suicide to unsuccessful employment histories. Problems such as arguing with one's supervisor and being unable to work with others reflect poor social skill acquisition and use.

The teaching of social skills, then, becomes imperative if we truly are committed to helping students achieve success in school and beyond. Teachers are a powerful influence on children, at times serving as their sole role models of acceptable social behavior. Historically, teachers have not engaged in purposeful teaching of social skills, but it has often existed as a "hidden curriculum" in that they set standards and hold students accountable for meeting them. Without a certain number of rules and expectations, classrooms couldn't run successfully. Without behavioral guidelines, group teaching would be impossible.

Unfortunately, many of our rules, guidelines, and expectations serve to control the behavior of students instead of empowering them to make responsible decisions. Although we need a certain number of compliance-based rules or skills to ensure smooth classroom operation, we can achieve the greatest good by helping students learn to make responsible choices about their own behavior. Doing so provides them with tools for meeting future challenges, in addition to helping them succeed in school today.

When a student is in the early stages of learning skills, a considerable amount of compliance is required in order for him or her to understand and benefit from your teaching. The student needs the "building blocks" of the basic skills to develop the higher-level skills that lead to self-reliance and self-efficacy. Once students begin to experience success using the basic skills you've taught, their beliefs about their capabilities to use those skills start to change. These beliefs or judgments about our abilities to influence the events that impact our lives are critical to our successes — more so than our actual skill levels (Mager, 1992). By giving students the basic tools of social interaction, we can shape success experiences and help them utilize learned skills to broaden and deepen their social skill repertoire.

## ▶ The Social Skills Curriculum

As described in Chapter 1, the Boys Town Education Model is made up of four components: Social Skills, Teaching Interactions, Motivation Systems, and Administrative Intervention. The Social Skills component tells us what to teach, while the Teaching Interactions and Administrative Intervention processes provide the vehicle for teaching.

Combs and Slaby (1977) have defined a social skill as "the ability to interact with others... in ways that are socially accepted or valued and at the same time are personally beneficial or beneficial primarily to others." In other words, a social skill is something that helps a person get along with others in ways that match the values of the society and that benefits that person or others.

Sixteen skills comprise the Boys Town Social Skills Curriculum. They encompass four main areas: Adult Relations, Peer Relations, School Rules, and Classroom Behaviors. The 16 skills are divided into two categories, **Basic** and **Advanced**.

## Basic skills

How to follow instructions

How to accept criticism or a consequence

How to accept "No" for an answer

How to greet someone

How to get the teacher's attention

How to make a request

How to disagree appropriately

## Advanced skills

How to give negative feedback

How to resist peer pressure (or say "No")

How to apologize

How to engage in a conversation

How to give a compliment

How to accept a compliment

How to volunteer

How to report peer behavior

How to introduce yourself

The seven basic skills have been designated as "basic" because of their level of complexity and because they come into play so frequently during the course of any given day. Since a large percentage of our daily social interactions are covered by these basic skills, they often are referred to as critical skills. Mastering these seven skills, along with "How to Engage in a Conversation," could significantly impact a student's ability to succeed in school. If students can adequately perform in these areas, they'll not only avoid considerable conflict with adults and peers, but also will have some prosocial skills that will enable them to make and keep friends. This does not mean that other skills are less important than the seven basic ones. The main difference is that basic skills might be used more often. Certainly, students need to know how to apologize and how to introduce themselves to others, but they probably will face more situations in which they will need to know how to greet others or accept criticism.

Each skill has been divided into discrete and observable steps. All 16 skills are outlined below. By limiting the number of steps in each skill and making sure that each step is measurable and observable, students will clearly understand what is expected of them and will be more successful using the skills. Teachers should teach skills consistently (i.e. using the same skill steps each time) in order to make student learning easier and to avoid confusion. This becomes especially important when students have more than one teacher instructing them in the Social Skills Curriculum.

# ▶ Teaching the Curriculum Skills

## Basic skills

### How to follow instructions

1. Look at the person.
2. Say "Okay."
3. Do the task immediately.
4. Check back.

### How to accept criticism or consequence

1. Look at the person.
2. Say "Okay."
3. No arguing.

### How to accept "No" for an answer

1. Look at the person.
2. Say "Okay."
3. No arguing, whining, or pouting.
4. If you don't understand why, calmly ask for a reason.
5. If you disagree or have a complaint, bring it up later.

### How to greet someone

1. Look at the person and smile.
2. Use a pleasant voice tone.
3. State your name and say "Hello."
4. Shake the person's hand.

### How to get the teacher's attention

1. Look at the person.
2. Raise hand.
3. Wait for acknowledgment.
4. After acknowledgment, ask question in a quiet voice tone.

### How to make a request

1. Look at the person.
2. Use a pleasant voice tone.
3. State request specifically.
4. Say "Please."
5. Say "Thank you" after the request is granted.

### How to disagree appropriately

1. Look at the person.
2. Use a pleasant voice tone.
3. Make an empathy or concern statement.
4. State disagreement specifically.
5. Give a reason.
6. Say "Thank you."

## Advanced skills

### How to give negative feedback

1. Look at the person.
2. Use a calm voice tone.
3. Make a positive statement or give praise.
4. State the problem specifically.
5. Give a reason why it's a problem.

6. Offer a solution.

7. Thank the person for listening.

## How to resist peer pressure (or say "No")

1. Look at the person.

2. Use a calm voice tone.

3. Thank the person or persons for including you.

4. Explain that you do not want to participate.

5. Offer an alternative activity.

6. If necessary, continue to refuse to participate.

## How to apologize

1. Look at the person.

2. Use a pleasant voice tone.

3. Make a specific statement of remorse.

4. State a plan for future appropriate behavior.

5. Ask the person to accept your apology.

## How to engage in a conversation

1. Look at the person.

2. Use a pleasant voice tone.

3. Ask the person questions.

4. Don't interrupt.

5. Follow up the person's answers with a comment, but don't change the subject.

## How to give a compliment

1. Look at the person.

2. Smile.

3. Use a pleasant voice tone.

4. Make a positive praise statement.

## How to accept a compliment

1. Look at the person.

2. Smile.

3. Use a pleasant voice tone.

4. Say "Thank you."

5. Do not disagree with the compliment.

## How to volunteer

1. Look at the person.

2. Use a pleasant voice tone.

3. Ask the person if you can help.

4. Specifically state the task you are volunteering to do.

5. Give a reason or benefit.

## How to report peer behavior

1. Look at the person.

2. Use a calm voice tone.

3. Ask to speak to the adult privately.

4. Give a specific description of the inappropriate behavior.

5. State the reason for the report.

6. Suggest possible solution or consequences.

7. Thank the adult for listening.

## How to introduce yourself

1. Look at the person.

2. Smile.

3. Use a pleasant voice tone.

4. State your name.

5. Shake hands with the person.

6. When departing, say, "It was nice to meet you."

Remember that not all of the expected behaviors may be clearly spelled out in the steps of each skill. Some specific teaching regarding the quality of a student's voice, the manner in which he or she uses eye contact, and other "paraskill" behaviors may be necessary to enhance a student's success. In other words, when teaching a social skill to a student, you need to teach the individual steps that make up the skill and the various behaviors that make up each step. For example:

## How to follow instructions

### Step
Look at the person.

### Behavior
Look directly at the person without glaring or making faces.

### Step
Say "Okay."

### Behavior
Answer right away. Speak clearly without sounding angry.

### Step
Do the task immediately.

### Behavior
Start doing the task within two or three seconds. Keep at the task until it's done. Ask for help if there are problems.

### Step
Check back.

### Behavior
Report what was done as soon as the task is completed. Correct anything that needs to be done again.

An excellent source for defining exact expectations for a variety of social skills is *Teaching Social Skills to Youth : A Curriculum for Child-Care Providers* (Dowd & Tierney, 1992). Many of the behavioral examples presented in this chapter were drawn from that text.

Although the Social Skills Curriculum consists of 16 skills, you can teach any skill by task-analyzing it and teaching it in a step-by-step manner. Start by deciding what you want the student to do. That is, begin with the end in mind. Once you know your end product, determine exactly what behaviors need to be included to get the desired result. Make sure each step is observable so you can tell whether the student is meeting your expectations. Include only critical steps, as you don't want the skill to be so long that neither you nor the student can remember all the components. For example, you may come up with the following steps for a skill you call "How to Be On Task":

1. Begin working as soon as assignment is given.

2. Continue working until assignment is completed or time runs out.

3. Get the teacher's attention appropriately if you need help or complete your work.

Remember that the level of skill performance will vary among students, depending upon their skill levels and target areas. You might expect a Merit student to respond to criticism by following the skill steps exactly, but your tolerances for a student who is just beginning the program would most likely be quite a bit different. For example, you may accept a new Daily Points student's response of rolling his eyes and looking away while hearing criticism if he previously argued loudly and turned away from you. His new behaviors indicate considerable improvement and progress. Even though the behavior does not match your "ultimate" expectations, you can continue to shape the student's behavior by individualizing your teaching.

## ▶ Introducing the Social Skills Curriculum

A social skills program can be taught like any other curriculum. Each skill should be taught individually at a neutral time (see Chapter 11, "Preventive Teaching") to help students experience success and gain fluency with the skills. At the same time, your students will be engaged in "on-the-job" training since you'll be addressing behaviors as they occur.

Prioritize your skills instruction by assessing the needs of your students. Skills that must be used frequently or are in need of improvement will probably be among the first ones you'll focus on. Keep in mind that the value of any social skill may vary according to who is assessing its importance. Your level of interest in fostering development of certain social skills may be much higher than that of your students. Whereas you may view a particular skill as central to effective classroom operation (for example, "How to Accept 'No'"), your students may have a different point of view. They may feel their status among their peers is endangered by performing the skill steps you've outlined. So, the manner in which you select and teach social skills should take the child's perspective into consideration, along with your own, for greatest impact and effectiveness (Dowd & Tierney, 1992).

Following your needs assessment, you'll teach the social skills much like you would any other content area. To be effective, you'll teach and practice the skills, then assess, redirect, and reinforce student efforts. By setting aside a regular block of time to preteach and practice skills, you'll send the message to students that learning social skills is as important as any other subject in school.

Equally critical to the success of the program is your consistent follow-up with each student. Immediate and contingent reinforcement and Corrective Teaching emphasize the importance of the Social Skills Curriculum and take advantage of the "teachable moment." Addressing behavior as it occurs enhances the learning environment by making the learning relevant and immediate.

Remember that praise should occur four times as often as Corrective Teaching for change to take place most quickly. Noticing positive behaviors not only sends the message that you are aware of the "good" things your students do, but also helps you build and maintain relationships with each student.

When teaching social skills, **your** behavior is extremely important. Whether praising appropriate behavior or effort, or teaching alternatives to inappropriate behavior, your demeanor and disposition should be supportive and calm. Establishing eye contact with the student, using the student's name, maintaining a pleasant or neutral voice tone and facial expression, placing yourself on the student's physical plane (i.e. both sitting or both standing), and keeping a comfortable distance between you and the student all contribute to the quality of the interaction. Your behavior sets the tone of the interaction and greatly impacts the outcome of your attempts to teach social skills. (See Chapter 10, "Effective Praise," for additional discussion.)

Finally, use the teaching techniques described in Chapters 11 through 14 to effectively motivate behavioral change. The sequences are designed to facilitate social skills learning by maintaining a teaching focus. Without each of the specific components, your interactions could become vague, irrelevant, or punitive. If you remember that the emphasis is on teaching, your chances of impacting students' behavior improve considerably. Clear, consistent social skills teaching, like clear and consistent academic teaching, can only increase the likelihood of student learning.

## ▶ Summary

The 16 skills in the Boys Town Education Model form the basic curriculum for teaching social behavior. Skills are made up of a number of observable steps and are categorized as Basic or Advanced. Any behavior can be broken down into components and taught in a systematic manner to meet each student's needs. Skills should be taught preventively so that students know what a teacher's expectations are, and in response to behaviors as they occur. Teaching sequences and strategies will be presented in later chapters.

# CHAPTER EIGHT

# Observing and describing behavior

The foundation of effective teaching is the ability to observe and describe behavior. This skill helps you determine what effect you have on your students and how their behavior affects you. It also helps you identify what skills to teach students and what behaviors make up each skill.

The goal of observing and describing behavior is to accurately verbalize what is happening in a given situation. In fact, the best descriptions are those that mirror a person's behavior so clearly that the behavior could be repeated or reenacted by someone who hadn't observed the behavior firsthand.

Changing the inappropriate behaviors of students and teaching new, appropriate behaviors is made easier by the ability to observe and describe behavior.

## ▶ Observing behavior

The first step in observing and describing any behavior is to watch and listen carefully. Determine who was involved in the situation and attend specifically to the following areas:

**What the person is doing**. Look at both large and small body movements, such as running, walking, kicking, throwing, hand gestures, and body posture.

**Facial expressions** help you determine a student's feelings. Look for expressions — smiles, scowls, grimaces, stares, or rolling of the eyes or eye contact.

**What the person is saying**. Listen carefully to specific words and how they are said. Tone of voice and inflection can sometimes be better indicators of what a youth is feeling than the words that are used. Also notice giggles, groans, moans, or sighs.

**Frequency, intensity, and duration of the behavior**. These characteristics often determine whether a behavior is appropriate or inappropriate. Laughing with a friend in the hallway may be appropriate; laughing with a friend during study hall may be inappropriate. Monitor whether the behavior occurs too frequently or not frequently enough, whether it escalates in intensity, and whether it lasts too long or not long enough.

**When and where the behavior occurs**. What events and circumstances happen before the event takes place? What time of day does it occur and where does it take place?

**The absence of behavior**. Was there a behavior that should have occurred but did not? For example, did the student fail to look at another person during conversation, or not answer a question when asked, or fail to raise his hand before speaking in class?

▶ **Describing behavior**

After closely observing behaviors, begin forming a mental picture of what occurred – almost like an instant replay of the behavior. Your goal is to describe what happened as accurately as possible. Concentrate solely on what behaviors occurred. An accurate picture of the situation is needed before any successful intervention is attempted. Don't make any judgments on a student's intentions or motives.

Make your descriptions:

1. Specific

2. Behavioral

3. Objective

**Specific** — Avoid using adjectives that are general or vague. You may feel a student has a "bad attitude," but what behaviors did the student engage in that gave you this impression? Similarly, a "good job," may indicate general satisfaction, but what specifically was good about it? The goal of being specific is to give students messages that are easily understood and that convey exactly what you mean. A "good job" may be more accurately described as using complete sentences on an essay test, completing a difficult classroom assignment on time, or putting all supplies where they belong without being prompted. The more specific you can be, the more the student is likely to understand, thereby having the opportunity to repeat positive behavior or change negative behavior.

One way to describe behavior accurately is to concentrate on using action verbs instead of adjectives. For example, terms like "You ran," "You growled," or "You yelled" describe actions and are easy to understand. They are not as open to interpretation as descriptions that rely solely on adjectives, e.g. good, bad, unfriendly, antisocial, etc.

**Behavioral** — Break behaviors down into specific components. For example, being "antisocial" could be described as not speaking when spoken to, not joining in study groups with other students, not going to extracurricular events, and so on. In this way, the student has three specific areas where he or she could learn new social skills.

**Objective** — Judgmental terms can harm a relationship by damaging a student's self-esteem or triggering an emotional reaction. Terms like "stupid," "bad," and "terrible" should be avoided. Also, keep any negative emotions under control. Concentrate on using a calm, matter-of-fact approach when describing behavior. Stay objective and students will be more likely to view you as concerned, pleasant, and fair. For example, instead of saying, "You were disrespectful to me," you could say, "When I asked you for your book, you scowled and gestured with your finger."

When describing verbal behavior, you may sometimes need to repeat exactly what a student says (within ethical and moral limits, of course). If you cannot offer an exact quote, begin your description with "You said something like...." Carefully and specifically describing verbal behavior helps you remain objective and concentrate on observable events and behaviors.

## ▶ When to observe and describe behavior

Naturally, observing and describing behavior is an ongoing process whenever you are working with your students. However, there are times when you will want to "zero in" on certain behaviors. These times include:

**When the student's behavior is inappropriate.** This could include any form of misbehavior or problem behavior, such as not following an instruction, arguing, or complaining.

**When the student's behavior is particularly appropriate.** This is a special time to "catch 'em being good" — to focus on behavior that you want to occur again. Many of us usually are so locked in to dealing only with problem behaviors that we often neglect to find something to praise and then tell the student about it. Describing what your students are doing correctly helps develop relationships and reinforce positive behavior.

**When you want to teach a new skill.** Describing new behaviors helps students learn quicker and progress through academic and social curricula more rapidly. And, after teaching a skill, accurately describing what was done — both correctly and incorrectly — gives the student feedback on his or her performance that is valuable in internalizing the skill you are teaching.

The ability to observe and describe behavior is a valuable skill. Accurate, objective descriptions help establish expectations and ensure successful and comfortable learning experiences for the student.

## ▶ Integrating behavioral descriptions and skill labels into the Teaching Interaction

**The Teaching Interaction** — a nine-step method used at Boys Town to teach skills to youth — will be explained in detail in Chapter 12. For now, it is important to present an explanation of how observing and describing behaviors fits into this teaching method. Clearly describing behavior and labeling skills help you teach your students a great deal in a short time. Clear, behavioral descriptions and skill labels are integrated into most of the components of Teaching Interactions.

An example of using skill labels and behavioral descriptions in the first four steps of a Teaching Interaction follows. Learning how to specifically describe behavior and label skills while using these steps will provide clear, focused, and non-judgmental teaching to your students. Explanations for each step also are provided.

### Example

**Situation:** Chris, a new student, is working on the computer during study hour. His teacher asks Chris to open the window to let some fresh air into the classroom. Chris sighs, doesn't look at the teacher, but gets up and walks to the window. The use of the first four components might sound something like this:

### Initial praise or empathy

**Teacher:** *"Chris, you did a good job of getting right up to open the window. I know it's hard to follow instructions sometimes, especially when you're working on the computer."*

**Explanation:** Specific, descriptive praise was given for "getting right up...." The general skill was identified in the context of the empathy statement, "I know it's hard to follow instructions...." Whenever possible, the initial praise should be related to behaviors that are part of the skill that is being praised or taught.

### Description of the inappropriate behavior

**Teacher:** *"But just now when I gave you that instruction, you sighed and you didn't look at me or say anything to let me know you heard or that you would help out."*

**Explanation:** Note that the general skill category of "Following Instructions" is repeated and the observed inappropriate behavior is described. Also, note that the teacher avoids vague and judgmental descriptions such as, "You weren't very cooperative..." or "You didn't seem too happy when I asked you to...."

### Consequences

**Teacher:** *"So please take out your school card; you have earned 1,000 negative points for not following instructions. In a few minutes, you'll have a chance to earn some of those points back by practicing how to follow instructions."*

**Explanation:** The use of the consequence provides an opportunity to clearly and concisely label the skill and the behaviors that are the focus of the interaction. It also indicates that the youth can earn back some of the points by practicing the skill.

### Description of the appropriate behavior

**Teacher:** *"Chris, let's talk about following instructions. Whenever anyone gives you an instruction, whether it's a teacher, your parents, or your employer, there are several things you should do. You need to look at the person and answer him or her by saying 'Okay' or 'Sure' to let the person know you're listening and will follow through. Be sure to ask questions if you don't understand. Do the task and then check back with the person when it's completed."*

**Explanation:** The teacher helps the youth generalize the skill to other situations by explaining the antecedent condition, "Whenever anyone gives you an instruction...." Then, the teacher provides a step-by-step, behavioral description to help the student learn the skill. During an actual interaction, the teacher would pause frequently to ask the student if he or she understands, has any questions, etc.

## ▶ Summary

Educators can be pleasant and effective by following the guidelines for describing behavior (carefully observing antecedents, behavior, and consequences); labeling skills and describing the behaviors related to them; and skillfully integrating these techniques into the components of the Teaching Interaction.

# CHAPTER NINE

# Rationales

Many students don't understand the relationship between their behaviors and the consequences or outcomes of their behaviors. That is why supplying rationales for students plays such an important part in the teaching you do.

A rationale, by definition, is a fundamental reason. We use rationales in many ways everyday to convince ourselves or others of the benefits or drawbacks of maintaining or changing a behavior. For example, the rationale for practicing a sport is that you probably will do better in a game. The rationale for being on time for work is that your employer may take that into consideration when deciding whether to give you a raise. The rationale for dieting is that you may lose weight.

The Boys Town Education Model uses rationales to explain to students how a behavior is linked to its results. In a Teaching Interaction, a rationale is a statement that describes the possible benefits or negative consequences a youth might receive from engaging in a certain behavior. It also may point out the effect the behavior could have on others. For example, you might tell a student that the reason she should study hard is to improve her grades. A student who is calling other children names might be told that no one will want to play with him if the name-calling continues. Or, you might tell a youngster he should follow instructions so he can save time, and have more free time to do fun things.

To maximize the effect rationales can have on behavior, they should generally focus on the benefits of behaving appropriately or refraining from inappropriate behavior. By identifying students' goals and tailoring rationales to match these goals, you can powerfully impact student behavior. For example, if a student is motivated to improve her grades, a teacher may provide the rationale that accepting (and implementing) feedback about assignments may help her master the content and receive higher grades on tests or future assignments. For the student whose present goal is to drop out of school as soon as possible, however, such a rationale wouldn't be meaningful. Rather, rationales for staying in school that are related to getting a job or daily living issues would be more appropriate.

Rationales that emphasize negative consequences are occasionally necessary. For example, pointing out the negative outcomes associated with fighting may be the most meaningful and direct tie to the behavior. Frequent use, however, could make the rationales begin to sound like warnings or threats. Positive rationales usually work better to encourage appropriate behavior.

## ▶ Importance of rationales

Many children do not fully understand the relationship between their behavior and subsequent events. For example, D.S. Eitzen (1974) conducted a survey of the attitudes of predelinquent and delinquent adolescents and found that they didn't understand that their behavior determines what happens to them. Instead, they often see themselves as "victims of fate," or blame other people for their problems (Jones & Jones, 1990). For example, a student who gets

caught cheating on a test and consequently suffers a failing grade may blame the teacher for catching him or her rather than seeing the consequence as a logical outcome of the behavior. The relationships between events must be carefully taught. By using rationales, you can help students understand the link between their behavior and the various consequences that may result (Downs, Black, & Kutsick, 1985) and shift the locus of behavior control from outside "forces" to the student.

## ▶ Types of rationales

Rationales fall into three main categories: benefits to the students, negative outcomes, and concern for or the effect on others. In general, rationales that focus on benefits or positive outcomes are the most meaningful to students, so they should be used more frequently than others. Certain situations, however, may dictate the use of a negative outcome rationale, as was discussed earlier in this chapter. Ultimately, your goal for all students is to teach them to consider the implications of their behavior on others. As such, you need to work toward incorporating rationales that focus on concern for others. At the same time, you must understand that this type of rationale initially may have little or no impact on a student.

A benefits rationale answers the questions of "What's in it for me?" or "How can it help me?" These may reflect the benefits or positive outcomes that might logically occur when a student engages in appropriate behavior or avoids engaging in inappropriate behavior. For example, a benefit statement may be, "When you can get a teacher's attention appropriately, you'll be more likely to get the help you need quickly and can then finish your work faster." A rationale for avoiding inappropriate behavior might sound like, "When you don't tease others, they're more likely to want to be around you and include you in games or activities." Both subtypes of rationales point out a potential gain or benefit to the student. Benefits rationales, as mentioned earlier, tend to be the most powerful or meaningful to children. This is especially true for students who are less developmentally mature or who are new to a social skills program.

A negative consequences rationale, on the other hand, states the potential negative outcomes associated with engaging in inappropriate behavior. "How can I be hurt?" or "What price might I have to pay?" are questions that are answered by a negative consequences rationale. Examples include: "When you don't turn assignments in, you get further behind, your grade drops, and you could even fail the class," or "If you argue when you're corrected, you may not get the help you need and may repeat the same mistakes," or "If you don't smile and return someone's greeting, the person may think you're unfriendly or rude, and may begin to avoid you instead of trying to be your friend." Although negative consequences are sometimes the most logical ones to point out, frequent use may be interpreted as verbal warnings or threats. This type of rationale, therefore, should be used selectively.

A concern-for-others rationale states the effects a youth's behavior may have on other people. In addition to teaching care and respect for those who could be affected by the student's actions, this type of rationale incorporates the notion of consideration for the rights and property of others. Examples include: "If you call out to get a teacher's attention, you could disturb others who are trying to complete their assignments," and "When you tease other students, they may take you seriously and their feelings could be hurt." As mentioned earlier, concern-for-others rationales may not be effective at first. Many students, because of age, developmental level, or personal needs, are unable to consider the rights, feelings, or needs of others. Therefore, a gradual introduction of this type of rationale into the teaching process, especially as the child is demonstrating behavioral gains, may be the most effective approach.

## ▶ Benefits of rationales

Although the most important reason for using rationales may be that they help teach the relationships between behaviors and resulting consequences, there are other benefits.

Using rationales also helps adults build positive relationships with children. Pikas (1961) and Willner, Braukmann, Kirigin, Fixsen, Phillips, and Wolf (1977) found that youth prefer adults who give rationales and explanations with their disciplinary requests. For example, the statement, "You can't watch television right now because your homework is not finished," contains a rationale; a youngster would prefer it over, "You can't watch television right now."

Rationales also can help with compliance. Elder (1963) found that youngsters are more likely to comply with their parents' requests if the parents provide explanations for their rules and requests. For example, a parent might say, "If you save your money from your paper route, then together we can buy you a new bike." This statement contains a rationale implying that the youngster cannot have a new bicycle now and why he or she should save money. Elder also found that when parents provided rationales for rules and requests, their children were more likely to be more confident in their own ideas and opinions. This confidence, along with the youngsters' understanding of the relationship between their behavior and the consequences, can help youth make better decisions.

Because rationales help youth understand the relationship between their behavior and the subsequent consequences, children can gain insight about the importance of learning new skills to replace old behaviors. As a result, children become less dependent on external rewards and reinforcement to motivate behavior change because they can see how their behavior determines what happens to them.

With regard to Teaching Interactions, Willner et al. (1977) and Braukmann, Ramp, Braukmann, Willner, and Wolf (1983) found that youngsters prefer Teaching Interactions in which adults provide explanations as they teach alternative, more appropriate skills. They found that when adults use rationales, youth are more likely to view them as fair and like them. Thus, given the importance of school climate and teacher-student relationships in improving student behavior and academic performance, using rationales is critical to effective teaching.

## ▶ Components of rationales

Effective rationales are characterized by several elements:

**1. They point out natural or logical consequences**. Rationales should point out consequences that naturally or logically occur as a result of a behavior. Natural consequences are those that tend to occur without human intervention, or those that are not within the youth's direct control. For example, "If you run down the sidewalk on a rainy day, you could slip and hurt yourself," or "If you tip back in your chair, you may fall." Logical consequences, on the other hand, are linked to behavior but are determined more by a student's actions or others interacting with the student. For example, "When you greet someone with a smile and say 'Hello,' the person is more likely to want to spend time with you and be your friend," or "If you prepare for a test by studying over a period of time, instead of studying only the night before, you'll probably get a higher grade."

**2. They are personal to the youth**. Rationales need to be geared to the individual interests of each youngster. This means carefully observing and talking with students to determine their interests, favorite activities, and likes or dislikes. Then, rationales can be specially tailored to each youngster. For example, if an eighth-grade student enjoys playing basketball and hopes to play on the high school team someday, his or her teachers can formulate rationales that help the student understand how following instructions or accepting criticism is beneficial. This may include taking criticism from the coach, accepting a referee's decision, or listening to the coach's instructions during practice. Similarly, for a youth whose motivation to graduate is low, rationales that stress the importance of paying attention in shop or computer class to learn skills that will help get him or her a job after leaving school may be far more effective than talking about higher education.

**3. They are specific and brief**. Usually, one good rationale is enough to accomplish the purposes of a Teaching Interaction or praise statement. You should be brief and to the point when providing a rationale, and avoid trying to convince the youth with numerous reasons. Long explanations may confuse a student; you're more likely to keep a youth's attention with a brief, specific rationale. Even if the tone of the rationale is positive, a lengthy explanation will be perceived as lecturing and punishing.

**4. They are believable and short-term**. Rationales are more effective when immediate, rather than long-term, consequences are emphasized. For example, an effective rationale for following instructions without arguing might be, "You will have more free time if you quickly follow instructions instead of wasting time arguing." Pointing out this short-term, believable consequence is generally preferable to providing a remote consequence such as, "When you have a job, you will be more likely to get a promotion and a raise if you can follow instructions."

Rationales also must be believable, which means they must be age-appropriate and personalized. For example, you might tell a nine-year-old who enjoys recess, "Putting your things away when I tell you, instead of waiting for the bell to ring, means you will get to have all of recess time to play." But for a college-bound 17-year-old, a more pertinent rationale may be, "If you study hard and do well on your college entrance exams, you might earn a scholarship, which will make paying for college a lot easier."

**5. They are developmentally appropriate**. Rationales that describe short-term, believable consequences are generally the most meaningful for youngsters who are new to a social skills program, or who are less developmentally mature. However, as a youth matures and begins to internalize the gains he or she has made, it also is important to use rationales that point out long-term consequences and include statements of concern for others.

Long-term rationales point out more general consequences related to a youngster's behavior — consequences that will occur at some point in the more distant future. It is important for youngsters to understand how their behavior may affect their employment, their ability to take care of themselves, and their capacity to develop and maintain relationships. For example, a long-term rationale that could be used when teaching a student how to accept criticism might deal with the youngster's ability in the future to get along with a spouse or to keep a job. Similarly, you need to provide rationales that point out how a student's behavior affects others. Such "other-oriented" rationales should focus on sensitivity and concern for others. Children need to understand that their behavior leaves an impression on other people, and that those impressions reflect on them and everyone in the school. For example, an other-oriented rationale for not getting into arguments at a shopping mall with kids from different schools would be, "The stores may ask all students to leave the mall because of the behavior of just a few boys or girls." Rationales can point out how the behavior of each child affects others, and how it can benefit or harm the other students and the school's reputation.

## ▶ **W**hen to use rationales

Rationales are used in each of the specific teaching situations described in Chapters 10-13. However, they can be used any time teaching occurs. Rationales enhance the teaching of social skills and make learning more relevant and meaningful to a youth by establishing a purpose or reason for the learning.

During the course of a day, there will be numerous informal occasions for you to provide rationales. Students may ask your opinion or you may offer advice or a point of view. Including rationales at every opportunity is extremely helpful.

Briefly, rationales are used in the following contexts:

**1. When teaching skills**. Rationales should be used in all phases of teaching. When introducing academic concepts or skills, use rationales to establish the relevance of the material to "real-life" situations or future or past

learning. When students are told why specific information is being studied, they demonstrate greater understanding and satisfaction about why they should learn what they are asked to learn (Porter & Brophy, 1988). Similar effects may generalize to social skills learning.

When you're introducing a new skill during Preventive Teaching (Chapter 11), rationales help students understand why they should learn a skill not currently in their repertoire. Rationales that focus on both short- and long-term benefits and cover a broad spectrum of situations can be generated by you and the student(s).

Rationales help reinforce the use of appropriate skills. They provide reasons why students should continue to engage in positive behaviors and are important to use in Effective Praise interactions (Chapter 10).

Rationales are extremely important when teaching correctively during a Teaching Interaction. Explaining why a student should change a particular behavior and focusing most often on the benefits of doing so will help the student realize the cause-effect relationship between the behavior and its outcomes. Understanding this relationship empowers students by helping them learn how to take control of their own behaviors.

**2. Whenever disagreements occur between educators and students**. Stating why you disagree gives students a chance to "buy into" or at least understand your point of view. Students also view you as more open-minded and fair. Providing a rationale also models appropriate or desired behavior to students.

**3. During problem-solving situations**. When you are helping students generate potential solutions to problems, providing rationales helps them evaluate their options. Rationales may help students make better decisions by considering the possible benefits or problems associated with each solution.

**4. During daily conversations**. Students often ask their teachers or other staff members for explanations or advice. Rationales help students understand the logic behind the explanations or advice.

Although you hope students will understand your rationales and find them meaningful, the goal of using rationales is not to get students to agree with your reasons. You want to students to understand the rationales, but they do not have to agree with your point of view.

Perhaps most importantly, teachers and others working with youth need to remember that rationales alone do not effectively change behavior. Consistently describing behavior and supplying consequences, coupled with good reasons for initiating or maintaining behavior change, will result in the most positive outcomes.

## ▶ Summary

There are three main types of rationales: benefits to students, negative outcomes, and concern for others. You decide which type is best for each student by considering such variables as development level, personal needs, and the situation at hand. Rationales are used in all the teaching tech-niques of the Boys Town Education Model, but are extremely helpful in a variety of other formal and informal contacts with students.

Keeping rationales brief, personal, and developmentally appropriate will enhance their effectiveness. By themselves, however, rationales will not effectively change behavior. They must be paired with specific teaching and consequences to have the greatest impact.

# CHAPTER TEN

# Effective praise

**P**raise is a powerful tool for changing and improving the behaviors of your students. It is crucial to the development of positive relationships between you and your students and is very important in strengthening appropriate behavior. Effective Praise interactions allow you to individualize your teaching of social skills by sincerely and enthusiastically recognizing each student's efforts and progress.

### ▶ What Is Effective Praise?

Effective Praise is a four-step teaching process that is planned and purposeful. It is specific, genuine, and contingent on positive behavior. Effective Praise interactions should be totally positive because you recognize appropriate behavior and pair spe-

cific descriptions with positive consequences. This means you should look carefully for opportunities to praise and reinforce a student's efforts toward positive behavior — to "catch 'em being good." Seizing the chance to praise appropriate behavior increases the odds that the desired behavior will occur again.

---

### Steps to Effective Praise

1. Description of appropriate behavior

2. Rationale

3. Request for acknowledgment

4. Positive consequence

---

# ▶ Benefits of Effective Praise

Effective Praise helps develop positive relationships between you and your students. Many students have had difficulty developing constructive relationships with adults in authority, or in making or keeping friends. Effective Praise interactions contribute substantially to helping each child learn and grow because you are recognizing the incremental gains being made by each student.

Many students will begin engaging in behaviors that are noticed by others in order to gain approval. Although many of these behaviors may be seen as prosocial by adults, you must guard against developing students who are merely obedient or compliant, and instead work toward developing a sense of responsibility in students. By helping them realize the benefits they will receive, students will begin to develop an internalized set of values and motivation that will result in a sense of personal power (Miller, 1984). Students who act only to please others remain motivated by external factors, have trouble connecting outcomes to their behavior, and may be ill-prepared to function in the changing world (Bluestein, 1988).

A study by Willner, Braukman, Kirigin, Fixsen, Phillips, and Wolf (1977), found that youth preferred being taught by adults who gave positive feedback, set clear expectations with reasons to back them up, and showed enthusiasm and concern. Similarly, studies have shown that students are more positive and friendly with others in their classrooms and develop more positive

"attitudes" when they experience warm and accepting relationships with their teachers (Serow & Soloman, 1979). By design, Effective Praise interactions can meet student needs and facilitate development of relationships.

Effective Praise increases learning and students' behavioral options. As you focus on what a student is doing well, you become more aware of the student's positive behaviors, creating a positive cycle of interactions. The more you're aware of what the student does "right," the more opportunities you have to address and increase positive behavior change. By reinforcing skills that fit societal norms, students increase their repertoires of behavioral responses and begin choosing those that are more readily accepted by others.

# ▶ How to use Effective Praise

Effective Praise should be used contingently. That is, praise should only be given after a desired behavior occurs, not as a general motivator. By providing praise after a student has demonstrated a particular behavior, you attribute success to the student's effort. This, in turn, implies to the student that similar success can be attained again. It helps students see that they are in charge and in control of their own behavior.

Effective Praise should always specifically describe which behaviors are being recognized and reinforced. Simple, direct statements enhance a student's understanding of what is being praised, and lend credibility to the interaction. Recognizing developmental levels and individual needs when praising students personalizes the interactions and shows students you're sincere.

## ▶ When to use Effective Praise

Use Effective Praise abundantly to reinforce new skills. When students are learning something new, they need reinforcement every time they use the skill correctly. Continuous reinforcement builds and strengthens skills. By reinforcing the use of a skill that is just emerging, you increase the likelihood that the student will use the skill again. Utilizing these opportunities to teach greatly adds to a student's repertoire of appropriate behaviors.

Effective Praise also is used when you are attempting to strengthen existing positive behaviors or build the fluency of a skill. As a student demonstrates more frequent and appropriate use of a skill, you should use an intermittent schedule of reinforcement to maintain it. Specifically describing the progress a student makes while mastering a skill helps the student become more natural and spontaneous when using it.

It is important to note that general, nonspecific praise also can be used to maintain a skill. Once the behavior seems fairly constant, you can begin to fade out the use of specific descriptions until the positive behavior can be sustained through the use of general statements, such as "Good job," "Nice work on the project," and so on. The eventual goal of Effective Praise is to develop and maintain behavior through social interactions.

Not giving any praise at all may lead the student to stop using the desired behavior. Behavior that was previously reinforced may diminish or cease if it isn't occasionally recognized and addressed. In general, behavior is best maintained when intermittent reinforcement is used.

## ▶ The steps of Effective Praise

Before discussing the steps of Effective Praise, it is necessary to emphasize an important aspect of this and other interactions you will have with the students. Whenever you talk with students about their behavior, you communicate not only with your words, but also with your actions. **How** you talk with someone is thought to be considerably more important than **what** you actually say. Because of this, you should pay close attention to factors called "quality components." Basically, these components refer to your positive verbal and nonverbal behaviors. They include looking at the student, using a pleasant voice tone, saying the student's name, smiling, using appropriate humor, and showing enthusiasm. Touching, such as a pat on the shoulder, also can be used (but with obvious caution). Of course, your use of touch will be based on many factors and will vary from one student to another.

Quality components establish and maintain a productive climate for learning. In general, everyone is more receptive to teaching when approached positively. You should not only begin any teaching episode with positive behaviors, but also make sure to maintain them throughout the interaction.

You should feel comfortable and natural when using quality components; students will not respond well to an adult who appears insincere or "robotic." When used naturally and spontaneously, quality components can greatly improve the relationships between you and your students.

Here are the steps of Effective Praise:

**1. Description of appropriate behavior:** Effective Praise combines specific behavioral statements with your general praise and enthusiasm. Descriptions of appropriate behavior increase the student's level of understanding and the likelihood that he or she will repeat the behavior. These statements help students realize exactly what behaviors fall within the acceptable range. They also help students focus on their accomplishments and progress.

As you make descriptive praise statements, accurately label the skill being taught. For example, "Thanks for looking at me and saying '**Okay**' when I asked you to take out your book. You did it right away without bothering others. You did a good job of **following instructions**." Labeling skills and providing specific behavioral descriptions increase the odds that students will successfully learn new ways of behaving and be able to generalize the skill to future situations.

List the skill steps performed correctly by the student. For example, "When I told you that you couldn't use the calculator, **you looked at me, said 'Okay,' and then calmly asked for a reason why**. You did a good job of accepting a 'No' answer."

As with any clear description of behavior, describe the circumstances surrounding the behavior — what happened, who was there, when it happened, how it happened, and so on. Again, clear descriptions help teach your youth how to generalize appropriate behavior to similar situations.

**2. Rationale:** Students benefit from learning about the consequences of their behavior. A rationale emphasizes this cause-effect relationship. Realistic, individualized rationales let students know why a specific behavior is beneficial to them or others. To your benefit, students will view you as more concerned and fair. Rationales also can help with compliance — students are more likely to do as they're asked when given a reason for doing so. And finally, rationales increase the pleasantness of interactions and are a key to building relationships with students. For example, "When you accept a `No' answer like you just did, others will think of you as someone they can work with. Maybe they will try to say `Yes' to your requests whenever they can."

**3. Request acknowledgment:** Check to make sure the student is paying attention and understands your rationale by asking for acknowledgment. Although this is a specific step in the sequence, requests for acknowledgment should take place frequently during any teaching. Ask questions such as, "Do you understand?" or "Does that make sense?" or "Do you follow me?" Requesting acknowledgment creates a dialogue; that way, you don't have to lecture.

**4. Positive consequence:** Positive consequences help promote constructive behavior change when paired with specific skill teaching. Tell the student that he or she has earned positive points or positive consequences for engaging in the specific appropriate behavior. Make sure the size of the reinforcer is appropriate — just large enough to maintain or increase the desired behavior. Pairing a positive consequence with a specific description of the behavior strengthens the student's understanding of the link between his or her behavior and the outcome. It also promotes more rapid behavior change.

**Example**

Nate is a seventh-grade student in your class. He is currently on the Daily Points System. You have been working with him on turning assignments in on time because he has had considerable difficulty in this area. Today, Nate turned in his homework from last night and just finished his math assignment with the rest of the class.

**1. Description of appropriate behavior** — "Nate, you've really been working hard! First thing this morning, you handed in your homework, and just now you finished your math paper right on time. Great job!"

**2. Rationale** — "Finishing homework and other assignments helps you learn better and faster. By doing assignments on time, you can practice what you just learned and get more of the assignment right because it's fresh in your mind. Then you can move on to the next thing."

**3. Request acknowledgment** — "Do you see why finishing your work on time is important?" (Nate says "Yes.")

**4. Positive consequence** — "For turning your assignments in on time, you've earned 1,500 positive points."

## ▶ General considerations

Your teaching has the greatest impact when it closely follows a behavior. If you can talk with a student as soon as possible after observing a behavior, you will capitalize on the best learning conditions. Relevant, immediate feedback enhances learning.

There may be times, however, when you don't observe a positive behavior, but still can praise the student for the choices he or she made. In these cases, you'll need to rely on other sources of information, and talk with the student as soon as you can. For example, another teacher might tell you that she saw one of your students appropriately discussing a disagreement with another student instead of arguing or fighting. Or, the school van driver reports to you that one of your students calmly accepted feedback for misbehavior. In these situations, get as much information as you can, then praise the student for the appropriate behavior.

Most of the time, you will use the Effective Praise interaction privately with the student. Speaking individually with the student provides complete and personal attention. Although occasionally appropriate, public praise can be embarrassing to a student and have counterproductive effects. Public praise probably should be reserved for times when the entire class has demonstrated a skill or when you know a particular student will respond positively.

Positive interactions with students, including Effective Praise, should occur at least four times as often as you use corrective interactions. This 4:1 ratio enhances relationships, results in more positive behavior from your students, and helps build "reinforcement reserves" for students. Frequently telling students what they are doing well helps them focus on their positive behaviors. This can help them feel more competent and better about themselves. When Corrective Teaching does occur, students have both emotional and token reinforcement reserves to fall back on. The 4:1 ratio is a minimum standard; many children need higher ratios of positive to corrective feedback to show improvement.

## ▶ Summary

Effective Praise is a four-step planned teaching process that is used to recognize and reward a student's appropriate behavior. The way you use Effective Praise is very important. When given in a manner that is direct, personal, specific, and pleasant, it will seem natural and sincere. Noticing what each student does well will show that you are sensitive and responsive to the needs of all your students. Perhaps more importantly, your students will feel better about themselves and will be encouraged to work even harder in the positive, caring educational atmosphere you have created.

# CHAPTER ELEVEN

# Preventive teaching

New teachers often worry about whether they will be able to control their students' behavior. They hope that most children have received a gradual "education" on how to behave from their parents and other adults through modeling, discussions, praise, and discipline. Unfortunately, many students today have not been a part of such a natural process. In fact, they often have had inconsistent or dysfunctional models who have left them confused and socially unskilled. Teachers who effectively use Preventive Teaching, along with other consistent teaching techniques, can help these youngsters make up for skill deficits.

## ▶ Classroom management and Preventive Teaching

A synthesis of considerable research (Effective Schooling Practices, 1990) revealed strong evidence that when effective classroom strategies are employed, student behavior, attitudes, and achievement improve measurably. Two key elements of good management cited in the report are establishing and maintaining consistent expectations and developing positive teacher-student relationships. These factors have been found to be far more effective as classroom management techniques than those which seek to maintain control by focusing solely or primarily on student misbehavior. Unfortunately, teachers often tend to notice and deal with disruptive behavior as a way to maintain order in the classroom. The methods used to do this can have a significant negative effect on students. Jones and Jones (1981), for example, found that negative remarks by teachers are correlated with student dislike for school. Similarly, Becker, Engelmann, and Thomas (1975) reported that critical remarks by teachers tend to worsen student behavior rather than improve it.

More-successful approaches to classroom management involve techniques designed to prevent problems before they occur (Kounin, 1970). Kounin found that one way to minimize student disruption was to maximize the time they spend in active learning. Addressing and resolving minor incidents before they became major problems also decreased time spent on disruptive behavior. Kounin found that teachers can achieve more effective classroom management by:

**1. Watching classroom activity at all times**. Effective managers station themselves so they can scan the entire classroom and see each student. This enables them to spot and deal with minor problems before they become serious or disruptive. This form of monitoring also communicates to students that the teacher is very aware of what is occurring in the classroom at all times.

**2. Performing several tasks at once**. For example, the effective manager can lead a classroom discussion while monitoring those not involved in the lesson.

**3. Being prepared to teach**. This allows teachers to maintain a brisk pace and avoid lapses because of the need to check a manual or scan notes to see what to do next. Effective managers also maintain the "academic flow" by dealing with inattention without disrupting the class. Common techniques include establishing eye contact, asking the student a question pertaining to the subject, or regaining attention with a comment to the student.

Using direct classroom observations, Anderson, Everton, and Emmer (1980) expanded on Kounin's original research and found that classrooms ran smoother when teachers demonstrated these key behaviors and set expectations at the beginning of the school year. Teachers experiencing the most success spent quite a bit of time on classroom rules and procedures during the first few weeks of school, introducing them gradually to avoid overloading students with too much information. Effective managers went beyond merely informing students of rules and expectations. In short, they taught rules and procedures in the same manner as academic subjects — through modeling, discussion, practice, and feedback on performance. Additionally, consequences for appropriate and inappropriate behaviors were consistently applied.

Evertson and Emmer (1982), in studying teachers of junior high students, found many similarities in techniques used for effective classroom management. Teachers at the junior high level need to clearly inform students of classroom rules and procedures, emphasizing the "how to's" of desirable behavior; monitor student compliance with those rules, including consistent and more frequent intervention for inappropriate behavior; hold students accountable for their work; effectively communicate expectations and instructions; and maximize the use of classroom time.

Although the emphasis of this chapter is on how to use Preventive Teaching sequences for social skills instruction, you will note many similarities to techniques used for effective instruction of academic concepts.

# ▶ **P**reventive Teaching in society

Practical applications of Preventive Teaching can be found in a variety of social and daily living contexts. Preventive Teaching is used whenever particular skills or behaviors need to be learned to handle specific situations. For example, in fire drills, occupants of a building locate alarms and extinguishers, and practice using exit routes in order to help reduce the chances of serious injury in a fire. To prepare their children to walk to school, parents may schedule a practice walk in which they show the route to school, where and how to cross streets, and where to find "block homes" a child can go to for help if necessary. We teach children how to dial the "911" emergency number to report an accident, injury, or threatening situation, and provide them with rules about dealing with strangers. On-the-job training programs provide instruction in dealing with difficult customers, handling hazardous materials, using new equipment, and many other topics to prepare employees for situations they may face. By reviewing and practicing specific behaviors that match particular situations, greater success can be expected when the actual situation is encountered.

# ▶ **B**enefits of Preventive Teaching

Preventive Teaching in school provides many benefits to students and teachers. In addition to the general benefit of improving classroom management, as described earlier in this chapter, Preventive Teaching provides an excellent opportunity to build positive relationships between students and teachers. Preventive Teaching improves a student's chances of succeeding because skills are being learned at a neutral time, in the absence of problem behaviors. This means that the learning process is far less threatening, in part because of the presence of a comfortable, supportive, and relaxed environment. Students appreciate the inherent fairness, concern, and support involved in learning something that will benefit them or help them avoid future difficulties or problem situations. Because they've been given the chance to learn and practice new skills ahead of time, they can feel confident when they approach new situations. All of this allows students to experience a great deal of success without having to experience failure in the process.

Not only do students have the opportunity to succeed as a result of Preventive Teaching, but educators experience success as well. Preventive Teaching helps avoid confrontation by positively establishing expectations and tolerances, and gradually shaping students' skills. Preventive Teaching allows you to feel more relaxed and comfortable when introducing students to new or varied situations. For example, preteaching behaviors can help with the implementation of Individual Education Plans in that you teach your expectations, then help students change through effective use of praise and Corrective Teaching. Teaching expectations associated with field trips, assemblies, pep rallies, or other special events can provide you with the sense that you have prepared your students to succeed in those specific situations.

# When to use Preventive Teaching

Preventive Teaching can be used to focus on basic or advanced social skills and to prepare students for specific situations or circumstances. With new students, your focus probably will be on teaching or introducing the basic curriculum skills. As discussed earlier (Chapter 7, "Teaching the Curriculum Skills"), these "critical skills" occur at a high rate of frequency, so the student will have many opportunities to practice them. The process of learning new skills and mastering them can be reinforcing by itself because students are experiencing success and recognizing their own progress. When this occurs, the teaching/learning process can become self-perpetuating as students who are acquiring these basic skills become easier to teach. Mastering these basic skills thus facilitates the introduction of more advanced skills such as being honest, rational problem-solving, or demonstrating sensitivity to others.

In addition to focusing on basic and advanced curriculum skills, you also can preventively teach about specific or special circumstances like school rules, or how to act during an assembly or when a guest visits the classroom. Knowing each student's strengths and weaknesses helps determine other situations that call for Preventive Teaching. For example, if you have a student who is shy or withdrawn, and guests are scheduled to visit your classroom, you may preventively teach skills like how to greet others and how to engage in a conversation. By specifically teaching such skills ahead of time, you improve the student's opportunity to succeed.

In the case of a student who is having problems getting along with a youth from a different class, you may use Preventive Teaching to focus on the skill of getting along with others. This would be especially important in preparing for a joint field trip of the two classes. Depending on your students' skill level, you may want to use Preventive Teaching to help them learn alternatives to engaging in confrontations or losing self-control in response to various situations. For example, if you know that a particular student often becomes verbally aggressive when told "No," you should do a lot of Preventive Teaching on how to accept "No." You'll want to teach specific alternatives to the inappropriate response (i.e. verbal aggressiveness) and help the student see how change could be beneficial.

Preventive Teaching can be used throughout the school year. Although there are predictable, specific times when its use is very effective (as mentioned earlier), you should use the techniques anytime you feel it will help your students be more successful. Preventive Teaching sequences can be used to introduce new skills or to reintroduce or review previously taught skills. Reteaching a skill may be necessary when you notice that students are having repeated difficulties or when you want to strengthen a skill that will be necessary for an upcoming situation. In either case, by re-introducing the skill, you are helping your students to be more successful.

Preventive Teaching sessions can be used with individual students, small groups, or the whole class. Individualized Preventive Teaching typically focuses on a youngster's particular behavioral problems or addresses situations that are specific to the student. Small-group or whole-class instruction usually focuses on skills that all students need to know. Preventive Teaching to groups can be related to academic content or concepts, such as use of a microscope or types of punctuation, or to behavioral expectations like how to introduce oneself or how to act at an assembly. Group teaching allows you to efficiently teach necessary skills and allows for positive student interactions.

## ▶ Preventive Teaching sequences

Preventive Teaching comprises three stages: Planned Teaching, Preteaching, and Preventive Prompt. Planned Teaching is used to introduce a new skill to students at a planned, neutral time. Preteaching is used to reintroduce a skill prior to a specific event or situation in which the student will need to use the skill. A Preventive Prompt is a brief reminder to the student about the skill immediately before the event or situation occurs.

### Planned Teaching

Planned Teaching is a systematic introduction of a new skill to a student or group of students at a planned, neutral time. Planned Teaching should be used frequently, especially with new students, to help them learn and practice the social skills. The steps of a Planned Teaching sequence are shown in Figure 1.

## Figure 1

**Planned Teaching sequence (Stage I)**

1. Introduce skill
2. Describe appropriate behavior
3. Give rationale
4. Request acknowledgment
5. Practice
6. Feedback
7. Positive consequence
8. Establish future/follow-up practice

**1. Introduce skill:** To begin the Planned Teaching sequence, label the skill to be taught and carefully describe situations in which the skill may be used. A number of specific examples should be provided and students should have opportunities to contribute and ask questions. By describing the skill in a variety of contexts, you'll help students generalize the application of the skill to a variety of antecedent conditions or settings. A demonstration of the skill also may be an effective teaching tool during the introduction.

**2. Describe appropriate behavior:** Following the general explanation, you should specifically describe each step of the skill. In cases where you're teaching a set of behaviors that does not appear on the 16-skill curriculum list, analyze the overall behavior (e.g. "staying on task") into observable components and teach each step. Make sure you clearly state your expectations or criterion levels to achieve the best results. Students should have the opportunity to ask questions to help clarify your description.

**3. Rationale:** List a variety of benefits or pay-offs that may be derived from using the new skill. Students should be involved in generating rationales to enhance meaning and ownership.

**4. Request acknowledgment:** Including this step allows you to determine whether students understand why or how using a skill can be beneficial to them. Students don't have to agree with every rationale provided, but should acknowledge that they can understand the benefits involved. A second part of this step is to have students repeat the skill steps to you. Requesting group responses, mixed with randomly calling on individual students, may be an effective way to increase participation and attention. Depending on the skill levels of the students, you may want to use verbal or visual cues to prompt responses.

**5. Practice:** A practice session follows the description and rationale so the students can become more familiar with the skill and put theory into practice. The practice also provides an opportunity for you to monitor progress and adjust your teaching according to student needs. To maximize the amount of practice opportunities during group or whole-class instruction, you may use a variety of practice formats. Paired practice, in which students work in groups of two, provides a chance for everyone to participate. A number of individual students may be called upon randomly (or volunteers may be used) to demonstrate the skill so that you can spot check for accurate skill use (e.g. "Robert, choose one other student and greet him or her using the skill steps we've discussed."). You

also may want to ask for a volunteer to demonstrate the skill as the class observes and prepares to give positive feedback. The practice step should be given adequate attention to ensure thorough learning and success.

**6. Feedback:** Specific, descriptive feedback should follow the practice(s). If the lesson was structured well, most of your feedback should be positive, but there also may be opportunities for corrective feedback. Generally, the feedback should be given by the teacher or instructor to ensure its appropriateness. However, you may be able to allow students to give positive feedback to one another under carefully structured conditions. For example, "how to give positive feedback" may have been the focus of another preventive lesson, or your group of students may be mature or trustworthy enough to handle this responsibility. If you doubt your students' abilities to provide positive feedback, wait until later to involve them in this step.

**7. Positive consequence:** Planned Teaching always includes a positive consequence that is delivered when desired behaviors are observed. Noting and describing positive behaviors and determining consequences are generally easy when working with an individual student. Points, "positives," or "responsibles" may be provided for practicing a skill, accepting feedback, reporting on time to the Planned Teaching appointment, or any other number of positive behaviors demonstrated by the student. When teaching a group, positive consequences that are delivered to the entire group must be carefully selected to make sure that the reinforcement is contingent upon performance. Behaviors may include participating, staying on task, and practicing the skill. Individual efforts also should be recognized by privately discussing appropriate behaviors with the particular student(s). For example, a student who volunteers to demonstrate or practice the skill in front of others may receive positive consequences for doing so.

**8. Future/follow-up practice:** To close the Planned Teaching sequence, tell the student(s) about the next opportunity for practicing the skill with you. Establish a firm time for your next rehearsal or review of the skill. The follow-up sessions (Preteaching sequences) enhance and reinforce your initial teaching efforts by allowing additional exposure to the skill during neutral times.

## Preteaching

Preteaching is the second stage of Preventive Teaching. During the Preteaching sequence, the skill is reintroduced prior to a specific situation in which the student needs to use the skill. The Preteaching sequence is shown in Figure 2.

## Figure 2

## Preteaching Sequence (Stage II)

1. Reintroduce skill
2. Describe appropriate behavior
3. Rationale
4. Request acknowledgment
5. Practice (optional)
6. Feedback
7. Positive consequence
8. Inform student of upcoming situation

The Preteaching sequence is similar to the Planned Teaching sequence, but because many of the concepts are being reintroduced, it may not take as much time. Students should be more involved in the Preteaching sequence, providing descriptions of appropriate behavior (i.e. skill steps) and rationales. The practice portion of the Preteaching sequence is optional. The decision to practice should hinge on the student's needs, including how well the student remembers and understands the skill being taught. Feedback should, again, be positive and specific, and corrective, if needed. Students will earn a positive consequence for participating in a Preteaching sequence, as they did during Planned Teaching. Finally, students should be informed of a specific, upcoming situation in which they'll need to use the skill they've been practicing. For example, they may be asked to introduce themselves to a new student who will be enrolling in your class the following day. Or you may inform them that the school will be having a fire drill sometime within the next few days, and that they'll need to demonstrate their skills of quickly and quietly exiting the classroom and building. If the skill you've been teaching can be used in a variety of situations (e.g. accepting criticism, following instructions), you may inform students that you'll be planning different situations in which they can practice the skill they've been learning.

## Preventive prompt

The last stage of Preventive Teaching is a Preventive Prompt. The prompt is a brief statement about the use of a skill just prior to the event or situation in which a student will use it. Examples of preventive prompts include asking a student, "Do you remember the steps to following instructions?", just before instructing the student to clean the blackboard, or saying, "Remember the steps we talked about for leaving the building during a fire drill" as the alarm begins to sound.

## ▶ Summary

Preventive Teaching builds relationships and fosters skill development. It can be used to teach basic and advanced curriculum skills and to prepare students for specific situations or circumstances. Preventive Teaching can be used effectively with individual students, small groups, or an entire class. Consistent use of Preventive Teaching can decrease the seriousness and frequency of problem behaviors that occur in school. The three stages of Preventive Teaching — Planned Teaching, Preteaching, and the Preventive Prompt — should be used systematically to help students learn new skills and avoid inappropriate behavior, thus promoting more efficient skill learning and greater success.

# CHAPTER TWELVE

# The teaching interaction

The Teaching Interaction is a nine-step process used to address inappropriate social behaviors and teach prosocial alternatives. Consistent use of the Teaching Interaction allows you to effectively meet the individual needs of each student. Teaching Interactions also help you build and maintain relationships with your students. By teaching alternative behaviors in a calm and pleasant manner, you show your concern for students and enhance the effectiveness of your teaching.

## ▶ When to use the Teaching Interaction

When a student behaves inappropriately, you should use a Teaching Interaction to teach a new skill or strengthen a weak skill. Your primary goal is to teach alternative, replacement behaviors and reduce or eliminate inappropriate ones. Rather than suppressing inappropriate behavior, you focus on building self-management skills so students can make better choices about how they act. Consistent teaching, including opportunities to practice a new skill, makes learning more efficient because the time you spend addressing behavior is productive and relevant.

Simply addressing inappropriate behavior as it happens will not, by itself, promote positive change. To build and maintain prosocial behavior, you must reinforce students' efforts to use appropriate behavior at least four times as often as you address their mistakes. Frequent reinforcement lets students know you notice what they do well and increases the likelihood of the behavior reoccurring. (See Chapter 10, "Effective Praise.")

# ▶ Teaching Interaction components

The nine steps of the Teaching Interaction can, over time, help students learn better responses to potential problems. Corrective Teaching occurs in an atmosphere of genuine concern for students (Dowd & Tierney, 1992).

---

## The Teaching Interaction

1. Initial praise or empathy

2. Description of Inappropriate behavior

3. Consequence (positive correction statement)

4. Description of appropriate behavior

5. Rationale

6. Request for acknowledgment

7. Practice

8. Feedback (positive consequence)

9. General praise

---

When you approach a student to discuss an inappropriate behavior, it is important to be conscious of your behavior. Even though your focus is on teaching a new, appropriate behavior, you want to convey care and concern through your verbal and nonverbal behaviors. Thus, your teaching should always be accompanied by positive "quality components." These include looking at the student, using a pleasant voice tone, calling the student by name, having a pleasant or neutral facial expression, maintaining a comfortable distance between you and the student, and either sitting or standing so you are face to face with the student. Remember: Your focus is to teach, not control, the student. By using quality components, you help make the Teaching Interaction more personal and allow the student to maintain his or her dignity. Used throughout your teaching, these components make it more likely that a student will accept your feedback.

## Initial praise or empathy

The interaction begins with a positive statement related to the behavior you are teaching. Your praise will appear much more genuine if it is related to the teaching situation. For example, Desiree wants your attention. She waves her arm in the air and calls out loudly, "I need some help over here!" You could praise her for a number of behaviors: staying in her seat, raising her hand, asking for help, staying on task, looking at you. In another situation, you greet Dan as he enters the classroom. He looks away from you, makes an "X" with his fingers, and walks by you without saying anything. Although it appears that there were no behaviors that warrant praise, you could still praise Dan for getting to class on time that day or going promptly to his seat.

Initial praise reinforces approximations of the desired behavior and helps the student recognize progress. It enhances your relationships with students by showing them that you are aware of their accomplishments, even when they display inappropriate behaviors. Also, by focusing on something the student did well, you start the interaction on a positive note and are less likely to be seen as negative or punishing.

You also may choose to begin your interaction with an empathy statement. This lets the student know that you understand what he or she is experiencing. Like praise, empathy helps set a positive tone and makes students more receptive to your correction. Using Desiree's situation as an example, you may empathize with her needing your help by saying, "I can understand that you'd really like some help with your assignment." You may find that older students respond better to empathy than praise, as it may seem more genuine and less contrived.

Without the consistent use of this step, students may come to view you as punishing — someone who is quick to criticize mistakes and slow to recognize accomplishments. If this happens, students may begin to actively avoid you because you represent negative consequences to them.

## Description of inappropriate behavior

Specifically describe to the student his or her inappropriate behavior. Using objective, behavioral terms, describe antecedent events and student actions to structure your teaching. For example, in the earlier situation with Dan, you might say, "When you came in this morning and I said 'Hello,' you looked away, made an 'X' with your fingers, and rushed past me without saying anything." This description "sets the stage" for your teaching by providing the stu-

dent a clear picture of what he did and helping you decide what skill to teach.

Avoid using judgmental terms in your descriptions. Describe behaviors instead of perceptions. For example, instead of telling a student, "Why are you being so disrespectful to Sue? You were just trying to hurt her feelings, weren't you?", focus on the specific behaviors. Use a statement such as, "When you passed by Sue's desk, you told her she was a slob and then laughed at her." (See Chapter 8, "Observing and Describing Behavior," for a complete discussion of these concepts.)

Keep your descriptions brief and to the point in order to avoid badgering the student. Focus on the most overt or obvious behaviors, then move on. The purpose of this step is to increase the student's awareness of the behavior, so you can shift the emphasis to providing appropriate alternatives.

## Consequence (positive correction statement)

For engaging in an inappropriate behavior, the student should earn a negative consequence. The type of consequence — a point fine, a "negative," or an "irresponsible" — depends on which Motivation System level the student is on. (See Chapter 6 and Chapters 15 through 17 for specific information about Motivation System levels and consequences.)

Immediately following the consequence, offer a "positive correction statement." This statement tells the student that he or she can earn back some of the points that were lost. It gives students an incentive to correct their behavior by practicing an appropriate alternative behavior. It also demonstrates fairness by giving students control over the eventual size of the negative consequence. For example, when talking to a Daily Points student, you may say, "You can earn some of these points back in a moment by listening to me and practicing your greeting." With a Progress student, the positive correction statement may be, "You have a chance to earn some positives on your card by practicing with me."

## Description of appropriate behavior

Following the consequence, teach the student an appropriate alternative behavior by specifically describing what you want the student to do. This description not only helps the student understand your expectations, but also assists him or her in learning social skills that can be used in other settings. To promote this generalization, use words like, "A better way to greet someone...," or "Whenever someone gives you feedback...." Using this phrasing, rather than "I" statements such as "I'd like you to," focuses the student on self-management skills instead of teacher-pleasing behavior.

As part of your description, label the skill and list the behaviors that make up the skill. For example, "A better way to greet people is to look at them, smile, use a pleasant voice tone, and say something like 'Good morning.'" If necessary, you can demonstrate or model the behaviors in order to make the description clear for the student. (See Chapter 7, "Teaching the Curriculum Skills.")

## Rationale

Giving the student a rationale after the description of the appropriate behavior tells him or her why the skill should be learned and used. The rationale should be personal, skill-based, brief, and should explain the short-term benefits the student can receive by using the skill. This helps the student internalize the behavior. Your rationale also should explain the negative outcomes for not using the skill, or how the student's behavior affects others. (See Chapter 9, "Rationales.")

Rationales help students understand the link between their behavior and possible outcomes. This helps them learn to take responsibility for their behaviors, rather than blaming outside forces for what happens to them. It also empowers students by teaching them that their behavioral choices, in part, determine what may happen to them. For example, you may tell a student who is learning how to greet others and is interested in making friends, "If you say 'Hi' to people in the hall, it may help you start a conversation with them and they may want to get to know you better."

## Request for acknowledgment

Requests for acknowledgment should occur throughout the teaching process to gauge student comprehension and to promote student participation. This component follows the rationale so that you can determine whether the student understands the rationale. Questions like, "Does that make sense?" and "Do you understand?" are effective at determining student responsiveness.

Avoid asking the student questions like, "Do you agree?" or "How do you feel about that?"; these types of questions can lead to the student arguing with you. The important point here is not that the student agrees with you, but that he or she understands what you are saying.

It also is a good idea to have the student repeat the skill's steps before practicing. This is most beneficial to students who are just learning the skill, or students who have had repeated difficulties with certain behaviors. Rather than asking a question like, "Could you tell me the steps for greeting someone?" and risk getting a "No" answer, say something like, "Tell me how you're going to greet people now," or "Tell me the steps for greeting others."

## Practice

Having the student practice the alternative behavior provides an opportunity to immediately use the skill in a "low-risk" situation. Just as practice helps a student learn an academic concept, the practice step acts as a bridge between the initial inappropriate behavior and progress toward skill proficiency. The student's performance during the practice also gives you an idea of how well you taught the skill. This is the only time during the Teaching Interaction where you can assess your teaching effectiveness and determine whether reteaching is necessary.

In order for the practice to be most effective, you should set it up very clearly for the student. The student should know exactly what he or she is supposed to do, what skill is being practiced, and what you are going to

do. For example, in setting up a practice for greeting someone, you might say, "Dan, here's an opportunity to use greeting skills just like we talked about. This time, you'll look at me, smile, and in a pleasant voice tone say 'Good morning.'" Ask the student if he or she understands your instructions so the student knows what to do. Say something like, "Does that make sense?" Then give the student a cue to begin the practice to separate your setup from the actual practice.

Usually, the practice is related to the original teaching issue. That is, if the student had trouble accepting criticism about a term paper, you'd give him or her the same criticism in the practice. By practicing the skill within the original situation, you bring closure to the episode; this should result in more effective teaching.

Practice sessions can sometimes be more successful and helpful to the student if you use a similar but hypothetical situation. This is especially true if the original issue involved a very emotional or intense response by the student, or if it was disruptive to your class. For example, Darla is out of her seat looking out the window. You give her an instruction to sit down, but she remains standing for quite some time before going back to her seat. Now, when you teach the skill of "How to Follow Instructions," it would distract the class and Darla if you sent her back to the window during the practice. Instead, you could have her practice following another instruction, such as getting started on her assignment, opening her book to a certain page, or taking out necessary supplies for the class. All these instructions would lead Darla toward being back on task with the rest of the class. Similarly, if the original situation involved an intense student reaction, you may choose to practice the skill in a pretend situation first. After a successful practice, you then could return to the actual situation for a final practice of the skill.

Some practices will have to be done later, at a more suitable time. For example, a student who comes in to class late may have to practice being on time when she goes to her next class or when she returns to your class the next day. In any practice situation, if the student doesn't achieve predetermined criteria, he or she should practice again. Most of the time, the student will practice the entire skill as you have described it. However, for students who are just learning skills, you may be looking for only a few steps at a time. These students are in the "shaping" process; they require praise for approximations of the desired behaviors.

## Feedback (positive consequence)

Following the practice, provide the student with positive feedback about his or her performance. Your feedback should include specific descriptions of the student's behavior and the consequence (points, "positives," or "responsibles," depending on the student's Motivation System level). Depending on the student's original behavior and skill level, your specific description of the practice could include anything from a verbal replay to selected highlights. For example, Malcolm has been working on the skill of "Making a Request" for some time. Although he has learned most of the steps, he often forgets to say "Thank-you." When he successfully practices the skill using all the steps,

your feedback might be, "Great request! This time you remembered to say 'Thank you.'" If another practice is necessary, praise the student for any approximations of the behavior before asking him or her to practice again.

Praise, descriptive feedback, and positive card entries will increase the likelihood that students will engage in appropriate behaviors again. Your feedback also demonstrates concern, shows support for students' progress, and reinforces appropriate behavior. Finally, it contributes to and helps build relationships between you and your students.

## General praise

This step is as much for you as it is for the student. It is designed to positively redirect the student and end the interaction on a positive note. Rather than summarizing the interaction, simple and brief praise like "Nice job" or "Good work" is the most natural way to end your teaching. Any further mention of the student's behavior, even when stated in a positive manner, may serve to undermine your teaching efforts. Statements such as, "Now I know you'll be able to follow instructions" or "I'm sure you won't make the same mistake next time" can communicate unrealistic expectations, setting students up for failure.

## ▶ Sample Teaching Interaction

Dan is a fourth-grade Daily Points student. As he enters your classroom one morning, and you greet him, he looks away from you, makes an "X" with his fingers, and says nothing as he rushes past. After you get the rest of the class started on an assignment, you approach Dan at his desk to talk with him about his greeting.

**Initial praise or empathy:** *"Dan, I'm glad you made it to school this morning and I appreciate you looking up just now."*

**Description of inappropriate behavior:** *"When I greeted you a moment ago, you made an 'X' with your fingers, rushed past me, and didn't say anything."*

**Consequence (positive correction statement):** *"For not greeting me appropriately, Dan, you've lost 1,000 points.* (Dan enters the point fine on his card.) *Nice job accepting that consequence. Let's talk about how you can earn back some of those points."*

**Description of appropriate behavior:** *"Whenever someone greets you, whether it's a teacher or other kids at school, it would be better if you would look at the person, smile, use a pleasant voice, and say something like 'Hello.'"*

**Rationale:** *"Dan, when you greet people like that, they're more likely to see you as friendly and want to get to know you better. You could even end up with more friends."*

**Request for acknowledgment:** *"Do you understand what I'm saying?* (Dan says, "Uh-huh.") *Tell me the steps for greeting others."* (Dan gives all the steps of the skill.)

**Practice:** *"Good job, Dan. Let's try that greeting again. This time, I want you to greet me by using all those steps. We'll just pretend we're standing at the door like before."* (Dan successfully practices the skill.)

**Feedback (positive consequence):** *"Excellent! This time you looked right at me, smiled, and pleasantly said 'Hello.' For practicing your greeting, you've earned 500 points back."* (Dan enters the points on his card.)

**General praise:** *"Thanks Dan. Why don't I help you get started on your vocabulary review now."*

## ▶ General considerations

Throughout the interaction, you should recognize and praise appropriate behaviors, particularly those that have been difficult for the student in the past. When you notice and praise these behaviors, students are more likely to continue to be responsive to your feedback.

When you notice mild inattentive behaviors before or during a Teaching Interaction, briefly prompt the student to pay attention. Teaching social skills is not effective when the student is inattentive. For example, you could say, "Edwin, could you put your book down and look at me, please? Thanks." If the behavior continues, escalates, or reoccurs frequently, you should use techniques described in Chapter 13, "Ongoing Behavior."

As with any interaction with students, quality components (pleasant voice tone, neutral facial expression, etc.) can enhance your effectiveness and help build relationships.

## ▶ Summary

The Teaching Interaction is a flexible tool that can be adapted to meet students' varying needs. It is used to correct inappropriate behavior by offering alternatives, giving reasons, actively engaging the student in a dialogue, and using consequences. By modifying your language and adjusting the expectations for the student, you can successfully use the Teaching Interaction with students of all ages and skill levels.

# CHAPTER THIRTEEN

# Ongoing behavior

**T**eaching Interactions are used when a student engages in inappropriate behaviors. However, nearly all students will at times have trouble accepting your feedback while they are being corrected and will display behaviors that interfere with your teaching. This is called **ongoing behavior**, and is defined as inattentive or problem behavior that occurs during a Teaching Interaction and interferes with the student's ability to learn.

Dealing with ongoing behavior when it occurs benefits both you and the student. Rather than responding emotionally, you should view these behaviors as skill deficits, and as opportunities to teach students better ways to manage their behavior when faced with criticism. You will be better able to deal with ongoing behavior calmly and objectively once you "depersonalize" it by viewing it as a "teachable moment."

When a student begins to show signs of not accepting correction during a Teaching Interaction, it will be necessary to temporarily stop the interaction. You can't "teach over" the interfering behaviors during social skills instruction any more than you can when teaching a critical academic concept. Both require student attentiveness and responsiveness. Instead, you'll use techniques (explained later in this chapter) that are designed to help the student regain self-control before you continue teaching.

Ongoing behavior can take many forms, ranging from subtle to overt. Some examples include:

**Facial expressions** — looking away, glaring, rolling the eyes, frowning, and grinning.

**Verbal behaviors** — interrupting, arguing, swearing, talking to others, and mumbling.

**Body movements** — slouching, folding arms, turning and/or walking away, moving excessively, making noise with hands or other objects, gestures with fingers or hands, and resting one's head on a desk or hand.

**Other behaviors** — not answering when asked to respond, sighing, crying, and laughing.

Ongoing behaviors are the opposite of attentive behaviors, which generally include looking at you, responding to questions or instructions, sitting or standing quietly, and maintaining a neutral facial expression. Your expectations for each student engaging in these attentive behaviors will depend largely on the student's developmental level and his or her current level of skill acquisition.

## ▶ Preventing ongoing behavior

Although ongoing behavior from students is virtually inevitable, your efforts should focus on preventing it. You already have learned many techniques to prepare students for Corrective Teaching. The relationships you develop with your students are strengthened by your consistent use of these various teaching methods and make it more likely that students will accept your feedback.

**Preventive Teaching** — A student is more likely to meet your expectations if you explain them before you do Corrective Teaching. One of the first things you should preventively teach all students is how to accept criticism and consequences. All students will receive considerable feedback each day to help them develop a better repertoire of behaviors. Teaching them how to accept criticism contributes to their future success.

Students who have difficulties accepting criticism will need frequent prompting prior to your feedback to internalize that skill.

As students begin to consistently use the skill of accepting criticism, you should begin to move from simply requiring student compliance toward teaching self-management strategies. Teaching a range of skills (disagreeing or interrupting appropriately, anger control, giving negative feedback, expressing feelings appropriately, conflict resolution, self-monitoring, and reflection) will help students "read" social situations, review their options, and choose the best response (Dowd & Tierney, 1992).

**Praise** — Using various forms of praise helps maintain or increase desirable behaviors and build relationships with your students. Praise is your most powerful tool to change behavior. Students who are frequently reinforced for positive behavior are less likely to act out to get your attention. If a student has a large "reinforcement reserve" (i.e. points, positives, or social reinforcers from others or himself or herself), the student is less likely to react inappropriately to a consequence or criticism. It is your responsibility to help the student develop the reinforcement reserve by noticing his or her positive behaviors and rewarding them.

**Corrective Teaching** — The Teaching Interaction is used when minor misbehaviors occur. Intervening early, when behaviors are "small," will help students learn your expectations and tolerances, possibly preventing escalation of inappropriate behavior. Inconsistent use of the Motivation Systems consequences may "set up" students and teachers for ongoing behavior. For example, Juanita has trouble asking for help in both Mrs. Nelson's and Mr. McGuire's class. Although both teachers address her behavior, Juanita receives point fines only from Mrs. Nelson. Invariably, these inconsistent responses will confuse Juanita, and she may have difficulty accepting Mrs. Nelson's consequences, most likely thinking she is unfair.

## ▶ The process

Ongoing behavior can occur at any time during the Teaching Interaction, but it happens most often during certain steps. These include the "Description of the Inappropriate Behavior," "Consequence," "Request for Acknowledgment," and "Practice." During each of these steps, students are either receiving corrective feedback or being asked to participate in the Teaching Interaction. By knowing where ongoing behavior is most likely to occur, you can use preventive measures like prompts and praise to reduce the chances of it happening.

The following sections explain the various methods that can be used when you first respond to a student's ongoing behavior.

## Helping the student regain self-control

When ongoing behavior occurs, stop the Teaching Interaction and deal with the inappropriate behaviors. The following methods are designed to help shape behavior and promote student self-control.

**1. Coupling statements** — These are brief descriptions of inappropriate behavior paired with descriptions of a more appropriate alternative. Example: "You're slouched in your chair. Please sit up."

Observe what the student is doing and describe the most overt or bothersome behavior. For example, a student is arguing in a loud voice tone, waving his arms, and glaring at you. The behavior you should address is the arguing. Loud arguing is probably the most disruptive behavior, and you would have difficulty doing any further teaching until it diminishes or stops. You might say, "Instead of arguing, please be quiet."

Avoid vague or judgmental terms by keeping your descriptions specific. Use brief statements and matched behavioral pairs that include a description of both the inappropriate behavior and the appropriate alternative behavior. Avoid describing the absence of a behavior, since it doesn't give the student an alternative behavior that could replace what he or she is doing.

**Example:**

**(Specific)**

*"You're tapping your pencil on the table. Please set it down."*

**(Nonspecific)**

*"That's really obnoxious. Would you stop that?"*

**Example:**

**(Brief)**

*"You're standing. Please sit down."*

**(Lengthy)**

*"You're standing up with your hands on your hips, shaking your head from side to side, and moving your mouth without saying anything. Please sit down, put your hands in your lap, and keep your head and mouth still."*

**Example:**

**(Matched pairs)**

*"You're pacing. Please stand still."*

**(Unmatched pairs)**

*"You're pacing. Please stop pacing" or "You're pacing. Please be quiet."*

If you vary your word choice, you'll avoid badgering the student, which usually escalates negative behavior. Avoid overusing any one particular phrase, especially those that may set off a power struggle, such as "You need to..." or "I want you to...."

Although giving simple instructions is acceptable (e.g. "Please sit down"), coupling statements provide clear behavioral contrasts and make students more aware of what they're doing. Perhaps the most important function of a "coupling statement" is that it serves as a check on your emotions. That is, if you are focused primarily on observing and describing the student's behavior, you are less likely to react emotionally, thereby worsening the situation.

**2. Specific praise** — Provide the student with specific praise to reinforce any appropriate behavior you want to maintain. Praise

the student for any instructions he or she follows. For example, if you ask a student, "Instead of turning away from me, would you please face me?", and he follows that instruction, you should tell him, "Thanks for turning and looking at me."

Recognizing any effort the student makes and reinforcing behavioral approximations helps the student regain self-control and maintain desired behaviors. For example, if you ask a student who is yelling to be quiet, you should praise her when she lowers her voice (e.g. "Nice job of lowering your voice.").

By praising any of the student's prosocial behaviors, you increase the likelihood that the behavior will continue or be used more frequently. Reinforcing the student's progress in regaining self-control is a key to this shaping process.

**3. Rationales or "reality" statements** — Rationales help students understand the benefits of following your instructions. Pointing out the positive outcomes of regaining self-control helps students make better choices about their behavior.

**Example:** *"If you can calm down and be quiet, we'll be able to take care of this more quickly."*

Knowing what reinforces a student and including it in your rationale also can help motivate change.

**Example:** *"When you look at me and answer calmly, we are more likely to finish this discussion in time for you to have lunch with your friends."*

"Reality" statements can help explain to students what you expect from them in a given situation. Many students have found through previous experience that certain behaviors, though maladaptive, get them what they want, which sometimes is to be left alone. By persisting in those behaviors, students find they can frustrate adults and achieve that goal. Adults may abandon their efforts and unintentionally reinforce the maladaptive behaviors. "Reality" statements (e.g. "We're sure not getting much accomplished this way" or "Are you really getting what you want here?") let students know you won't go away and that you will help them resolve the issue, thus breaking the cycle of reinforcement.

**4. Empathy statements** — A statement that lets the student know that you understand his or her situation or experiences can help deescalate a problem behavior. Such a statement might start out like, "I know it's difficult to accept someone's criticism...." Often, simply recognizing that a student is experiencing something difficult can help alleviate some of the ongoing behavior.

**5. Positive correction statements** — If a student loses points for an inappropriate behavior, you should let him or her know that part of what was lost can be earned back by following your instructions. Simple contingency management often serves to increase desired behaviors. An example of a positive correction statement would be, "When you start following instructions, you'll begin earning back some of the points you lost."

Now let's put all of these steps together in an example classroom situation:

Heather is a seventh-grade Daily Points student who has been off task for several minutes. You asked her to get back to work, but she remained off task. You approach her and initiate a Teaching Interaction on how to stay on task.

### Start a Teaching Interaction

*"Heather, I know this assignment may be somewhat difficult for you, but just a moment ago, you were looking around the room, tapping your pencil on your desk, and yawning. For being off task, you've lost 1,000 points. Please take out your point card and..."*

Heather begins to argue about the consequence.

### Stop the Teaching Interaction

Attempt to help the student regain control through "coupling" statements, specific praise, rationales, and empathy.

### Coupling statements

*"Heather, you're talking loudly. You need to be quiet and listen right now."* (Pause)

### Praise and coupling statements

*"I appreciate your looking at me and staying seated, but you're still talking loudly; please be quiet."* (Pause)

### Rationale

*"You know, Heather, when you're quiet, we can get this taken care of a lot quicker and you can finish your essay a lot sooner."* (Pause)

### Empathy and coupling statements

*"I know you have some concerns about your assignment, but we can't discuss them when you're yelling. Please be quiet."* (Pause)

### Praise

*"Nice job lowering your voice, Heather. That way I know you're getting ready to calmly talk about this with me."* (Pause)

*"I appreciate you looking at me, and you're quiet now, too. Thanks, Heather."* (Pause)

### Acknowledgement

*"Looks like we can finish this now, okay?"*

(Heather acknowledges.)

How you use the components of this technique will depend on how a student responds. Always be aware of your own behavior — use a calm, modulated voice tone; avoid harsh, demanding instructions; pause often to allow the student to respond. You may even need to talk while the student is talking, but be careful not to "talk over" the student. If the student raises his or her voice, lower yours; the student may be influenced by your modeling, or may lower his or her voice to be able to hear you.

Avoid responding directly to demands or accusations (i.e. "getting into content") to prevent a power struggle between you and the student. Address the student's arguing by using the techniques discussed earlier in this section. Although a student may have a valid issue to discuss, addressing it now may reinforce an inappropriate way to bring up concerns with people. Consider this example: A student says, "You're so unfair! How come you like everyone else better than me?" You respond with, "I can see you have some issues you'd like to discuss with me and I'd be happy to set a time later today for us to talk (empathy). But instead of trying to talk about it now, you need to just be quiet and listen (coupling statement) so that we can finish this and move on with class (rationale)."

Continue this shaping process as long as the student demonstrates improvement. The more praise you provide for behavioral approximations, the more likely you are to see positive change. However, if the negative behaviors are escalating and you see no improvement, or the student is substituting one inappropriate behavior for another, you can begin using the office referral process that will be explained later in this chapter. Your goal is to keep the student in the classroom, if at all possible, so he or she doesn't lose instruction time.

## Completing the Teaching Interaction(s)

Once you have helped the student regain self-control and have reinforced all behavioral progress with specific praise, move on to completing your teaching. Since your goal is to teach the student the skills that best meet his or her needs, assess each situation and each student individually and teach accordingly.

There are three basic ways to continue and complete your teaching once a student has regained self-control. You may choose to: 1) teach in response to the ongoing behavior and the behavior that led to the original Teaching Interaction; 2) teach in response to only the ongoing behavior; or 3) return to the original Teaching Interaction. Whatever choice you make, you must complete a Teaching Interaction that includes consequences for the behaviors you address.

If you decide to **teach in response to the original behavior and the ongoing behavior (Example 1)**, you will complete two Teaching Interactions. This decision should be based on the student's need to learn both skills and his or her ability to cope with this amount of information. One interaction will focus on the original skill deficit. To determine the other skill, you need to consider these factors:

1. Always note the antecedents to the ongoing behavior. For example, if the interfering behavior occurred during the "Consequence" step, you may want to teach the student how to accept a consequence or how to disagree appropriately. If the student has difficulty when you ask him or her to practice, you may teach him how to follow instructions. Teaching how to accept criticism would be the logical choice if a student engages in negative behaviors during the "Description of the Inappropriate Behavior" step.

2. It's also critical to consider the student's individual needs. Ask yourself questions like, "What skill does this student frequently have trouble with?", "What skill will provide the greatest assistance in different situations?", and "What can I teach that will allow this student to better

manage his or her own behavior?" These questions will help guide your decisions, particularly with students who have progressed from needing compliance-based skills toward self-management skills.

3. Frequently, your second Teaching Interaction will be about accepting criticism or a consequence. Most ongoing behavior comes from students who are in the acquisition stage of social skills learning (i.e. Daily Points students). In order for these students to progress to higher-level skills, and consequently higher-level systems, they need to increase their fluency with the critical skills of "Accepting Criticism/Consequences," and "Following Instructions."

Once you've decided to teach two skills and have determined which skills to teach, move into the Ongoing Behavior Teaching Interaction. Tell the student that you will return to the original behavior, but first you need to discuss the ongoing behavior.

Proceed with your teaching in response to the ongoing behavior just as you would with any Teaching Interaction.

(For the sake of continuity, we will continue with the example involving Heather, the seventh-grader.)

**Example 1**

### Start the Ongoing Behavior Teaching Interaction

*"Before we can talk about staying on task, Heather, we first need to discuss how you just accepted that point fine."*

"When I tried to talk to you about being off task, you argued with me about the consequence. So, Heather, you lost 1,000 points for not accepting a consequence. Please write that on your point card."

**Heather enters the point fine.**

"Nice job, Heather. When I told you that you lost 1,000 points, you looked at me and wrote the fine on your card without arguing. When you can accept consequences that way, situations usually don't get worse. Make sense? For accepting that consequence, you earned 500 points back. Good work!"

**Heather enters the positive correction points.**

Now return to the original Teaching Interaction and include a preventive prompt to increase the student's chances for success at accepting the rest of your criticism/consequences.

"And you'll get another chance to practice accepting consequences because we need to finish talking about you being off task. Remember to accept the point fine, okay?"

Complete the original Teaching Interaction sequentially.

### Original Teaching Interaction

"Heather, because you were off task, you lost 1,000 points."

**Heather enters point fine.**

"Nice job of accepting that consequence, just like we practiced. You've earned 250 points for that."

**Heather enters positive correction points.**

"Let's talk about staying on task. What should you do to stay on task, Heather?"

**Heather gives skill steps.**

"That's right. That way you'll probably finish your essay and not have to take it home with you. Let's practice staying on task so you can earn back some more points. I'm going to go over to check Tyrell's work. While I'm gone, you can stay on task and finish your essay, okay? I'll be back in a minute to check your work."

**Heather practices staying on task by finishing her work.**

"All right, Heather! You earned 250 points back for practicing staying on task. Plus, you finished your work and don't have to take it home."

**Heather enters the positive correction points.**

"Super job. Now why don't you see if Jodi needs some help with her editing?"

Sometimes you may decide that the ongoing behavior represents a greater skill deficit and requires more attention than the original inappropriate behavior. In these situations, you may choose to **teach only to the ongoing behavior (Example 2)**. Previous experiences with the student, in addition to the current one, may indicate that the original issue served only as an antecedent to the "real" problem — accepting your feedback about any type of mistake. You can address the original issue at another time through a delayed practice or by using Effective Praise when the student demonstrates appropriate skill use. In Heather's example, you may notice her staying on task at another time and reinforce her use of the skill then.

## Example 2

### Ongoing Behavior Teaching Interaction

*"Instead of talking about staying on task, it looks like we need to discuss how you accepted that consequence. Just now, when I tried to talk to you about being off task, you argued with me about the consequence. You still need to get the point fine on your card. Remember that whenever you get a consequence, you should just look at the person, say 'Okay,' and put it on your card without arguing. Ready? Write on your card that you lost 1,000 points for not accepting a consequence."*

### Heather records the point fine.

*"Nice job, Heather. You accepted that point fine without arguing! When you can do that you have a lot more time to spend on your work. Does that make sense?"*

### Heather acknowledges.

*"Super. Since you accepted that consequence really well, you earned back 500 points."*

### Heather enters the positive correction points.

*"Now, why don't you get back to your essay. You only have one more paragraph to write. Let's see if you can finish it, okay? If you need my help on anything, just raise your hand."*

**Teaching in response only to the original behavior (Example 3)** will probably occur when the ongoing behavior is fairly brief and of low intensity. If you can help the student regain self-control with a few prompts, cues, and/or coupling statements, simply return to and complete the original Teaching Interaction. It's a good idea to "pick up where you left off," unless that involves describing what the student did inappropriately. If you "rehash" the inappropriate behavior, you may risk inciting additional ongoing behavior. When ongoing behavior occurs at the "Consequences" step, include a preventive prompt before you return to the original Teaching Interaction. This will prepare the student to accept the consequences appropriately.

## Example 3

### Start a Teaching Interaction

*"...but just a moment ago you were looking around the room, tapping your pencil, and yawning. For being off task, you've lost 1,000 points. Please take out your point card and..."*

### Heather begins to argue.

*"Heather, you're talking; please be quiet. (Pause) Great. You're quiet. Can you keep looking at me too, please? Thanks, Heather. Let's continue, okay? Remember to just look at me and say 'Okay' when you get that point fine."*

### Continue with the Original Teaching Interaction

*"Heather, please take out your point card and write down that you lost 1,000 points for being off task."*

**Heather enters the point fine.**

*"Nice job writing down that point fine, Heather. Now, let's talk about how you can earn some of those points back. Whenever you're given a task, get all the materials you need, start right away, continue until the task is completed, then let the teacher know when you're finished. If you can do that, you'll probably finish the work a lot quicker and move on to something you enjoy, like reading your novel. Does that make sense?"*

**Heather acknowledges.**

*"Okay, let's practice. I'm going to go and help Tyrell. While I'm over there, you'll need to practice staying on task by finishing that last paragraph. Okay? I'll be back in a while to see how you did."*

**Heather practices.**

*"Great job staying on task! You earned back 500 points and you got your essay finished."*

**Heather enters positive correction points.**

Teach the skill(s) that will be most beneficial to the student and structure your teaching to fit each individual situation. You may need to rearrange some steps or use positive correction points (up to half the number lost for Daily Points students) more frequently to maintain the student's attention, or to reinforce certain desired behaviors. In Example 2, you'll notice that the description of the appropriate behavior preceded the delivery of the consequence to serve as a preventive prompt. Sometimes the point fines or negatives students earn for their ongoing

behavior are larger than those illustrated. The size of the consequence is determined by the frequency and severity of the behavior. Please refer to Chapter 6 and Chapters 15 through 17 for specific discussion of these concepts.

View each student individually. Teach according to each one's needs and the behavioral outcome you are trying to achieve. Don't be too rule-governed or try to follow an exact procedure with every student and situation. Behavior is not an isolated or static event; exchanges occur in a dynamic context, with each aspect related to those that precede or follow it. By recognizing behavior as an interactional, developmental process, you can modify and customize your teaching to meet the needs of all students.

## ▶ Ongoing Behavior Teaching Interaction into Administrative Intervention

In the first part of this chapter, you learned how to prevent or de-escalate ongoing behaviors that interfere with the learning process. When these methods are effective, students regain self-control so you can complete your teaching and they can remain in your classroom. However, there will be situations when students won't respond to your efforts. When this happens, they need to leave the classroom to receive additional, individualized attention from an administrator. (See Chapter 14, "Overview of Administrative Intervention.")

In this section, we will discuss the process of referring a disruptive student to the office. Keep in mind that **you** decide when to begin the referral process. Your decision should be based on the severity and duration of the behaviors and whether the student is showing progress toward the goal of regaining self-control.

## Definition

The referral process is not a separate type of Teaching Interaction. It is not a fixed series of steps that is to be used at a designated point in time, or following a particular set of behaviors. Rather, it is a flexible teaching sequence designed to help the student recognize the severity and consequences of his or her behavior, and to provide behavioral alternatives. It includes many of the same techniques discussed earlier in this chapter, but also employs the use of consequences. The sequence is flexible because you can easily return to the original teaching agenda if a student regains self-control. The sequence is fair because you continue to communicate expectations and outcomes to a student throughout the process.

## Purpose and timing

The main purpose of the referral sequence is to help the student regain self-control while continuing your teaching focus. Using clear instructions, praise, and rationales helps students understand their options and make better decisions about their behavior.

The most logical time to utilize the referral sequence is when a student displays ongoing behavior that continues or escalates during a Teaching Interaction. If, at any time, a student's behavior is perceived as dangerous to the student or others, all steps should be bypassed and the student should immediately be referred to the office. Examples of behavior that would result in an immediate referral include, but are not limited to, verbal or physical abuse or assault, major destruction of property, and being under the influence of drugs or alcohol. Your school or school district probably has a list of major offenses that result in removal of a student from a classroom. Additional discussion of types of office referral behavior is found in Chapter 14, "Overview of Administrative Intervention."

## The process

Whenever you begin to discuss students' behavior with them, it is hoped that they will accept feedback and consequences without arguing, complaining, or demonstrating any other interfering behaviors. Unfortunately, this doesn't always happen. When disruptive behaviors do arise, you must deal with the ongoing behavior in order to teach needed skills. Little learning can take place if the student continues engaging in negative behaviors while you are trying to teach. Your main goal is to help the student regain control so he or she can remain in the classroom. As such, the first task is to help the student identify inappropriate behaviors and replace them with more appropriate ones. The following section explains each step in the office referral process. Examples are used to illustrate the steps.

**Give specific instructions:** Once you've recognized the student's ongoing behavior, you should provide clear descriptions of the negative behavior and alternative appropriate behaviors to help the youth make better decisions. As described earlier in this chapter, these paired statements should focus on correcting one behavior at a time. Describing too many behaviors can confuse the student and have a "badgering" effect that can escalate negative behavior. Descriptions should emphasize the behaviors that are the most overt and disruptive to your teaching at that moment. Examples include: "You're arguing. It would be better if you'd be quiet and listen"; "You have your head on your desk. I'd like you to sit up and look at me, please"; and "You're standing up. Please sit down." Coupling the inappropriate behavior with an alternative behavior lets the student know what he or she should and shouldn't do.

After each instruction, pause to allow adequate time for the student to respond. The pauses should be long enough to give the student a chance to calm down, but short enough that they don't reinforce inappropriate behavior. Don't expect immediate compliance; it's difficult for most people to follow instructions after they have lost self-control. Praise any approximations of desirable behaviors. These may be the specific behaviors you asked for, or any others you observe. The descriptions should be brief and specific. Let's look at an example of a classroom situation in which the referral process is used.

### Example

David is a ninth-grade student who is on the Progress System. While you're talking with him about forgetting his social studies homework, he begins to argue.

**Student :** David is standing by his desk, arguing loudly and pointing his finger.

**Teacher:** *"David, you're talking loudly. I'd like you to be quiet and listen."* (Pause)

**Student:** David lowers his voice, crosses his arms, turns his back to you, and continues arguing.

**Teacher:** *"Thanks for lowering your voice. You're continuing to talk. Please stop talking and listen."* (Pause)

**Student:** David continues the disruptive behaviors.

**Teacher:** *"It's great that you're standing still and staying right here, but you're still arguing. It would be better if you'd be quiet and listen."* (Pause)

Using empathy statements and rationales, as discussed earlier in this chapter, also may help the student regain self-control. Continue using a combination of these techniques as long as the student is making progress. However, if the student's ongoing behavior continues or escalates, you'll need to move on to the next step of the process.

**Give a moderate consequence:** Letting the student know that he or she has earned a moderate consequence indicates the seriousness of the behavior. A moderate consequence may motivate the student to stop the inappropriate behaviors and begin engaging in more appropriate behaviors. Within the Motivation Systems, a moderate consequence is 5,000 points on the Daily Points System, a moderate negative on the Progress System, an "irresponsible" for on-card Merit students, and a natural/logical consequence (e.g. loss of a special privilege or staying after school) for off-card Merit students. Please refer to Chapter 17, "The Merit System" for additional discussion of behavioral expectations of Merit students.

**Example**

**Student:** David is standing by his desk with his back to you. His arms are folded across his chest and he continues arguing.

**Teacher:** *"David, you've earned a moderate negative for arguing."* (Pause)

**Give specific instructions (paired statements, empathy, or rationales):** If the moderate consequence does not stop the student's ongoing behavior (and it sometimes will not), you should again provide some paired statements to help the student move toward more desirable behaviors. As mentioned before, your descriptions should focus on the most overt behaviors. If you have described one particular behavior throughout the process and the student hasn't improved that behavior, you may want to switch your focus to a different inappropriate behavior, as illustrated in the next example.

Your choice of strategies and the length of time you spend on this step will depend on what you know about the student and what you observe. Whereas paired descriptions are very helpful to one student, empathy statements or rationales may work

best for another. Some students may be able to regain self-control fairly quickly, while others will demonstrate slow, but steady improvement. In general, though, unless the student is beginning to demonstrate real progress toward regaining self-control, you'll need to start thinking about how the disruption is affecting the other students in your classroom. Giving the student too much attention at this point also may serve to reinforce the student's out-of-control behavior.

**Student:** David continues to stand by his desk. He turns around to face you and places his fists on his hips. He sighs loudly and begins to argue about the consequence.

**Teacher:** *"Thanks for looking at me, David. You're standing up. Would you sit down, please?"* (Pause)

**Tell the student a major consequence and office referral is possible:** If the student does not respond to your instructions, you should tell him or her that a major consequence and an office referral is possible if the ongoing behavior continues. This statement indicates the seriousness of the situation and the consequences that will follow if the behavior isn't stopped.

A major consequence would be a 10,000-point fine for students on Daily Points or a major negative for students on the Progress System. Letting students know about the consequences they will receive if they don't regain self-control helps establish a tie between the behavior and the consequences. The student should realize that he or she determines what happens next — either stop the negative behavior or earn the negative consequences. By understanding this basic concept — that they can control the outcome of a situation by controlling their behavior — students hopefully will choose to avoid the major consequence and the office referral.

**Example**

**Student:** David continues his ongoing behaviors.

**Teacher:** *"If you continue to not follow my instructions, you will earn a major negative, and will need to report to the office."* (Pause)

**Give a major consequence and refer the student to the office:** If the student continues to behave inappropriately after you have described the possible negative consequences, he should immediately be referred to the office. Your attempts to help the student regain self-control have not been successful, so in fairness to the student and the others in your classroom, an office referral is necessary. Once in the office, the student will receive additional one-on-one attention and teaching from an administrator in order to learn better ways of dealing with problems in the classroom and other situations. (See Chapter 14, "Overview of Administrative Intervention.") The combination of teaching and consequences should help the student learn self-control and what to do to avoid an office referral in the future.

When making the actual office referral, tell the student he has earned a major consequence and to report to the office. Ask the student if he can get there on his own or if he needs assistance. The student no longer has the option of staying in your classroom, but might not get up and leave on his own. In this situation, you'll need to follow predetermined procedures for getting help. In any case, the final decision on how a student reports to the office is left to the student, giving him another opportunity to make choices about his behavior. Choosing whether to report on his own or with assistance can affect the level of consequences that go with the office referral, as "Severity Ratings" often are used to characterize the level of the referred student's behavior. (See Chapter 20, "Systems Level Changes.")

**Example**

**Student:** David remains standing and continues to argue.

**Teacher:** *"David, you've now earned a major negative for not following instructions and you need to report to the office. Can you get there by yourself, or do you need some help?"*

Once you've made the office referral, the administrator assumes the responsibility of dealing with the student's behavior until the intervention sequence is completed. Inform the office of the referral by the prearranged method (e.g. intercom, telephone, student assistant). At the same time, let the office know whether the student needs assistance.

**Example**

**Student:** David says *"Fine!"* in a loud voice and leaves your room, slamming the door on the way out.

**Teacher:** Calls office via intercom. *"David Rogers has been referred to the office. He's on his way."*

**or**

**Student:** David sits down in his chair, crosses his arms, looks away, and says nothing.

**Teacher:** Calls office via intercom. *"David Rogers has been referred to the office. He needs assistance."*

Hopefully, the student will quietly leave the classroom and report directly to the office. Should he refuse to leave the classroom, your main concern still is with your other students. Trying to teach the student additional skills at this time would be unproductive, at best. Paying attention to his refusal may only serve to reinforce that behavior and give the student an audience in front of the other students. As long as he is not disturbing others, the student may remain in your class until an administrator arrives. (Of course, this is assuming that an administrator or crisis interventionist is in the building and will arrive within minutes of the referral.)

What if the student not only refuses to leave the classroom, but also is being disruptive or destructive? In these cases, your best option is to instruct the other students to leave the classroom with you. Moving your class to the hall, media center, or multipurpose room is preferable to attempting physical restraint or allowing the out-of-control student to demonstrate such behavior in front of an "audience." Leaving the student alone may help de-escalate the youth's behavior. And, you will ensure that the rest of the class isn't at risk of getting hurt. Consequences, including any necessary compensation, should be given by the administrator during the office referral process.

## ▶ General considerations

When you are dealing with a student who is engaging in ongoing behavior, monitor your own behavior very carefully. It is very easy to allow yourself to get caught up in the student's words and actions. You may feel angry, agitated, or frustrated when a student is not following your instructions or accepting your feedback. Therefore, you have to be aware of your own behavior. Concentrate on keeping a calm, nonthreatening voice tone and body posture. Responding with harsh, aggressive behavior, in all likelihood, will only escalate the student's negative behavior.

A calm, quiet voice tone models your expectations and may help the youth to regain self-control. Trying to "talk over" a student results in a cycle of each person speaking louder than the other, eventually leading to a shouting match and accompanying feelings of anger. You may have to pause and take a deep breath in order to avoid the impulse to speak loudly.

Remember that this is not a time to justify your role, explain fairness, or address the student's complaints or issues. Even though you may feel like responding to what a student is saying, don't get drawn into arguments or discussions. The easiest way to avoid this trap is to respond only to the behavior of **talking**, not to what the youth is saying. The overriding goal is to help the student calm down. Once this is accomplished, you can set a separate time for the student to discuss concerns with staff members.

There are many advantages to not arguing with a student. You'll not only avoid losing your own self-control and possibly escalating the student's behavior, but you'll also maintain your relationship with the student. You won't risk saying something hurtful or negative to the student if you keep your focus on the student's **behavior** of talking or arguing rather than on the words that are being said.

Maintain a safe, appropriate distance between the student and you. Stay at least an arm's length away; you don't want the student to feel "closed in" or physically pressured. If the student feels trapped, he or she may strike out or try to run away. Touching, in most cases, is not recommended when dealing with an agitated student. Any type of touch or certain hand gestures at this time may be perceived as aversive or threatening. Reaching out, pointing at the student, or clenching your fists may send strong, negative messages to the student. A less-threatening posture may be to keep your hands at your sides, in your pockets, or folded in front of you.

Always remember to allow a pause after you've given an instruction to the student. Pausing allows the student to hear, understand, and begin to comply with what

you've said. "Rapid-fire" instructions may confuse children and may escalate their negative behaviors. Counting to yourself between instructions may help you maintain an appropriate pace.

## ▶ Summary

You may find that your most powerful tool in preventing ongoing behavior is consistent teaching and recognition of a student's efforts. Clearly communicating your expectations and following up with praise and Corrective Teaching show your concern and fairness, and help build strong relationships with students. These relationships, in turn, may help students bring their behavior under control in stressful situations. At the very least, even if you are unsuccessful in helping a student remain in your class after he or she has lost self-control, the student's return to your room will be easier because your relationship with the student has remained intact.

In addition, you must view each student individually. Teach according to each one's needs and the behavioral outcomes you are trying to achieve. Don't be too rule-governed or try to follow an exact procedure with every student and situation. Behavior is not an isolated or static event; exchanges occur in a dynamic context, with each aspect related to those which precede or follow it. By recognizing behavior as an interactional, developmental process you can modify and customize your teaching to meet the needs of all students.

# CHAPTER FOURTEEN

# Overview of administrative intervention

So far, you have learned techniques for dealing with ongoing or "out-of-control" behavior. However, as described in the preceding chapter, you can face situations when a student can no longer stay in the classroom because of the frequency, intensity, or severity of the ongoing behavior. In these situations, the student is referred to the school office, where the principal or other staff member intervenes to help the student regain self-control. We call this process Administrative Intervention.

This chapter provides guidelines for determining when to refer a student to the office, an overview of Administrative Intervention, and an explanation of your role in the referral process. Specific information about office consequences is covered in Chapter 20 "Systems Level Changes."

## ▶ When to refer a student

The office referral process gives teachers a series of steps to follow when a student is unable to bring his or her behavior under control. This process, which was described in the previous chapter, should cover as many as 90 percent of the situations in which office referrals are necessary.

There are three main patterns of student behavior that can lead to an office referral. Two of the three are preceded by teaching; the third type results in an automatic referral. Let's take a look at automatic referrals first.

Automatic referrals occur whenever a student commits a **major infraction of a school rule** or engages in a **serious misbehavior**, particularly one that endangers the safety of that student or others.

This type of referral should be fairly infrequent because it represents behaviors of considerable magnitude. Depending on what the student does, little or no teaching may precede the referral. Examples include fighting; possession of weapons, drugs, gang-related paraphernalia, or other contraband; major destruction of property; being under the influence of drugs or alcohol; and physical or verbal aggression that is perceived as threatening. Such aggression would include striking out at you or another student, or getting physically close to someone and directly swearing at or threatening that person. You may need to use some of the techniques for calming a student that were described in the previous chapter but most of these situations also require help from others.

Again, the frequency of automatic referrals should be fairly low. If you find you are referring students quite often because of rule infractions, you may want to spend some time evaluating your school policies to see if they are too restrictive. Certainly, major misbehaviors warrant automatic office referrals to ensure the safety and well-being of all students and staff. However, the majority of students' inappropriate behaviors should be dealt with in the classroom. An example may help illustrate this point. In some schools, any swearing by a student results in an automatic office referral. The swearing may or may not be directed at any one person. As a result, some students, given their backgrounds and other difficulties, could find themselves in the office fairly frequently. But unless the behavior (swearing) is so serious that it disrupts or endangers others in the classroom, it may be much more beneficial to use direct skill-based teaching and consequences. By keeping the student in the classroom, you have an opportunity to teach alternative behaviors and the student will not miss valuable classroom time.

The second pattern of behavior that can result in an office referral is the most common of the three types. In this case, the student is engaging in **ongoing behavior** and has been asked several times within one Teaching Interaction to begin following instructions so that he can bring his or her behavior under control. Students most frequently are referred for ongoing behavior related to not following instructions, or not accepting criticism or consequences. Although the ongoing behavior could vary significantly in intensity, duration, and variety, it is not perceived as a threat to the safety of the student or others. Therefore, the teacher has the opportunity to teach alternative behaviors before referring the student to the office for additional help. Chapter 13, "Ongoing Behavior," includes techniques for helping a student regain self-control.

The third pattern of behavior resulting in an office referral is **minor misbehavior over time**. These frequent problem behaviors, which require repeated teaching, may occur many times during a single day or class period, or may continue over many days. When using the office as a "back-up" or increased consequence for repeated minor misbehaviors, remember these points:

1. The skill level of the individual student will, in part, determine your use of this office referral option. Although you may choose to refer a Progress or Merit student for repeated minor difficulties, such as not

having the proper school materials or inappropriately giving negative feedback, you probably would not refer a Daily Points student to the office for these same behaviors. A student on Daily Points most likely has many other target behaviors that need improvement, and these would take precedence over some of the higher-level "fine-tuning" skills. In other words, you should choose consequences and strategies that are in the best interests of each student, based upon his or her skill levels and needs. Otherwise, you may find yourself making too many referrals or falling back on your largest consequences for a variety of misbehaviors. This can dilute the system and frustrate your students.

2. Students should be told that an office referral is probable for continued difficulties. If the behavior continues over time, even with repeated teaching and consequences, you need to let the student know that the situation is becoming serious and that the next step will be an office referral unless some behavioral changes are made. For example, you have talked with a student for the fourth time during one class period about making inappropriate comments. Since the misbehavior is continuing, you feel that the teaching and consequences you've used have been ineffective. At this point, you may tell the student something like, "I need to let you know that if you make any more inappropriate comments to other students during this class period, you'll be referred to the office." This lets the student know what you expect of him or her and what will happen if misbehavior continues.

3. In general, this type of office referral is reserved for one behavior that occurs over time. Infrequently, however, you may tell a student that he or she will be referred to the office for engaging in any of a variety of inappropriate behaviors. This usually occurs when a student begins engaging in a inappropriate behavior as soon as you've finished a Teaching Interaction on a different skill. If this pattern occurs, you may need to increase the in-class consequences or tell the student that any other inappropriate behaviors will result in an office referral. Also, you should check your own behavior by assessing your tolerances for ongoing behavior. It may be that while you're teaching the student, he is doing things that indicate he is not accepting your feedback. Unchecked, these behaviors may escalate or result in "limit-testing" by the student. That is, a student may continue to engage in minor inappropriate behaviors to see how far he can go before you respond.

## ▶ The Administrative Intervention process

The Administrative Intervention process involves joint efforts and cooperation between the teacher and administrator. The main goal of the process is to help the student regain self-control and to teach alternative behaviors to replace those which resulted in the child's removal from the classroom. Although the immediate teaching agenda focuses on what happened in the classroom, the long-range goal is to teach skills that the student can use to control his or her behavior under any conditions, thereby avoiding negative outcomes such as office referrals, fights, or damaged relationships.

In addition to skill-based teaching, the process allows administrators and teachers to concentrate on building trusting, caring relationships with students. The teaching focus helps students understand that teachers and administrators are genuinely concerned about them, and that the students' behavior, not the students themselves, are at issue.

## Step one: Obtaining partial compliance

After a teacher makes an office referral, the student chooses to report in one of two ways: "in crisis" or "under partial compliance." Preferably, a student will choose to leave the classroom quietly and immediately. If the student goes to the office, is relatively quiet, and follows instructions, but still displays some negative behaviors, he or she is considered "under partial compliance." However, if the student chooses to remain in the classroom following the referral, does not report directly to the office, or reports to the office but is unable to sit quietly, he or she is "in crisis."

The administrator who is working with the student will use a variety of techniques to help the student regain self-control. The goal of this part of the process is to have the youth sit quietly in an assigned place the student and the administrator can talk. The student also promises to stay in his or her seat while the administrator goes to visit the teacher who made the office referral. The techniques used in the office are similar to those used when dealing with ongoing behavior:

**1. Praise** — Specific descriptions of a student's progress toward regaining self-control can help the student calm down. Praise is the first thing a student should hear from the administrator upon reporting to the office following a referral. For example, the administrator may say, "Thanks for coming to the office right away." Praise also is used when a student follows specific instructions or approximates desirable behavior.

**2. Coupling statements** — Using paired descriptions of behavior emphasizes appropriate alternatives to the student's current behavior. An example is, "You're talking. Please be quiet and listen."

**3. Simple instructions** — Giving simple instructions gives the student options for appropriate behaviors. Examples include, "Please sit down," and "Lower your voice, please."

**4. Empathy** — Students in crisis often need to know that someone understands their feelings and struggles. By using empathy statements such as "I know this is difficult," or "I understand that you're upset," the administrator can help de-escalate the student's behavior. Empathy statements are often paired with rationales.

**5. Rationales** — "Process-oriented" rationales are most frequently used during a crisis situation. Statements such as, "The sooner you can quiet down and listen, the sooner we can resolve your issues," let students know that regaining self-control can result in positive outcomes for them. Such rationales should be worded carefully so students don't get the impression that their problems or their "side of the story" will be discussed **immediately.** Since this type of rationale implies that the student will have an opportunity to share information, an appropriate time should be set aside for this (typically, after the teaching portion of the Administrative Intervention process has been completed).

**6. Physical monitoring** — While talking with the student, the administrator should be relaxed and move slowly, keeping a safe and comfortable distance from the student to avoid escalating the negative behavior. The goal is to help the student regain control to the point that he or she is able to sit in the place set aside for the office intervention. The administrator helps guide the student to this place by standing between the door and the assigned area. If the student tries to leave the office area, however, the administrator should move away from the door and let the student leave. Generally, administrators should not block the student's path or restrain the student in any way since physical restraint and management most often escalate behavior. If a student chooses to leave the office area, the administrator should move aside, then follow the student within the school building. In situations where the student might be in danger by leaving the building, an administrator may need to follow or physically keep the student inside. Some schools are near busy streets or highways, and some children may not understand the danger of running out of the building into the street. Administrators should continue to follow set policies about students who leave the school building without permission, but should also be prepared to use physical techniques to keep stu-

dents safe. The National Crisis Prevention Institute in Madison, Wisconsin is one organization that can provide training and information about physical management. Decisions as to the appropriateness of these techniques are left to the trained individual.

The administrator works with the student, using a combination of these techniques, until the student is relatively quiet and sitting in the designated spot. At this point, the administrator asks for a verbal commitment from the student that he or she will stay seated in the chair the whole time the administrator is gone. Getting this commitment is necessary for the process to continue, as it represents a "trust bond" between the student and administrator. If the student is not ready to give that commitment, the administrator will not leave. Rather, the administrator will continue working with the student, pointing out continued progress toward the goal, rationales for the process, and potential outcomes of the student's behavior.

The way the administrator asks for the verbal commitment is very important. The wording should specifically ask for the student to stay seated the entire time the administrator is out of the office. By clearly stating this expectation, and having the student agree to it, the administrator can avoid problems that may occur in his or her absence. Consider the potential differences in a student's behavior by changing a few words when gaining a verbal commitment: "I need to know you'll be in this chair when I get back," versus "I need to know that you'll remain seated the entire time I'm gone, and that you'll be here when I get back." Asking the student to stay seated the whole time the administrator is gone does not ensure anything, of course, but it does leave the responsibility and choice of behavior with the student.

If the administrator has any concerns about leaving the student alone in the office because of safety issues, the child would not be left unattended. Rather, another adult would keep an eye on the student during this period of time. Depending on the student's level of compliance, it may be easier to move an adult near the student than to have the student move closer to an available adult.

## Step two: Checking with referring teacher

After the student agrees to remain seated, the administrator leaves the office and meets with you (the referring teacher). At that time, the administrator fills out an office referral form (Figure 1) with the information necessary to accurately complete the intervention process. If possible, you should jot some quick notes following the referral so you can provide specific details of your interaction with the student. This information helps the administrator focus on appropriate alternative behaviors to replace those that led to the office referral.

You should be prepared to respond to a number of questions about the referral:

**1. Antecedent events** — What circumstances surrounded the behavior? Who was involved? Where and when did this occur?

**2. Behavioral responses** — What did the student do or say? How severe was the behavior? How often does this type of behavior occur? Has it happened frequently in the past?

**3. Consequences** — How did you intervene? What type of teaching did you attempt? Were any consequences delivered?

**4. Additional information** — What else can you add to help the administrator work with the student?

The administrator uses this information to determine the type of referral **(serious misbehavior/major rule infraction, ongoing behavior, or minor misbehavior over time)** and the skills to teach during the intervention process. The administrator then returns to the office and begins working with the student to gain specific compliance.

## Step three: Intensive Teaching

Upon returning to the office, the administrator should praise the student for staying seated and for anything else the student has done appropriately. If it appears that the student did not stay seated during the administrator's absence (for example, items missing or askew), appropriate consequences for the behavior are given later in the intervention process.

The administrator's goal during Intensive Teaching is to de-escalate the student's disruptive behavior to a point where the student can once again follow instructions. Hopefully, the time the administrator was away has helped the student gain addi-

**Figure 1**

# Office Referral

STUDENT _____ CLASS/TIME _____ REFERRED BY _____

*CIRCLE ONE:*

MAJOR MISBEHAVIOR/          CONTINUED MINOR MISBEHAVIOR          FAILURE TO ACCEPT
INFRACTION OF SCHOOL RULE          OVER TIME          CRITICISM/CONSEQUENCES

SPECIFIC DESCRIPTION OF PROBLEM BEHAVIOR:

TEACHER INTERVENTION(S):

ADDITIONAL COMMENTS:

*Was 10,000 point penalty entered on card?* _____ *Yes* _____ *No* tional self-control. However, if the student continues with partial compliance, the administrator consistently uses the techniques described earlier to help the student achieve this level during Intensive Teaching.

During Intensive Teaching, the administrator shapes the student's behavior using coupling statements, specific praise, empathy, and rationales — the same techniques you use when dealing with ongoing behavior and the administrator uses when de-escalating a crisis situation. The administrator works with the student until he or she displays behaviors that indicate a readiness to follow instructions and accept feedback. Acceptable behaviors include being quiet, paying attention, and sitting up straight.

## Step four: Teaching Interaction

Once the student is displaying appropriate behavior, the administrator starts a Teaching Interaction on the referral behavior. The Teaching Interaction follows the same steps as the one you have learned, but may include extra practices, more discussion, and some problem-solving.

Consequences for the office referral and any other outstanding contracts (see Chapter 20, "Systems Level Changes") are given within the context of the Teaching Interaction. If the student's behavior resulted in any other consequences during the office intervention (e.g. damaging the office, prolonged out-of-control behavior), these also are given at this point. In addition to point fines and potential restitution, each office referral requires notification of parents, an apology to the referring teacher, and completion of all missed classroom assignments.

Throughout the teaching process, the administrator works hard to maintain a sense of fairness and understanding, while helping the student learn better ways to handle difficult situations in the classroom. One goal of the process is to preserve and strengthen the teacher-student relationship; that is, during the intervention, the administrator supports the teacher's decisions while also attending to the student's issues. If an administrator has concerns about the appropriateness of the referral, he or she will talk with the teacher at a separate time.

After all consequences have been delivered, the administrator can allow the student to discuss problems or feelings related to the office referral. At this point, the student has successfully completed the office intervention (except for the apology) and should be able to discuss concerns and feelings rationally. The student and administrator may spend some time problem-solving, working through issues that may have contributed to classroom difficulties, or talking about the student's "side" of the referral. By delaying discussion until this time, the student probably will be more successful in conveying concerns appropriately.

## Step five: Prepare and practice apology

The student and the administrator work together on the apology to the referring teacher. The administrator asks questions and helps the student formulate an appropriate apology. A number of practices follow to ensure that the student will be successful when delivering the apology to the teacher. Practices also help the student accept responsibility for his or her own behavior by emphasizing the response chosen by the student. When the administrator feels reasonably confident that the student can successfully make the apology, he or she will return to your classroom to update you on the student's progress and determine if this is a good time for the student to return and give the apology.

## Step six: Check with the teacher

When the administrator returns to your classroom, he or she will talk to you about the office intervention and the upcoming apology.

The administrator also will discuss strategies for helping the student return to class successfully. He or she will let you know that the consequences associated with the referral were taken care of, and that no further mention of them is necessary. Reminding the student about negative behavior could result in repeated problems, whereas praise for appropriate behavior will increase the student's chances for successfully returning to class. The administrator may ask about the classwork the student missed while in the office, and encourage the student to talk with you about it.

## Step seven: Student delivers apology

After you and the administrator have determined when the student should make the apology, the administrator and sdtudernt will return to your classroom together. Before returning, however, the administrator probably will have the student practice the apology one more time.

You will be asked to step outside the classroom so the student can apologize away from other students. The administrator will determine whether the apology is acceptable because he or she has been working with the student and has set the expectation level for the student. If the apology does not meet these expectations, the administrator will take the student back to the office for additional teaching and practice. If the apology is acceptable, the administrator will make a statement of approval (e.g. "Nice job, Jan."), or will ask the student if he or she is ready to return to class. You can then welcome the student back to your class and provide immediate praise for some aspect of the student's behavior.

Following up with frequent praise is also important. By praising the student's efforts, you'll help him or her learn about maintaining relationships even in the face of conflict. Your attention to positive behaviors also communicates that you recognize the attempts the student is making to "start anew."

## ▶ Summary

You have a crucial role in determining the success of the Administrative Intervention process. The following summarizes your main responsibilities.

1. Consistently maintain low tolerances for inappropriate behaviors and teaching methodologies.

2. Notify appropriate personnel when you have referred a student to the office. Know the proper procedures for notifying the office (e.g. use of intercom, telephone, teacher assistant, or student).

3. Be prepared to clearly describe the antecedent events and student behavior that led to the office referral. Take quick notes following the referral if that will help you be more accurate.

4. Be prepared to provide information about any classwork the student misses. This will ensure that the student is accountable for all assignments.

5. Be ready to accept the student back into your class and to reinforce the apology. You may not always feel ready to have the student back, but the student should be allowed to return following successful completion of the Administrative Intervention process. You can share your specific concerns with the administrator at the time he or she checks back with you (Step Six), but the administrator makes the final determination about the student's return to the classroom.

6. After the student returns, reinforce any positive behaviors and efforts. The tone and quality of your interactions may well determine how successful the students reintegration into your classroom is.

# CHAPTER FIFTEEN

# The daily points system

Daily Points is the first level of the Boys Town Motivation Systems. As described in Chapter 6, each of the three levels of the semi-token economy is designed to meet students' changing and emerging needs as they gain fluency with social skills. The main goals of the Motivation Systems are to shape appropriate student behaviors, provide students with the support they need to be successful, and fade students off the artificial contingencies of the system as they gain proficiency and move through the three levels.

Students determine their rate of progression through the levels of the Motivation Systems. They make decisions about their own behavior and, consequently, are somewhat in control of the number of tokens (points) they earn. They decide how to spend their points — whether on bonds, tan-gibles, or activity reinforcers. These decisions determine how long a student stays on any one level of the system, including Daily Points.

All students new to the Motivation Systems program begin on Daily Points. It is an effective level for students who have had limited success in "mainstream" school settings. Many students who have had difficulty in school are not intrinsically moti-vated and need a structured, "external" system of reinforcement to help them develop a self-directed repertoire of life skills. A major goal of Daily Points is to provide immediate, consistent, and frequent reinforcement of social and academic behaviors that should meet the needs of students in the acquisition stage of social skills learning.

Not all students are best served by the Daily Points System. But since it is difficult to initially judge their level of need by reading files, giving tests, or interviewing them, each student begins at Daily Points. A student can move to the next level fairly quickly by demonstrating skill fluency in the classroom, thus reaching the level most appropriate to his or her needs. Specific details of this process are presented later in this chapter and also are discussed in Chapter 16, "The Progress System."

## ▶ General description

Students on the Daily Points System directly earn points for appropriate behavior and lose points for inappropriate behavior. They learn basic social skills to help them "get along" in school each day. The skills can be generalized to settings outside school, and the teaching process helps students begin to make connections between their behavior and the consequences which may result. The frequency and immediacy of basic social skills teaching are key principles of the Daily Points System.

Daily Points, like the other levels of the Motivation Systems, is a "flexible" economy. Students earn and lose points, depending on the behaviors they exhibit. Since students on Daily Points are acquiring and beginning to use new skills, you should expect them to have many learning opportunities during the school day. This means they will lose points for social skills errors, but will have the chance to earn many points back by practicing alternative behaviors with you. This concept of "positive correction" allows students to earn back points, which keeps the system flexible and also provides immediate

opportunities for the student to learn replacement or alternative behaviors.

Although there is no "ceiling" on the number of points a student can earn each day, a total of about 30,000 positive points reflects a "good" day. By frequently reinforcing desired behaviors (maintaining at least a 4:1 ratio of praise to Corrective Teaching), students should be able to earn enough points each day to purchase something from the privilege menu. (See Chapter 19, "Purchasing and Menus," for complete discussion.)

Students spend their accumulated points on tangibles, privileges, or "bonds." Bonds are abstract exchange units used to purchase the next level of the Motivation Systems. Each bond costs 6,000 points, and students must obtain 100 of them to "buy up" to Progress. Students determine how often and how many bonds they buy. This allows them to move through Daily Points at their own pace, reflecting their needs for immediacy and structure. Often, students new to the Daily Points System don't buy many bonds because they are abstract and don't represent an immediate reinforcer. As students mature behaviorally, they learn to delay the need for immediate reinforcement and begin to see the advantages of moving to a less-restrictive system. At this point, students may begin to spend more of their points on bonds.

Frequent social skills teaching is a hallmark of the Daily Points System. Students should have 25 to 30 positive interactions a day to ensure sufficient opportunity to learn prosocial skills. As when learning any new skill, whether it be two-digit addition, hitting a baseball, or greeting someone, students need a high level of feedback, practice, and reinforcement to gain fluency and proficiency.

Daily Points students generally work toward learning basic or "critical" skills. By gaining proficiency with these, students may find increased success in many situations and environments. Please refer to Chapter 7, "Teaching the Curriculum Skills," for additional discussion of the Social Skills Curriculum and teaching decisions. Suggestions for goal-setting and targeting will be presented later in this chapter.

## ▶ Mechanics of the Daily Points Sheet

All earned points are recorded as individual entries on the three-page Daily Points Sheet. The first page (Figure 1) is for positive social and academic points. Point penalties are recorded on the second page (Figure 2), and school staff comments and homework assignments are written on the third page (Figure 3).

### Page one: Positive points

The left side of the first page is reserved for recording academic performance, not social behavior. Students should be reinforced for completing in-class and homework assignments and for participating during class time. Additionally, students can earn points for "bonuses" or extra effort related to academic work.

The nature of academic reinforcement will depend on the student's current level of performance. You should consider where the student presently "functions," then shape behaviors from that point of reference. New students, for example, may earn academic points for "showing up" each day and participating at a fairly minimal level. Because of many past negative school experiences, students need to be reinforced for any behaviors approximating desired outcomes. By noticing and reinforcing positive steps, students can learn that school is a rewarding place. Although, at first, you may feel as though you are communicating low expectations, you will continue to shape each student's behavior by expecting improvements over time.

Points on the academic side of the card are earned in increments of 500 and 1,000. Generally, students earn the maximum number of points if they are in class all period and meet their individualized criteria (discussed earlier with them). Students usually receive the smaller number of points for "Participation" and "Assignment Completion" if they are in class for only part of the period. Again, the number of points earned will depend on the individualized expectations of performance for each student. All students can earn between 15,000 and 20,000 points each day for academic behaviors.

The right side of the front page reflects positive social interactions. Entries are made for appropriate use of target skills and "other" behaviors observed during the day. (See also "Teaching Social Behavior to Daily Points Students" later in this chapter.) Although entries generally are made in 500-

**Figure 1**

# Daily Point System

_____  
_Name_

_____  
_Date_

| Points Possible | Points Earned  T.I. | | Period | Class |
|---|---|---|---|---|
| 500-1000<br>500-1000<br>500-1000 | _____ _____<br>_____ _____<br>_____ _____ | Class Participation<br>Assignment Completion<br>Bonus/Homework | | Reading |
| 500-1000<br>500-1000<br>500-1000 | _____ _____<br>_____ _____<br>_____ _____ | Class Participation<br>Assignment Completion<br>Bonus/Homework | | Language Arts |
| 500-1000<br>500-1000<br>500-1000 | _____ _____<br>_____ _____<br>_____ _____ | Class Participation<br>Assignment Completion<br>Bonus/Homework | | Math |
| 500-1000<br>500-1000<br>500-1000 | _____ _____<br>_____ _____<br>_____ _____ | Class Participation<br>Assignment Completion<br>Bonus/Homework | | Social Studies |
| 500-1000<br>500-1000<br>500-1000 | _____ _____<br>_____ _____<br>_____ _____ | Class Participation<br>Assignment Completion<br>Bonus/Homework | | Science |
| 500-1000<br>500-1000<br>500-1000 | _____ _____<br>_____ _____<br>_____ _____ | Class Participation<br>Assignment Completion<br>Bonus/Homework | | Music |
| 500-1000<br>500 | _____ _____<br>_____ _____ | Class Participation<br>Bonus | | P.E. |
| 500-1000<br>500 | _____ _____<br>_____ _____ | Class Participation<br>Bonus | | Art |
| 500-1000<br>500-1000<br>500-1000 | _____ _____<br>_____ _____<br>_____ _____ | Class Participation<br>Assignment Completion<br>Bonus/Homework | | |
| 500-1000<br>500-1000<br>500-1000 | _____ _____<br>_____ _____<br>_____ _____ | Class Participation<br>Assignment Completion<br>Bonus/Homework | | |
| 500-1000<br>500-1000<br>500-1000 | _____ _____<br>_____ _____<br>_____ _____ | Class Participation<br>Assignment Completion<br>Bonus/Homework | | |
| 500<br>500<br>500<br>500<br>1000<br>500 | _____ _____<br>_____ _____<br>_____ _____<br>_____ _____<br>_____ _____<br>_____ _____ | Bus<br>AM Homeroom<br>Personal Appearance<br>Lunch<br>Recess/Other<br>PM Homeroom  (clean room,<br>    accounting, study time) | | |

CLASS ROOM SUB TOTAL        _____

SOCIAL SUB TOTAL        _____

1. POINTS EARNED        _____

2. POINTS LOST        _____

3. TOTAL TODAY        _____  T.I. _____

Bank Book Balance: _____

Bonds: _____

Describe social behaviors here.  
(100 - 1,000 points per entry.)

|  | **Target Areas** | **Points  T.I.** |
|---|---|---|
| **1.** | _____ | _____ |
| | _____ | |
| | _____ | |
| | _____ | |
| | _____ | |
| **2.** | _____ | _____ |
| | _____ | |
| | _____ | |
| | _____ | |
| | _____ | |
| **3.** | _____ | _____ |
| | _____ | |
| | _____ | |

**Behaviors Observed Today**

_____  
_____  
_____  
_____  
_____  
_____  
_____  
_____  
_____  
_____  
_____  
_____  
_____  
_____  
_____  
_____  

SUB TOTAL _____

_____  
_Parent Signature_

_Revised 8/90_

**Figure 2**

# Point Penalties

| **ADULT RELATIONS** | | **TI** | **TI** | **TI** | **TI** |
|---|---|---|---|---|---|
| Not Following Instructions | 1,000-10,000 | | | | |
| Not Accepting Criticism | 1,000-10,000 | | | | |
| Not Accepting "No" | 1,000- 5,000 | | | | |
| Swearing/Disrespectful Language/Voice/Comments | 1,000-10,000 | | | | |
| Not Greeting | 1,000- 5,000 | | | | |
| Inappropriate Gestures or Facial Expressions | 1,000-10,000 | | | | |

| **PEER RELATIONS** | | | | | |
|---|---|---|---|---|---|
| Swearing/Disrespectful Language/Voice/Comments | 1,000- 7,000 | | | | |
| Inappropriate Gestures or Facial Expressions | 1,000- 7,000 | | | | |
| Teasing | 1,000- 7,000 | | | | |
| Arguing or Threatening | 1,000- 7,000 | | | | |
| Hitting or Fighting | 1,000-10,000 | | | | |

| **CLASSROOM BEHAVIORS** | | | | | |
|---|---|---|---|---|---|
| Not Having Proper Permission/Interrupting | 1,000- 5,000 | | | | |
| Not Attending to Classwork/ Homework | 1,000-10,000 | | | | |
| Noise or Rowdiness | 1,000- 5,000 | | | | |
| Carelessness (Materials & Furniture) | 1,000- 5,000 | | | | |

| **SCHOOL RULES** | | | | | |
|---|---|---|---|---|---|
| Late for School or Class | 1,000- 5,000 | | | | |
| Chewing, Smoking, Candy, Gum, Etc. | 5,000-10,000 | | | | |
| Cheating, Lying, or Stealing | 5,000-10,000 | | | | |
| Not Returning Card | 1,000- 5,000 | | | | |
| Loss of Point Sheet | 9,000 | | | | |

**Figure 3**

## School Staff Comments

What did this student do well today (include social and academic skills)?

_____

_____

_____

_____

_____


What areas does this student need to work on (include social and academic skills; describe major point lossed, i.e., 5,000 or more, and any referrals to Principal)?

_____

_____

_____

_____

_____


Ask this student about: _____

_____

_____

_____

_____


Homework assignments for tomorrow (if any): _____

_____

_____

_____

_____

and 1,000-point increments for ease of calculation, there are exceptions to this guideline that will be thoroughly described in "Determining Point Values," later in this chapter.

Following each Effective Praise interaction, and under your direction, students enter the description of the positive behavior in the appropriate "Target Area" or under "Behaviors Observed Today." At least 50 percent of entries should be in targeted areas to ensure adequate practice of these skills.

When guiding students as they write on their Daily Point Sheets, use words such as "You have earned..." or "Enter..." to help them take ownership of the behavior and process. Statements such as "I'll give you..." or "I'll let you have..." imply that you hold all the points and power to distribute them as you see fit. The words we choose can communicate strong messages — either that the student is in control of his or her own behavior and is responsible for those choices, or that the teacher controls all possible options and outcomes. By helping students develop a sense of ownership, they begin to make internally motivated choices about their behavior instead of responding each time to externally-manipulated contingencies.

An example of helping a student write points on the card may sound like this:

"Shawna, you did a great job of following instructions. You looked right at me, said 'Okay,' and took the books up to the shelf. You've earned 500 points for following instructions. Go ahead and write that on your card."

The teacher initials each entry on the card to validate it. Only entries with accompanying teacher initials are counted at the end of the day when a student "totals up" his or her card.

The bottom-left side of the card summarizes the daily point totals and current status of a student's account book and bonds. All positive points (both academic and social) are entered and added together, then a net total is determined by subtracting the number of points lost, which are recorded on page 2 of the Daily Points Sheet.

As mentioned earlier, students having a "good" day on the Daily Points System earn approximately 30,000 points. Students never end a day "in the hole." Even if the net sum is a negative number (i.e. the student earned more negatives than positives), a zero balance is entered for the day. Students are never penalized by having a negative balance go into their bankbook, and the negative total is never carried over from one day to the next. Any student may experience occasions when negative points outweigh positive points, but if this occurs with any level of frequency, you may need to evaluate whether you missed opportunities to reinforce appropriate behavior. Other "troubleshooting" guidelines and questions are discussed at the end of this chapter.

A student's daily point total is entered into a bankbook, which provides a running total of the student's accumulated points. (See Chapter 18, "End-of-Day Conference.") It functions much like a checkbook, reflecting point "deposits" and purchase "withdrawals." The total number of bonds purchased by the student also are tracked in the bankbook.

## Page two: Point penalties

The second page of the Daily Point Sheet is for recording point penalties. Students earn negative consequences for engaging in inappropriate behaviors related to four concept areas: Adult Relations, Peer Relations, Classroom Behaviors, and School Rules. The various categories are subdivided into specific skills or behaviors that don't always exactly match curriculum skills. However, the preprinted entries do provide more specificity which enhances learning for students.

For example, Tanya demonstrated problems with peer relations when she called another student an "idiot" after he'd answered a question incorrectly in class. Her behavior doesn't necessarily "fit" any of the specific social skills, but clearly matches the category of "Swearing/Disrespectful Language/Voice/Comments" within the "Peer Relations" concept area of the Daily Points Sheet.

Students enter the point penalty for the misbehavior to help them take responsibility for it. Negative consequences are earned in increments of 1,000 points, with the highest single point penalty being 10,000.

Only one point penalty is earned for each teaching episode. For example, if a student doesn't follow instructions to put supplies away, your teaching focuses on following instructions, as does the point penalty. The student would not receive another negative consequence for improper use of or carelessness with supplies; rather, the issue of supplies would be dealt with within the Teaching Interaction on "Following Instructions." A similar situation might involve you giving criticism to a student about an assignment. She curses and argues, then folds her arms across her chest. Rather than earning consequences for each of the discrete behaviors, she would receive only one consequence in the area of "Adult Relations" — "Not Accepting Criticism."

Generally, the size of a point penalty is determined by the frequency, severity, and duration of the behavior. Initial point losses generally start at the low end of the point penalty range assigned to each category of behaviors and then progress upwards as repeated teaching is necessary. Some inappropriate behaviors carry fairly large minimum point penalties. These are typically viewed as fairly serious misbehaviors, such as smoking, cheating, and stealing. Students who lose their point sheets receive an automatic 9,000-point penalty; this is to discourage students from "misplacing" or "losing" their point sheets. This level of fine is generally greater than any other group of penalties that may have appeared on the student's Daily Points Sheet, making the "loss" a less desirable option.

Repeated misbehavior can lead to an office referral. For example, Tom, a fifth-grade student, has had problems accepting criticism from you three times in one day. Tom's negative consequences have increased with each Teaching Interaction, but the behavior continues to recur. You may tell Tom that he'll earn an office referral if he has any more difficulties accepting criticism that day. In such situations, you need to decide whether an office referral consequence is appropriate for the student. Consider individual skill levels and needs when making decisions about consequences, just as when you determine targets and point values.

Major misbehavior also can result in an office referral. A student who receives a single fine of 10,000 points automatically is referred to the office. This is **not** a cumulative 10,000-point fine; it is one episode or behavior resulting in a major consequence. Examples include fighting, major destruction of property, possession or use of contraband, and threatening behavior. Additional discussion can be found in Chapter 14, "Overview of Administrative Intervention."

The exception to the one-penalty-per-incident rule is when ongoing behavior occurs during a Teaching Interaction. (See Chapter 13, "Ongoing Behavior.") For example, as you point out to a student that he was not following instructions, he begins to argue loudly and then walk away. You now have two separate issues to teach — accepting criticism and the original problem of following instructions. Since there are two teaching agendas, there will generally be two distinct consequences. If the ongoing behavior continues, the student may be sent to the office, where all consequences will be handled.

Students who have earned negative consequences always need the opportunity to demonstrate appropriate skill use (positive correction). On the Daily Points System, students can earn back up to half the number of points they originally lost for their inappropriate behavior. Giving students a chance to earn back points helps you teach and strengthen the use of prosocial alternatives by having them practice desirable skills.

It helps students see that losing points isn't the "end of the world," and that by trying to correct a mistake, they can get back some of what they lost. Opportunities for positive correction also help maintain student-teacher relationships; students are more apt to view you as fair and less punitive. All this helps students respond more appropriately to your teaching.

## Page three: School staff comments

The third page of the Daily Points Sheet is designed to increase communication between the school and the student's parents or guardian. Providing daily comments on this page is ideal, but it should be used at least two to three times each week. Comments should reflect areas of considerable effort or concern. They can support point entries or be used as "stand alone" statements. For example, "John volunteered to read his book report!" could be used to expand on a point entry of "Volunteered," whereas "Mary should leave her Walkman at home" may or may not have followed Corrective Teaching and a point penalty, depending on previously set expectations, school rules, and the like.

The easiest and most effective way to use this page is to write comments on the sheet as events occur. Your comments are more likely to be accurate and descriptive, and the student receives the praise or corrective feedback immediately. Like other sheet entries, be sure to initial your comments to validate them.

The first section of Page Three is used to note positive behaviors demonstrated by the student. Comments can be related to both academic and social behaviors. Noticing and taking time to write comments about positive behaviors can benefit your relationships with students and their parents. Many of the parents of the students we work with are bombarded with negative reports about their children. We should strive to maintain the same levels of positive-to-negative feedback with parents as we do with our students. In this way, parents are more likely to be receptive to our suggestions and supportive of our efforts. Your comments not only should contain accurate information, but also should reflect your level of enthusiasm about the student's progress or effort. Writing "Great job on today's test!" helps the student and parent re-create your intent apart from the actual situation.

The second section — "What areas does this student need to work on?"— can be used to communicate present concerns or recurring problems. You also can list problems that may lead to future difficulties, if they are not addressed. For example, "Robert has been interrupting and teasing others," could represent ongoing difficulties and build into a larger problem for him if not addressed. Most entries in this area should reflect fairly significant concerns. Moderate to major point fines (5,000 to 10,000) should also be explained in this section.

"Ask (student's name) about..." may be used as a request to parents to reinforce any activity, social skill, or academic concept needing attention. You can write about areas the student needs to work on (but that aren't necessarily major concerns), but try to write positive information whenever pos-

sible. Use comments like, "Ask Jenny how she handled the problem with her friend today," or "Ask Tony about the interesting talk he gave on baseball cards." Hopefully, the parent will be able to use this information as a springboard to an interesting and "upbeat" conversation about the student's day at school.

The final section on Page Three lists homework assignments for that evening. Be specific when giving assignment details so students can accurately enter the information. They are responsible for recording the assignment; you are responsible for verifying its accuracy and initialing the entry. When homework assignments are listed on the Daily Points Sheet, the likelihood of confusion and "forgetting" are lessened. Parents, too, can help students take responsibility for completing homework by checking these entries and setting "study times" at home.

## Getting the card returned

A student on Daily Points takes his or her point sheet home each night to have it reviewed and signed by his or her parent or other designated adult. The student returns it to you the following morning. The parent's initials indicate he or she has reviewed the card and, hopefully, discussed the main points with the child. Parents should be encouraged to use the Daily Points Sheet as a communication tool, too. They should feel free to write a comment or note to you on the sheet, knowing you'll receive it first thing in the morning. Since students know about this two-way communication, they'll be less likely to try to manipulate information.

Occasionally, you may have difficulty getting the sheet returned to you. Uninvolved or unsupportive parents may contribute to these difficulties, but students should, ultimately, be responsible for returning their sheets. You may try giving the student positive points for returning the sheet or negative points for "forgetting" it as a "front line" strategy. If points don't help motivate behavior, you may want to talk with the student and parents about their ideas for getting the sheet signed.

If, after exploring all other options with the student and parent, you're still not getting the sheet back regularly, you may need to help the student identify a "significant other" who can sign the sheet and reinforce the student for his or her hard work each day. This adult may be the principal, coach, counselor, or other support staff such as the school custodian. If you use this arrangement, you should still collect sheets from the student and periodically talk with the parent about the student's progress in school. You may choose to send the sheet to the parent or review it in a conference session. Parents have the right to be updated on their child's performance and progress, so you need to communicate with them as regularly as possible.

## ▶ Teaching social behavior to Daily Points students

Probably the most critical teaching concept associated with the Daily Points System is shaping. Students are on Daily Points because they need to build a repertoire of skills to help them "get along" in a variety of contexts and situations. They need to learn basic skills and strategies to help them act and interact appropriately. One of our goals, then, is to target skills critical to the student's success and well-being — not only for the relatively short period of time they spend in school, but in preparation for adult life.

Determining target behaviors requires analysis of many factors. Although our goal is to help students become self-reliant and empowered, they also need to acquire skills that will help them "fit" within the parameters of broadly recognized social acceptability.

Many of these skills are somewhat "compliance-oriented," but form the basis or prepare the learner for more advanced skills. Therefore, students must develop basic skills such as accepting criticism, following instructions, and accepting consequences to develop some level of self-control so they can benefit from other instruction.

Target behaviors should be chosen according to individual student needs. You may want to start by taking an inventory of all the problem behaviors a student exhibits, then review them to determine relevancy and significance to the student's overall needs. You may consider, among other things, how frequently a student engages in each specific inappropriate behavior, how much the behavior interferes with the student's learning or ability to interact with others, whether any of the behaviors are dangerous to the student or others, and whether any of the behaviors are related to one another (e.g. the student swears in response to requests, frustration, instructions, feedback, and peer-initiated interactions).

Kaplan (1991) suggests applying the "So what?" test to determine whether behavior is maladaptive and should, therefore, be targeted for change. He proposes using the criteria of harm (present or potential) to the student or others in social-emotional, physical, or academic areas as an indication of need. By asking "So what?" about a student's behaviors, thereby identifying the notion of harm, you can target areas of true worth. A student who is frequently off task will suffer academically because little learning will take place. This represents a present academic harm. The student who demands or takes materials in class instead of requesting them potentially risks alienating himself from others and denying access to materials to others. Even if the behavior is not harmful to self or others in one setting (e.g. a "self-contained" classroom for students with behavior disorders), it may be harmful in another environment or setting. Rude, demanding behavior in a regular classroom or job setting, for example, could result in removal from the class or loss of a job. Kaplan (1991) states that we should attempt to intervene in potentially maladaptive behaviors just as we do with presently "harmful" behaviors.

Once you've completed your inventory, you should be able to prioritize treatment goals or targets for the student. Remember, however, that for students to be motivated to change, they'll need to see the relevancy of the skills being targeted for them. As such, it will be important to help students understand the benefits associated with this change and recruit their help in establishing their goals.

Students new to the Daily Points System shouldn't necessarily be viewed as capable of learning and employing all components of each skill we teach under "one-trial learning" conditions. That is, it will most likely take many teaching episodes and considerable practice for students to become fluent with even the more basic social skills. In fact, skills will probably need to be broken down, taught, and reinforced in a step-by-step fashion for most students.

Inherent in the concept of shaping is beginning with the student's current level of performance (i.e. "where the student is 'at'") and building from that point. As stated by Kaplan (1991), shaping is "the process of gradually changing a person's behavior by reinforcing progressively closer approximations of the target behavior." Shaping focuses on changing aspects of the student's behavior, not on the events which precede or follow the behavior. It should be used whenever there is a significant gap between the student's present level of functioning and the expected level (i.e. target behavior or skill). To help students close this gap, we need to positively reinforce their movement toward the goal behavior(s). We can accomplish this by carefully monitoring their progress, reinforcing behavioral approximations, and adjusting our criteria as we see positive change. (See also Chapter 5, "Principles of Behavior.")

Two examples of how shaping is employed to reach target behaviors will be presented in this section. Principles of differential reinforcement, successive approximations, and shifting criteria for reinforcement are of key importance and will be included in the examples.

**Example 1**

Gerard is a new fourth-grade student in your class. After observing the various behaviors Gerard demonstrates, you decide to work on the skill of "following instructions" because of its broad scope of classroom application. Gerard currently says "Okay" when you give an instruction, but does not look at you or do what you ask.

You ask Gerard to get started on his journal writing. He says "Okay," and picks up his pencil. Since this is an approximation of doing what you asked, Gerard should earn positive points for following instructions. Teaching does not stop at this point, however. You'll want to guide him to begin writing in his journal and may tell him you'll check his progress shortly. You'll need to return to him fairly quickly — perhaps within a minute or so — to ensure that he's engaging in the behavior you're teaching and to positively reinforce him.

Your goal is to reinforce Gerard every time you see him beginning a task after he receives a verbal instruction. Whenever you ask him to do something and he responds by saying "Okay" (present level of performance) **and** starting the task (successive approximation), reinforce him with positive points. Gerard begins to learn this paired response to instructions, using both steps nearly all the time. He may be ready to learn another step at this point. You can double-check his readiness by moving to a variable schedule of reinforcement. If Gerard can maintain the present behavior on this new schedule, he is most likely ready to move on. With many students, you can be somewhat

less methodical. You may instead, after an arbitrary period of time, let the student know the new expectation for the skill. In Gerard's case, you'd let him know that in order to earn points, he'll need to look at you in addition to the other two steps he currently performs. This, of course, would follow teaching and practice attempts.

As Gerard begins demonstrating fluency by saying "Okay" and starting the task, you begin shifting the criteria for reinforcement. That is, you begin reinforcing Gerard's behavior only when you see all three steps of the skill, and no longer view the combination of saying "Okay" and doing the task as full use of the skill.

Obviously, "doing the task" is the most critical component of following instructions and we should feel pleased when students reach this level. However, our goal is to teach social skills as life skills, and the component of looking at the person conveys attentiveness, which is important in many situations or environments.

There probably will be times when working with Daily Points students that you'll need to tolerate and even positively reinforce inappropriate behaviors. This will occur when the student is working toward achieving a target behavior (for example, accepting criticism by looking at you, saying "Okay," and not arguing) but is not yet fully capable of engaging in the skill "to the letter."

**Example 2**

Sandy is a new eighth-grade student in your class. Whenever you give Sandy criticism, she curses loudly at you. Sandy presently looks at you periodically while you talk with her, but acknowledges your feedback only by swearing. You decide to work toward decreasing the intensity and frequency of Sandy's swearing in response to criticism. Since Sandy currently looks at you a bit, you want her to continue using that component. You may start by reinforcing the "looking" behavior, then teach her to "be quiet" as the next step for accepting criticism. Later in the day, Sandy has an opportunity to accept criticism about her off-task behavior. This time, rather than swearing loudly, she swears "under her breath." You may choose to positively reinforce this "quiet" swearing because it is an approximation of the target behavior, or you may use a small negative consequence followed by a larger positive one. This would send the message that the swearing is still considered inappropriate, but is much better than the behavior seen previously.

With each opportunity Sandy has to accept criticism, she should be moving closer to the goal. Every time she demonstrates behavior that approximates the target, Sandy should receive praise. The praise may or may not be accompanied by points, depending on her progress and individual needs, but you should always provide the social reinforcement by describing her improvements specifically.

Once Sandy can accept criticism without swearing or using other negative statements, you'll want to establish new criteria, such as saying "Okay," nodding her head, or looking at you more consistently while you talk with her. You determine the

next step by considering what may be the easiest to achieve or is the most critical to the skill.

Any time you employ shaping, carefully observe the outcome by watching the student's response. Be sure the increments you choose match the student's capabilities. If your steps or approximations are too far apart, your students will probably not experience much success. In this case, add new steps to get students from one level of approximation to the next.

Sometimes, however, you may encounter the reverse of this situation — you may create a series of expected approximations based on observed behavior, only to find the student is fully capable of using a complete skill once you made the expectations known. The general rule, then, is to use shaping procedures whenever needed to teach skill components to students, but be sure shaping is necessary. By recognizing students' individual needs, starting "where they're 'at,'" and reinforcing positive approximations, you keep your focus on teaching alternatives and praising students instead of punishing them.

## ▶ Determining point values

Students on the Daily Points System generally earn 500 or 1,000 points per interaction for positive behaviors. The Daily Points Sheet indicates increments of 100, but values less than 500 are seldom used, primarily because of the difficulty of the math calculation when many different point values are used. Beyond this, positive correction points, — usually half the number of points lost because of an inappropriate behavior, — calculate out in 500-point increments.

One exception to the 500- and 1,000-point increment guideline is when positive correction is used for more that one behavior. For example, Ron loses 1,000 points for leaving his desk without permission. Since one of his target areas is accepting consequences, and he accepted the consequence without arguing, you want to reinforce his use of that skill. Ron also practiced the skill with you. In order to acknowledge both areas, the positive points must be divided between the two skills, not to exceed half of the total points lost. Therefore, Ron may earn 250 positive points for accepting a consequence and 250 positive points for practicing the skill of "Getting the Teacher's Attention to Ask for Permission."

Determining how many points a student should earn for positive behaviors depends, primarily, on how much effort the student had to put forth to use a skill (i.e. the level of difficulty). You should consider factors such as whether the student used the skill in a new situation (representing generalization), or demonstrated better performance than previously seen (e.g. used a complete skill instead of just a few components). Think about how many points the student probably needs in order to continue engaging in the particular behavior (principle of size). Keep in mind that you don't want to inflate the economy by awarding too many points too frequently. For example, if you are reinforcing a new behavior on a continuous schedule, your point values shouldn't be excessive.

For example, Chris is a sixth-grade student who has been on Daily Points for three weeks. He follows instructions without too many problems, regularly greets adults, and knows how to get the teacher's attention. He has some difficulty accepting "No" and frequently argues when given criticism. Chris's target skills are "Accepting Criticism," "Accepting 'No,'" and "Making Appropriate Requests." This morning, Chris greeted you as he came into the classroom, then sat down and got out his writing. When he realized he didn't have a pencil, he raised his hand, waited to be recognized by you, then asked, "May I borrow a pencil, please? I guess I lost mine."

Given this scenario, you have many options. Chris could earn points for a variety of behaviors, including properly getting your attention and making a request. He could, theoretically, earn or lose points for being prepared with materials, since he took out necessary materials to start the morning assignment, but didn't have a pencil. You would have to make decisions about what behaviors to reinforce or teach based on Chris's past performances or patterns and your general expectations. If, for example, Chris forgot or "lost" his pencil every day, you probably would have already done some teaching about this behavior. If, on the other hand, Chris rarely comes to school without a pencil, you'd probably choose to loan him one without any consequence. The other behaviors he demonstrated were clearly positive ones. Without question, you would reinforce Chris for his appropriate request, knowing this is a target or "forming" skill for him. Chris needs frequent recognition of this behavior to strengthen his use of the skill. The other skills he used also could be acknowledged, either through points and praise, or praise alone, depending on how much reinforcement Chris needs to maintain these skills.

Point penalties are typically earned in increments of 1,000, ranging from 1,000 to 10,000. Some skill categories have "upper limits" of point penalty values, while more serious misbehaviors start at higher levels. (Refer to Figure 2 for this information.) The student's current level of performance and the seriousness of the behavior will determine the number of points lost. Typically, the first time each day a student demonstrates an inappropriate behavior, he loses points at the low end of the scale (usually 1,000). For each additional problem he has with that behavior, the point losses increase. This is a general guideline, not an absolute rule. You need to watch the student's behavior in response to teaching and consequences to determine the effectiveness of your interventions.

There may be a time when you use the same point penalty for a particular inappropriate behavior, just as there may be a time for initially using a higher consequence. For example, Aubrey is a new ninth-grader in your class. Because she has such difficulty accepting criticism, you teach her that skill frequently throughout the day, perhaps limiting the point penalties to 1,000 each time. You should closely monitor the point penalties Aubrey earns so as not to "bury" her in negative consequences, while trying to shape her approximations of the desired behavior.

Always remember to allow for positive correction — an opportunity to earn back up to half the number of points lost — following a point penalty for engaging in inappropriate behavior. If, for example, a student loses 1,000 points for not accepting your "No" answer, she would be able to earn 500 points back, either for practicing the alternative appropriate behavior, accepting your criticism, or a combination of both. When the point fine is larger, the number of positive correction points also is larger. If Claudia earns a 4,000-point penalty for teasing another student, you have 2,000 points to use for positive correction to reinforce her prosocial behaviors (e.g. practicing making positive comments to peers, apologizing to the other student, accepting a consequence).

## ▶ Summary

The Daily Points System is the first level of the Boys Town Motivation System. Students in this system earn positive points for appropriate behavior and lose points for inappropriate behavior. Students can use positive points to buy privileges and bonds, which allow the students to progress to a higher Motivation Systems level.

A student's Daily Points Sheet illustrates his school day. The entries on the card reflect the student's behavior, but only those behaviors you choose to address. Thus, it is critical to the students' success that you focus your teaching efforts on their treatment goals. No two students have identical needs; the success of this system depends on the individualization of your teaching. The skills you teach will vary from student to student and each student's Daily Points Sheet will reflect that variation.

# CHAPTER SIXTEEN

# The progress system

Progress is the second level of the Boys Town Motivation Systems. Achieving this level represents an increase in social skill knowledge and use. Students who move to Progress from Daily Points are considered to be in the fluency-building stage of skill learning. That is, they have acquired and demonstrated an understanding of the basic skills and are now ready to refine and expand upon their current repertoire. Refining "old" or basic skills and learning new, advanced skills are difficult and complex tasks. Consequently, students often spend the longest period of time on the Progress System.

Students on the Progress System also are developing an awareness of the benefits and power associated with skill acquisition. They experience many situations in which their behavior (i.e. the responses they chose) determines the outcome of the event. The cumulative effect of these experiences, coupled with consistent teaching, has led the student a step closer to self-directed behavior. Consequently, some of the artificial and structured aspects of the Daily Points System need to be faded out to match the emerging needs of the Progress-level student.

Perhaps the most apparent difference between Daily Points and Progress is the nature of the reinforcers. Obviously, the way rewards and penalties are recorded for each of the levels is substantially different, but the conceptual "shift" of deferring the immediacy of points represents the larger change. Specifically, feedback on the Progress level is provided in terms of "positives" and "negatives" instead of point increments. In a sense, the reinforcement of points (and what they represent) is delayed until the end of each day, when the earned tokens are translated into points. Complete discussion of these concepts will be presented later in this chapter.

▶ ## Moving to the Progress System

Students "buy up" to the Progress level by spending earned points on abstract exchange units called "bonds," rather than on tangible or activity reinforcers. Generally, purchased bonds are kept track of on paper. A running total of the number of accumulated bonds is kept in each student's bankbook to verify purchases and monitor the student's movement toward the Progress level. Some schools have chosen to create actual, tangible bonds for students to buy. This can be of substantial help to students who need more concrete evidence of their purchases.

Students must purchase 100 bonds at 6,000 points each to move up from one level of the Motivation Systems to another. Given that students on Daily Points can earn about 30,000 points on a "good" day, it would take at least 20 school days for a student to have accumulated enough bonds to move to Progress.

6,000 points x 100 bonds =

30,000 points per day for 20 days

Although moving to Progress is mathematically possible within this time frame, students seldom advance that quickly. A system advancement within 20 school days assumes that the student has had relatively few difficulties acquiring social skills and has chosen to spend all his or her points on

bonds. Most students like or need to spend points on more tangible reinforcers.

Students who do not need immediate or concrete reinforcers, or who come to our programs with a fairly broad repertoire of social skills may not require the structure of the Daily Points System. For these students, and as an incentive to all new students, a "one-time-only" special is offered to move to Progress for half the amount of bonds. Commonly called the "Blue Light Special," this method allows students to move to Progress by purchasing only 50 bonds at 6,000 points each. To be eligible for the "special," students must keep their cumulative point losses at or below 5,000 points for the first 10 consecutive days of their enrollment in the program.

Offering this alternative allows students to strive for the most appropriate level of the system in a fairly short time. The principle is similar to academic "advanced placement" tests which allow students to bypass certain courses by demonstrating proficiency in them. Students who truly exceed the expectations and need for structure provided by the Daily Points System should have little difficulty attaining this standard. Other students may be motivated to "beat the system" and will utilize their skills to try to quickly move to the less restrictive Progress level. Opening up such opportunities to all students allows them to take control of their own program. They can determine their rate of movement from the first level to the next, which in turn gives them power over their privileges and other reinforcers.

In some settings, students also must complete 10 consecutive school days without an office referral immediately prior to moving to Progress. Students may simultaneously accrue bonds and work toward completion of the time-based requirement. That is, while a student is buying bonds toward Progress, all the consecutive days he successfully completes (by using skills to avoid an office referral) count toward this requirement. If a student has purchased all 100 bonds, and is referred to the office after nine successful days in class, for example, he would need to begin his consecutive days "string" again. He would not, however, lose his bonds. Those are his to keep and use again to move to Progress. Additional information about moving up and down within the Motivation Systems is provided in Chapter 20, "Systems Level Changes."

Moving to Progress has many benefits and advantages. The physical appearance of the Progress Card is more appealing to many students because it is smaller and less obtrusive than the Daily Points Sheet. Points are negotiated each day, to a maximum of 40,000. This represents an increase in earning power and gives the student greater control or "say" in the overall interpretation of the quality of his day. Progress students also are eligible for increased privileges and status. Some events and activities may be reserved for Progress and Merit students only, depending on how many skills they have acquired and how often they use them. Other privileges may be negotiated on an individual basis.

Allowing students to have input into their own program results in greater motivation and investment on their part. Students are aware that Merit status can be attained only from the Progress level. No

"skipping" of levels occurs, so achieving Progress puts students closer to the third level and, ultimately, full inclusion in the regular education program.

## ▶ Mechanics of the Progress Card

The front of the Progress Card is divided into three main sections (Figure 1). The top of the card is used for identification and "bookkeeping" information such as the student's name, the current date, bankbook balance, and bond status. It also is used to record information specific to that day's card, such as the total number of positives, the card's "rating," how many points were negotiated, and initials of the teacher and student.

The middle section is reserved for the student's "target" or goal behaviors. Space is provided for specifying up to four goals, but students generally work on no more than three target behaviors at a time. More than three can become overwhelming, because students would have to improve too many areas at once. Although some of the Progress student's target areas may still reflect needs in basic skill acquisition (e.g. accepting criticism, making requests appropriately, etc.), they should begin to include more advanced or complex skills at this stage. Examples may include accepting consequences, self-reporting, and introducing oneself to others. As on the Daily Points level, at least 50 percent of social skills teaching that occurs should be in targeted areas. For additional information on targeting behavior, see Chapter 7, "Teaching the Curriculum Skills," and Chapter 15, "The Daily Points System."

**Figure 1**
FRONT OF PROGRESS CARD

# Progress Card

Name _____     Points Negotiated _____

Date _____     T.I. _____     S.I. _____

Total Positives = [ ]     Rating =     _____ excellent
_____ good
_____ fair
_____ in need of improvement

| Goal Behaviors I am working on | Positive + | | | Negative - | | |
|---|---|---|---|---|---|---|
| | Major | Moderate | Minor | Major | Moderate | Minor |
| | | | | | | |
| | | | | | | |
| | | | | | | |
| | | | | | | |
| Behaviors That Appeared Today | | | | | | |
| | | | | | | |
| | | | | | | |
| | | | | | | |
| | | | | | | |
| | | | | | | |
| | | | | | | |
| | | | | | | |
| | | | | | | |
| | | | | | | |

_____
*Parent Signature*

The third section on the front of the Progress Card is for recording other behaviors that occurred during the day. Any behaviors, other than targeted areas, which were observed and need to be noted will be recorded in the third section.

Keep in mind that considerable fading of the system will occur while the student is on Progress. The fading process will include a decrease in the number of interactions and the number of entries made on the card. Specific guidelines regarding this process will be discussed later in this chapter.

All targeted behaviors (and other behaviors) need to be worded positively, just as they were on Daily Points. For example, rather than entering "not swearing" as a targeted behavior, a positively stated alternative may be "appropriate language." You, then, are able to observe and reinforce the presence of a behavior (i.e. using appropriate, nonoffensive words) in a variety of situations rather than the absence (not swearing) of an undesirable behavior. Finding appropriate alternatives to problem behaviors helps students learn new ways to behave. Merely stating the absence of a behavior provides no direction or choice for the student.

Unlike the Daily Points Sheet, the front side of the Progress Card is used for recording both appropriate and inappropriate skill use. Appropriate behaviors are recorded in the "Positive" columns, while inappropriate behaviors are noted in the "Negative" columns. Each category of behaviors is coded as "Major," "Moderate" or "Minor."

The size of the consequences for appropriate and inappropriate skill use is determined by many factors. When you observe a student using a skill appropriately, you'll want to take into consideration how much effort has been involved. That is, depending on the student's fluency with the particular skill or the context in which it occurred, different levels of difficulty can exist. An example may help clarify this:

Mike is a seventh-grade student on the Progress level. He has shown considerable fluency greeting people he knows well, but less fluency when greeting people he doesn't know very well. From time to time when Mike greets you, in order to help him maintain his greeting skills, you reinforce that behavior. Since you know Mike's ease with this type of greeting, a minor positive may adequately reinforce this behavior. On another occasion, you observe Mike greeting school guests who are visiting several classrooms. Because these people were not familiar to Mike (i.e. a different context), you may choose to use a slightly larger reinforcer to increase the chances of him engaging in that behavior again. This time, you may choose to use a moderate positive because you know the behavior in the second context was more difficult for Mike.

Another example is provided to point out how different behaviors may fall under the same skill name, but result in varying levels of consequences for a student:

Jackson is a fifth-grade student who has been on Progress for six weeks. He has purchased about half the bonds he needs to move to Merit. During class one day, Jackson focused on his assigned work and successfully ignored another student who was giggling and talking. You chose to reinforce Jackson's appropriate behavior by praising him (social reinforcement only). Later that day, when another student was calling names and being somewhat verbally abusive toward Jackson, he chose to walk away from the situation, rather than respond in kind. You talk with Jackson about how well he dealt with the situation, and he earns a major positive for ignoring peer behavior.

Similarly, varying levels of consequences may be used with different students because of each one's general level of mastery. For example, Jenny may have little or no difficulty volunteering to help under any conditions, whereas Robert is fairly reluctant to initiate such behavior. The levels at which you reinforce these students will be markedly different because of their current performance levels. Looking at each student as having unique and individual needs will help you determine the most appropriate levels and schedules reinforcement.

Determining the level of consequences for inappropriate behaviors is similar to the process described above. In addition to weighing factors related to individual needs and levels of performance, consideration of the behavior itself needs to come into play. Specifically, the severity of the behavior and the frequency with which it occurs will help you decide whether to use a minor, moderate, or major negative. Low-intensity behaviors that occur infrequently probably call for the use of minor negatives, whereas frequent occurrence of a particular behavior or high-intensity behaviors may require the use of moderate or major negatives. Remember that the size of the negative consequence should

match the behavior and should be just large enough to effect change. For example:

Anne is a ninth-grade student who has been on Progress for 12 days. While you are talking to her about math corrections, she begins to roll her eyes and sigh. You talk to Anne about her behavior, and the inappropriate behavior stops. Anne may earn a minor negative for not accepting criticism. At another time and under similar circumstances, Anne raises her voice when you talk with her. She then begins to argue and swear while receiving criticism. You teach in response to Anne's ongoing behavior, and are able to help her regain self-control. This time, Anne may earn a moderate negative (or even a major negative, depending on her target behaviors, skill level, etc.) for not accepting criticism, along with a negative consequence for the original problem related to voice tone. (Please note that a second negative consequence is only given in relation to ongoing behavior.)

As described in this example, some behaviors may warrant using a major negative as a consequence. Major negatives, however, should be reserved for fairly significant behavior because they are the largest card-based consequence and because of the way they are interpreted when you and the student negotiate the number of points earned each day. The negotiation process is explained in more detail later in this chapter.

Major negatives also are earned as a result of an office referral. Anytime a Progress student is referred to the office for inappropriate behavior, one of the consequences will be a major negative on his or her card. When a student receives a major negative, it signifies fairly serious misbehavior and **sometimes** can result in an office referral. Referrals, however, **always** earn a student a major negative, which is given by the administrator working with the student in the office.

Positive correction on the Progress Card differs from Daily Points. The "half-back rule" no longer applies because of the way positives and negatives are translated into points. On Daily Points, students can earn up to half the number of points lost as a result of inappropriate behavior by demonstrating appropriate behaviors (usually accepting feedback and practicing the skill) during the Teaching Interaction. On Progress, the number and degree of positives "earned back" by the student will depend on the same factors as those guiding your decisions about other positive card entries. Specifically, consider how difficult the behaviors were for the student or how much effort was involved to "turn the behavior around." For example:

Angie is a Progress student who has "Accepting Consequences" as a target skill. After completing a project, she leaves her supplies laying out. Angie earns a minor negative for leaving out supplies, and accepts that consequence without arguing or making excuses. She may earn a moderate positive for accepting a consequence and, perhaps, a minor positive for putting the supplies away. To help Progress students begin experiencing logical outcomes of their behavior, they should be focusing on compensatory behavior when negatives are given. In this example, Angie earned negatives on her card, but also cleaned up her supplies.

The back of the Progress Card (Figure 2) is similar to the "Academic" side of the front page of the Daily Points Sheet. Students write in each of their classes under the column "Class," and teachers initial, write a comment, or make some other notation under each of the headings: "Completed Work," "Participated in Class," and "Bonus Work." Teachers should make these entries at the end of each class period so their comments or notations reflect the entire class period. As on Daily Points, this area is not intended to reflect social behavior; rather, it should give a general "picture" of the student's academic performance that day. General guidelines for marking each area follow:

Completed Work — The student finished class assignments.

Participated in Class — The student's level of participation met expectations.

Bonus Work — The student completed some work that exceeded class expectations for the day. The work was particularly worthy of special notice.

Space also is allotted for "Homework" or "Comments." Students write their homework assignments for each class, and teachers initial the entries. Teachers may write comments on these lines, as well, to offer some additional praise for behavior. For example, a teacher may choose to note "Volunteered to read first" on a student's card, reflecting both social and academic behavior, or "95% on today's quiz!" to emphasize outstanding performance.

**Figure 2**
BACK OF PROGRESS CARD

## Academic Performance

| Class | Completed Work | Participated in Class | Bonus Work | Homework or Comments |
|-------|----------------|------------------------|------------|----------------------|
|       |                |                        |            |                      |
|       |                |                        |            |                      |
|       |                |                        |            |                      |
|       |                |                        |            |                      |
|       |                |                        |            |                      |
|       |                |                        |            |                      |
|       |                |                        |            |                      |

| | |
|---|---|
| A.M. Homeroom | Lunch |
| Personal Appearance | Recess/Other |
| Other | P.M. Homeroom |
| Bus | |

**Comments**

Labeled spaces at the bottom of the card should be initialed to indicate that the student met criteria in the applicable areas: "A.M. Homeroom," "Personal Appearance," "Opening Exercises," "Lunch," "Recess" and "P.M. Homeroom." Spaces also are available for "Additional Comments" at the bottom of the card. Teachers and parents can write notes in this area to communicate information to one another.

## ▶ Negotiating for points

Each school day, students have an end-of-day conference. During the conference, Progress students review their cards with the teacher and negotiate for their point totals. Unlike students on Daily Points, who simply calculate point earnings and losses, Progress students learn to interpret their daily performance more holistically. They learn to generate rationales for why they deserve a certain point total and they compromise in the negotiation process. Negotiating for points is unique to the Progress System.

The negotiation process includes several steps. First, students must determine the point range in which they are eligible to negotiate. To do this, a student needs to count up all the positives and negatives on his or her card. The teacher double-checks the number of entries, then together with the student determines the ratio of positives to negatives. For example, Joe earned 31 positives and three negatives on his Progress Card. Joe's ratio is slightly greater than ten to one (10:1). Once the ratio is calculated, the card is reviewed to determine if the student earned any major negatives. These two factors deter-

mine the rating ("Excellent," "Good," "Fair," or "In Need of Improvement") and the number of points that can be negotiated. (See Figure 3 for complete details.)

After the rating and range has been established, the student and teacher negotiate the number of points the student will receive that day. Students are pretaught the skill of "How to Negotiate" so they enter the process with enough knowledge to participate adequately. The student should do most of the talking during the process. This allows for considerable practice of the skill and gives the student much responsibility for the outcome. There are no specific or established point values for any marks or comments on the Progress Card.

## How to negotiate

1. Look at the person.

2. Use a pleasant voice tone.

3. Listen to the other person's points without interrupting.

4. State your position specifically and clearly

5. Give rationales for your position.

6. Be willing to accept the other person's rationale.

7. Thank him/her for their willingness to compromise.

Figure 3

# Negotiating Points for Progress: Guidelines

| Rating | Point Range | Criteria |
|---|---|---|
| Excellent | 39-40,000 | No negatives but may have some activities not completed to satisfaction. |
| Good | 35-38,900 | No major negatives and a ratio of eight or more positives for each minor or moderate negative. |
| Fair | 25-34,900 | One major negative and a ratio of eight or more positives for each negative.<br><br>or<br><br>No major negatives but a ratio of less than eight positives for each minor or moderate negative. |
| In need of improvement | 0-24,900 | Two or more major negatives.<br><br>or<br><br>One major negative and a ratio of less than eight positives for each negative. |

The negotiation process involves give and take and the use of rationales to justify the final point total. Although notations on the "Academic" side of the card do not correlate directly to the ratio or rating, they give the student reasons to justify asking for the maximum number of points available.

There are many goals and advantages of the negotiation process for Progress students. It allows and reinforces students to self-evaluate and reflect on their behavior. It helps students learn the connection between their behavior and the resulting consequences. It teaches students two life skills: negotiating to compromise (instead of giving up or demanding), and compensating for their mistakes. Students learn that compensating does not mean erasing or completely undoing their errors, but that consequences may be lessened and relationships maintained when mistakes are corrected or not repeated.

An example of the process so far may sound something like this:

**Teacher:** *"Bob, are you ready to total up your card?"*

**Student:** *"Sure, I just finished counting up my positives."*

**Teacher:** *"Okay. How was your day?"*

**Student:** *"Pretty good, I think. I had some trouble in Science and P.E., but overall I think I did okay."*

**Teacher:** *"That's good to hear! What was your ratio?"*

**Student:** *"It was 37:3 — That makes it more than 12:1, and means I had a good day, right?"*

**Teacher:** *"Right. You don't have any major negatives, and each time you earned a negative, you made up for it by earning at least eight positives. Tell me what you think your card is worth."*

**Student:** *"Well, only one of my negatives was in a target area, and all three negatives were minors. I even apologized to Sam after I called him a name. I think 38,000 would be fair."*

**Teacher:** *"It seems to me you've been having trouble with the same skills all week, so I'd say 38,000 is a little high. What about 37,000?"*

**Student:** *"I guess I can see your point, but look how I earned lots of positives in the same areas where I got negatives. All the negatives I got were in the morning, too — I really tried hard to do better this afternoon. Look at these bonuses I got in English and Math. How about 37,500?"*

**Teacher:** *"You've given some good reasons. I think 37,500 sounds about right. Let's write that on your card and in your account book. "*

Once the point total has been negotiated, the student enters that number on the front of the card. He and the teacher initial the card, then talk about goal behaviors for the next day. Goals for Progress students should not change very often if they are appropriate to the student's needs. As with

Daily Points, the student takes his Progress Card home to have it reviewed and signed by his parent(s) or guardian. The student then brings the signed card back to his teacher the following day. The remainder of the exchange between student and teacher may sound like this:

**Teacher:** *"Let's get your card ready for tomorrow."*

**Student:** *"Okay. I guess I should still have the same goals for tomorrow."*

**Teacher:** *"Well, you seem to be having some difficulty with each of them, so I'd say that's a pretty good idea. Why don't you go ahead and write them in on tomorrow's card."*

**Student:** *"Thanks for your help Mrs. King. Could you initial my new card for P.M. Homeroom?"*

**Teacher:** *"Sure. Why don't you work on your journal now until the bell rings."*

**Student:** *"Okay. Thanks again."*

Remember, negotiating is a learned skill and should be taught and practiced to help students become comfortable and fluent with it. As with any other skill, you shouldn't assume students know how to negotiate, especially when it involves compromise. Teaching the skill in a variety of contexts and giving feedback on a student's performance will help the student master the skill and prepare him or her to use it in future situations.

## ▶ Fading the system

Students who are new to the Progress System continue to receive a high level of social skills teaching. As with Daily Points, new Progress students will experience 25 to 30 interactions a day. To help "wean" students away from the artificial nature of the Motivation Systems, however, the system must begin to be faded as students gain skill proficiency.

Artificial reinforcement, in the form of points or other marks on a card, does not exist in the "real world." Students need to become accustomed to naturally occurring or logical consequences of their behavior. If they are taught to respond only to artificial reinforcers, behavior will not be maintained when the reinforcers are suddenly removed. Students won't experience the benefits of engaging in alternative behaviors if their source of reinforcement is taken away. The system also must be faded so students can begin responding to social reinforcement, and eventually be able to realize and provide their own reinforcement. Gradually fading the system, helps keep students from "opting back in" after mainstreaming because they miss the continuous reinforcement they got while on the Motivation Systems.

One way to fade the artificial constraints is to tie the number and frequency of interactions to the student's bond status. As students purchase bonds toward Merit, their skill proficiency also should be improving. During this time, you will need to use fewer and fewer token reinforcers, replacing them with social reinforcement and praise. Corrective Teaching, too, will require a move away from tokens, and begin to incorporate more natural or logical contingencies. The following guidelines will help you systematically fade the system.

1. For the first 25 bonds a student purchases, teaching and card entries should occur with about the same frequency as Daily Points (25 to 30 interactions a day). This is approximately four positive interactions per class period. Target skills should be different than those the student worked on while on Daily Points, but maintaining this frequency should help with the transition to the less restrictive Progress System.

2. From 26 to 50 bonds, students should receive about three positive social interactions per class period (20 to 25 each day). Some of the student's target skills should be relatively more complex, but others can remain the same.

3. From 51 to 75 bonds, your social interactions with students will occur roughly twice per class period (approximately 15 per day). The feedback that is written on the card is fairly limited by now, and you should be seeing relatively little inappropriate behavior.

4. For the last 25 bonds (76 to 100), social interactions in conjunction with card entries are infrequent. You should now be down to approximately one per class period (six to 10 per day). At this point, the student is demonstrating considerable skill refinement and use, and your interactions are beginning to more closely approximate the "real" classroom environment.

These guidelines should help you monitor the frequency with which you interact with Progress students. At the same time you are fading the artificial nature of the system, you need to use other strategies to help the student through the transition.

As the artificial reinforcers are being faded out, continue to socially reinforce positive behaviors. Doing so will help the student maintain the prosocial behaviors you've helped establish. Failing to notice appropriate behaviors could lead to their extinction.

Teaching in response to inappropriate behavior should continue to include positive correction. However, as students gain fluency with social skills and as they begin to accrue a substantial number of bonds, the positive correction should reflect intermittent use of logical consequences. Making this shift helps students prepare for regular classroom contingencies. For example, Sharon was several minutes late to your class today and missed the opening activity. It took her a few more minutes to orient to class and get into her small group, causing the group members to lose a little time on the assignment. Rather than earn a negative on her card for not being on time, Sharon may need to stay in for a few minutes at lunch or have extra homework assigned to complete the opening activity. She also may need to apologize to the other members of her group for keeping them from beginning the assignment on time. For following through on the apology, and for completing the work on her own time, you may decide to not count Sharon's assignment as being late.

Progress students with more than

50 bonds should not be displaying many inappropriate behaviors. If they are, their status on Progress may be at risk. Visiting with the student and sharing your concern for his status may be a logical first step. You and the student may be able to problem-solve or determine some of the contributing factors to his change in behavior. If, for example, a student seems to need some extra structure, you may suggest that he not buy any more bonds at that point. You could then increase the number of interactions you have with the student for awhile, and later begin the fading process again. Should a student continue to have multiple difficulties, he could be faced with an office referral resulting in a system reduction to Daily Points.

To determine a student's rating for the day, you should continue to use the eight to one (8:1) ratio. Although "high bond" Progress students are earning considerably fewer card notations than "low bond" students, the expectations for appropriate behavior are increased. That is, students should be engaging in very little inappropriate behavior and they should be able to achieve the ratio, even with the limited number of card entries being made. Expectations and the use of logical consequences will only continue to increase as students move to Merit. Without ample preparation on Progress, students will not successfully make the transition to the next higher level. The principle of increased expectations and stronger contingencies can be seen in most any system. Generally, as one "moves up," whether in school, social organizations, or in a job, performance expectations are increased while many supports are withdrawn.

## ▶ Summary

The Progress System is designed to help students achieve considerable fluency with social skills. It also serves to "wean" students from the artificial reinforcers and structure of the Motivation Systems. As such, students probably will be on Progress longer than any of the other levels. While students are on Progress, they begin to understand more about their own behavior. They learn to take more responsibility for what they do, in that the concept of compensation is introduced. Students learn that although they cannot necessarily erase negative behaviors, they can sometimes lessen the effects of their errors by compensating for them.

On the Progress System, students experience a shift in the frequency of social interactions they receive and in the quality of the consequences. By building skills and becoming accustomed to logical contingencies, the Progress student moves closer to achieving inclusion into the regular classroom.

# CHAPTER SEVENTEEN

# The merit system

The Merit System is the third and highest level of the Boys Town Motivation Systems. It is designed to help students master and maintain the skills they have learned on the previous levels without many of the artificial reinforcers used on those levels. Rather, students learn to maintain and refine skills through natural and logical contingencies. Attaining Merit should be an indication that the student has developed an internalized set of rules and rationales that will guide his or her behavior. Since a major focus of the Progress System is to help students become less reliant on external, artificial means of reinforcement, the Merit student should be ready to achieve this goal. Considerable attention has been devoted to fading the structure of the systems during Progress, and this process continues while the student is on Merit.

## ▶ Benefits of the Merit System

By the time a student reaches the Merit System, the youth has demonstrated the ability to focus on his or her behavior and to delay or diminish the need for artificial reinforcers. The student has shown the ability to demonstrate appropriate behavior over time and under more "realistic" conditions (i.e. less-frequent praise for positive behaviors), and has developed a greater repertoire of prosocial skills.

Being on the Merit System brings with it many benefits. These extra privileges help motivate Progress students to attain Merit status. They also serve as ongoing reinforcers to students who have achieved Merit status. Benefits, other than those that follow, should be determined by individual schools and teachers in order to respond to the perceived interests of their students while staying within budgetary and time limitations. Examples include:

1. Privileged time, such as arriving at and being dismissed from school five minutes early.

2. Spending lunch time in a "Merit Center." The center may be equipped with games, comfortable chairs, a tape recorder, and other desirable objects. Students would be responsible for the upkeep of the center.

3. Attending special school events for free. While students on Daily Points and Progress would need to pay points for events such as a movie, Merit students would be admitted free.

4. Going on special trips. Merit students may be chosen to go along on planned outings, such as to the bookstore with the media specialist to help pick out new materials.

Aside from the tangible or activity reinforcers Merit students receive, many find reinforcement by being on the highest level of the Motivation Systems. Other students may look up to them and they may be perceived as the leaders of their classes. As Merit students continue to improve and refine their skills, they increasingly look forward to full inclusion in the regular education program.

## ▶ Moving to Merit System

To advance to the Merit level, a student must purchase bonds and satisfy other requirements set by the managing teacher or school. A student must buy 100

bonds at 6,000 points each to move from Progress to Merit. No opportunity exists to "buy up" for half the cost, as was available to students moving for the first time from Daily Points to Progress. This helps ensure adequate time for skill learning on Progress before moving to a less-structured level.

In addition to purchasing bonds, a student must have completed 10 consecutive days without an office referral just prior to moving up. The student can buy bonds toward Merit and work toward his or her 10 referral-free days at the same time. That is, if a student is currently buying bonds to advance to Merit and also is staying out of the office, his or her 10 days will be counted retroactively as soon as he has bought all 100 bonds.

Students also are expected to complete a Merit Service Project before attaining Merit status. Guidelines regarding the type of project should be determined by each school and teachers may provide some input to help the student decide on a project. Projects should be some type of service to others, whether peers, teachers, school, or community. Examples include peer tutoring, creating bulletin or special message boards, school beautification, school tours for guests, and organizing or working with others on a school drive for charity.

Schools also may require students to fill out an actual application for Merit. These applications are developed by school personnel and reflect the developmental levels and needs of the students. An example of a Merit application form is provided in Figure 1. If your school decides to use an application process, you should consider the following suggestions:

**Figure 1**

# Application for Merit System

Name_____ Homeroom_____

I, _____ am applying for Merit status. I have reviewed Merit expectations with my homeroom teacher and have not had an office referral for 10 days. I understand that in order to sign a Merit Contract, I need to complete the project or meet the goals specified by the Merit Review Committee.


_____        _____
Student's Signature                Homeroom Teacher Signature

_____
Date

Homeroom Teacher Comments: _____

_____

_____


## Merit Review Committee

Application approved: _____ Not approved: _____ Date: _____

Goal and/or Service Project: _____

_____

_____

Progress System students must maintain "Good" or "Excellent" ratings prior to the expiration date otherwise this agreement will be void. Any office referrals prior to the completion of this agreement will void the agreement and require a new Merit Application to be submitted no sooner than 10 school days following the referral.


Expiration Date: _____

Date Completed: _____     _____

                                                 Homeroom Teacher Signature

**1. Use a committee to review applications and to help determine service projects**. The committee should include teachers and students. Committee members may suggest that a student improves certain behaviors prior to being allowed to move to Merit, but the committee generally focuses on decisions related to service projects.

**2. Use clear time lines for completing applications and communicate them to the students**. Time lines may vary from one student to the next, as they should reflect specific and developmental needs. If, for example, the committee sees that Nikki has had a few recent problems giving negative feedback to peers, she may be asked to demonstrate improvement in that area. Specific time lines should be stated to Nikki so she knows exactly what is expected of her. Similarly, clear time lines should be set for completing the Merit project. You may need to help the student with time management because many service projects will have a series of steps that will need to be completed on schedule in order for the whole project to be finished as expected. For example, Jerome (with considerable assistance from school personnel) is heading up a canned foods drive for the fifth-grade class. He needs to meet with teachers and the principal to establish dates and prizes. He also needs to help design the flyer that students will take home explaining the drive. He must obtain tubs for the collected food from the janitor. He and the principal will tally the number of cans from each class and will determine the winner. Helping Jerome set time lines for each step will be critical to his success.

**3. The student's homeroom or "core" teacher may be the logical person to facilitate the application process**. The student applying for Merit should initiate the process, but would most likely meet with his main teacher to discuss and fill out the application.

Upon completion of the Merit application process, the student signs a contract which clearly states expectations and privileges associated with Merit status and penalties for contract violations. Depending upon the school site, the student should meet with either an administrator or an assigned teacher to review and sign the contract. At this time, all aspects of the Merit Contract are explained to the student to ensure full understanding of the expectations. A sample Merit Contract is shown in Figure 2.

The behavioral expectations of a Merit student are quite high. However, a student who has achieved Merit status should demonstrate behavior similar to any other student in the regular education program. Merit students are expected to utilize social and problem-solving skills to avoid behavior that could result in an office referral. They should be able to advocate for themselves and others when disagreements, conflicts, or decision-making situations arise. They also should be responsible for their own behavior, as much as is developmentally appropriate, in the concept areas of adult relations, peer relations, school rules, classroom behaviors, and community relations.

Should a Merit student violate the terms of the contract, certain penalties can be imposed. The consequences will depend on the severity of the behavior and any other identified individual needs. Penalties include, but are not be limited to:

## Figure 2

# Merit System Contract

This agreement is entered into between _____ and _____
                                              (student)                        (school administrator)

on this date _____ . _____ has purchased the necessary
                                                        (student)

bonds, and has not had an office referral for the past ten school days.

Under this contract, it is agreed that the student shall remain on the Merit System as long as the following conditions are met:

1. The school staff does not find it necessary to refer the student to the office for:

   - a serious misbehavior or infraction of a school rule;
   - failure to accept feedback or refusal to follow instructions when confronted or corrected;
   - a repetitive pattern of minor misbehaviors.

2. The student carries the daily Merit Card for 10 successive school days.

3. The student who is no longer required to carry the daily Merit Card obtains feedback from all teachers and meets to discuss progress with his/her homeroom teacher each week.

*     *     *     *     *

While on the Merit System, the student will have available the following privileges:

1. 30,000 point allowance each day;  160,000 point weekly allowance for students who are off card.
2. Inclusion in special events or activities as announced.
3. _____ .
4. _____ .
5. _____ .
6. _____ .
7. _____ .
8. _____ .
9. _____ .

Penalty for violation of this contract may result in the following:  return to or extended time on the Merit card, reduction to the Progress System, reduction to the Daily Points System, and/or in-school suspension.

We understand and agree to the terms of this contract.


_____            _____
            (Administrator)                                      (Student)

cc:  File
     Parent
     Homeroom Teacher
     Student

1. Return to or extended time on the Merit Card. (See next section, "Point Allowances.")

2. Return to the Progress System.

3. Return to the Daily Points System.

4. In-school suspension.

5. Compensatory activities.

## ▶ Point allowances

Once a student moves to Merit, he or she carries a card for 10 consecutive school days. While on the Merit Card, a student receives a daily, **noncontingent 30,000-point** allowance. The points allow the student to continue to purchase tangible and activity reinforcers while being "weaned" from the structure of the Motivation Systems. Although students receive fewer points on Merit than they can earn on Progress, they actually need fewer points. Merit students no longer buy bonds and are eligible for a variety of activities without "paying" for them.

After 10 days, the Merit student goes "off card" and no longer receives a point allowance. This represents one of the final steps in the fading process and prepares the student for full inclusion in the regular education program. Students begin to become accustomed to not receiving points and privileges for using social skills. In some schools, students may work in the school store or office to earn the opportunity to purchase tangible or activity reinforcers. The purchasing process may be based on barter or negotiation, or the student may earn a certain amount of play money in exchange for his work. Additional discussion regarding the management of off-card Merit privileges is presented in the "Mainstreaming" section of this chapter.

## ▶ Mechanics of the Merit Card

While students are on a Merit Card, they continue to receive feedback about their behavior. Card entries and feedback are used fairly infrequently, and are geared to help students move away from the structure of the card.

The Merit Card is divided into three main concept areas (see Figure 3 and 3a):

1. Identification and "bookkeeping" information

2. Social skill/behavior feedback

3. Target behavior menu

**1. Identification and "bookkeeping" information:** Different parts of the card are reserved for information about the student and his or her status. The student writes his or her name and the current date at the top of the card and enters the name of each class in the appropriate class period along the left side of the card. Spaces for morning and afternoon homeroom, and lunch/recess also are provided.

Homework assignments for each class period are entered under the appropriate heading. Students write in notes about

**Figure 3**

Front of Merit Card

## Merit Card

NAME _____

DATE _____

Class _____

| | Responsible Behaviors | Irresponsible Behaviors | Homework Assignment | Area of Extra Effort |
|---|---|---|---|---|
| HR | | | | |
| 1 | | | | |
| 2 | | | | |
| 3 | | | | |

Circle target behavior:

1. Follows instructions
2. Obtains permission
3. _____ (Peer relation skill)
4. Uses greeting skills
5. Accepts feedback
6. Uses appropriate language
7. Stays on task
8. Completes assignment
9. Participates in class

Bank Book Balance _____

10. Arrives on time
11. Volunteers
12. Personal appearance
13. _____ (Other target behavior)

_____ Parent Signature

## Figure 3a

Back of Merit Card

| Class | Responsible Behaviors | Irresponsible Behaviors | Homework Assignment | Area of Extra Effort |
|---|---|---|---|---|
| 4 | | | | |
| Lunch / Recess | | | | |
| 5 | | | | |
| 6 | | | | |
| 7 | | | | |
| HR | | | | |

Revised 10/89

© 1991 FFBH

homework to help them remember assignments and prepare for the next day's lesson.

Other "status" information appears just below the "Extra Effort" column where the student's bankbook balance is recorded. This information tells the student how many points are available for purchases. There also is a space on the front of the card where a parent, or another adult who is responsible for the student, can sign the card, signifying that he or she reviewed the card.

Cards usually are filled out during the end-of-day conference. The mechanics of the end-of-day conference are discussed in Chapter 18, and will help clarify how and when cards are prepared.

**2. Social skill/behavior feedback:** Most of the space on the Merit Card is devoted to feedback. Columns headed "Responsible Behaviors" and "Irresponsible Behaviors" are for recording positive and negative entries. Numerical entries matching the social skills listed in the "Target Behavior" area are made for teaching opportunities and praise interactions.

Not all behaviors will fit the skills listed on the card. Since most Merit students are working on higher-level skills than those listed in the target menu, you'll need to write out or abbreviate the skills or behaviors you observe. For example, Martin (a Merit student) is working with two other students in a cooperative group when the other two begin to argue about an answer to one of the problems they are working on. Martin uses the skill of paraphrasing and reminds the others how to criticize ideas instead of people. You

later talk to Martin about how well he was able to use conflict resolution skills and have him enter that information under "Responsible Behaviors." Individualizing your feedback to all students is critical and you should strive to personalize each interaction by accurately labeling the skill you hope to reinforce or teach. Never limit the scope of your feedback to a Merit student because of the preprinted information on the bottom of the card.

Actual notations on the card should be fairly limited. While you want to make sure that Merit students receive some reinforcement for skill use and appropriate amounts of teaching in response to skill deficits, too much reliance on card use will disrupt the "fading" process. Rather, much of the social reinforcement you provide should take the form of general praise statements to more realistically replicate classroom environments. In the earlier scenario, for example, you may have chosen a general praise statement to recognize Martin's mediation of the potential problems in his group. Positive consequences, if any, would then be natural or logical, such as a few minutes of free time on the computer or in the reading center, to coincide with the amount of time Martin saved by keeping the others on track during their group assignment.

Other factors, such as delaying your feedback until the end of the class period or a logical break in the instructional day, also will help students begin the transition to regular classroom operation. When teaching is necessary, Merit students should participate in discussions about their behavior. Having the student reflect on his or her behavior and generate alternatives and rationales is certainly more appropriate and beneficial at this stage than providing all the information yourself. Logical consequences of the student's behavior should be used in place of card notations whenever possible.

You should continue to use the "Extra Effort" column as you do on the other levels of the Motivation Systems. Specifically, include notations of student behaviors that are exceptional and worthy of special attention. Martin's situation is an example of a possible "Extra Effort" entry, depending on his general skill levels and target behaviors.

**3. Target behavior menu:** During the end-of-day conference, the teacher and student determine target behaviors for the next day or week. As with other levels, many factors are taken into consideration when deciding targets. For example, a review of the student's current or recent cards may reveal a pattern of irresponsible behaviors indicating a need to work on a particular skill. Conversely, the student may not be having any problems with routine skill use, but in order to prepare him for mainstreaming or future events, you would target more advanced or difficult skills.

As an example, let's say you wanted to prepare a Merit student to assist with class management with a substitute teacher. You may want to target skills such as volunteering, prompting peers, and disagreeing appropriately to help ensure smooth classroom operation. Demonstrating such skills while you are present would indicate the student's ability to use them in one context, while utilizing them in your absence would demonstrate ability to generalize the skills to other situations. Remember, as a general rule, that since students are on the Merit Card for a brief period of time, very few actual changes will be made in their target behaviors.

Once targets are determined, they are circled or written in on blank targeting lines (numbers 3 and 13) on the Merit Card. The student generally makes these entries to enhance ownership. Like the other levels of the Motivation Systems, you should attempt to focus more of your teaching on target areas than nontarget skills. Targets should, in fact, comprise the majority of your actual card entries for the Merit student.

## ▶ Merit Weekly Review

After successfully completing 10 consecutive days on the Merit card, a student may move off card. Although some social reinforcement and skill teaching still occurs, the nature and frequency of the interactions continue to change. The student is no longer carrying a card, so notations of responsible and irresponsible behavior cannot be recorded. Rather, natural and logical consequences completely replace the artificial contingencies.

Once a student attains off-card status, he or she no longer receives points. Instead, the student has access to privileges anytime, with teacher permission. This not only fades all remnants of the artificial system, but more closely resembles a regular classroom situation. (See the "Mainstreaming" section later in this chapter.) A student generally must spend all accumulated points before moving off card. You should encourage the student to make purchases during his or her final on-card days because unused points are forfeited. You can be somewhat flexible with this time line; however, students who no longer need the structure of the Motivation Systems should not be able to keep and use accumulated points to purchase systems-related privileges. This includes participating in auctions and other "specials" that serve as motivators to students on lower Motivation System levels.

At the end of each week, the off-card Merit student asks to get together with each of his or her teachers, asking for summative feedback about his or her behavior. This information is recorded on a Merit Weekly Review (Figure 4 and 4a). Each classroom teacher rates the student's behavior in the areas of Adult Relations, Peer Relations, Classroom Behaviors, and School rules. Ratings are made on a three-point scale:

> 1 = frequent concerns
>
> 2 = occasional concerns
>
> 3 = no concerns

Teachers are asked to write comments in terms of the student's behavioral strengths and weaknesses to support and more fully explain their numerical ratings. For example, Shanice's math teacher marked her card on Friday afternoon as follows:

| | |
|---|---|
| Adult Relations: | 2 |
| Peer Relations: | 3 |
| School Rules: | 3 |

| | |
|---|---|
| Classroom Behaviors: | 2 |

**The teacher's comments revealed:**

## Strengths

*Nice work accepting criticism and asking permission. Also for being to class on time, ignoring peers, and being responsible with materials.*

## Areas of improvement

*Shanice can improve Merit skills by completing homework assignments and accepting "No."*

Many teachers keep notes on 3 x 5 cards to help them remember specifics about a student's behavior. For example, Shanice's math teacher based some of his ratings on the information he jotted down during the course of the week:

11/17 — Shanice, not accepting "No" (computers)

11/19 — Shanice, forgot homework

11/20 — Shanice, incomplete homework

Keeping notes makes it easier to be specific and accurate when filling out the weekly review. Without notes, you may run the risk of attributing some behaviors to the wrong student or not having any suggested areas of improvement. Neither situation benefits the student, as teaching and learning opportunities are lost or irrelevant.

**Figure 4**

Front of Merit Weekly Review

# Merit Weekly Review

NAME _____

WEEK _____

| TEACHER | SOCIAL SKILLS<br>1 - OCCASIONAL CONCERNS  2 - MINOR CONCERNS  3 - NO CONCERNS | STRENGTHS | AREA(S) of IMPROVEMENT |
|---|---|---|---|
| | ADULT RELATIONS- 1 2 3 | | |
| | PEER RELATIONS- 1 2 3 | | _____ CAN IMPROVE MERIT SKILLS BY: |
| | SCHOOL RULES- 1 2 3 | | |
| | CLASSROOM BEHAVIORS- 1 2 3 | | |
| | ADULT RELATIONS- 1 2 3 | | |
| | PEER RELATIONS- 1 2 3 | | _____ CAN IMPROVE MERIT SKILLS BY: |
| | SCHOOL RULES- 1 2 3 | | |
| | CLASSROOM BEHAVIORS- 1 2 3 | | |
| | ADULT RELATIONS- 1 2 3 | | |
| | PEER RELATIONS- 1 2 3 | | _____ CAN IMPROVE MERIT SKILLS BY: |
| | SCHOOL RULES- 1 2 3 | | |
| | CLASSROOM BEHAVIORS- 1 2 3 | | |
| | ADULT RELATIONS- 1 2 3 | | |
| | PEER RELATIONS- 1 2 3 | | _____ CAN IMPROVE MERIT SKILLS BY: |
| | SCHOOL RULES- 1 2 3 | | |
| | CLASSROOM BEHAVIORS- 1 2 3 | | |
| | ADULT RELATIONS- 1 2 3 | | |
| | PEER RELATIONS- 1 2 3 | | _____ CAN IMPROVE MERIT SKILLS BY: |
| | SCHOOL RULES- 1 2 3 | | |
| | CLASSROOM BEHAVIORS- 1 2 3 | | |

## Figure 4a

Back of Merit Weekly Review

ADULT RELATIONS- 1 2 3
PEER RELATIONS- 1 2 3
SCHOOL RULES- 1 2 3
CLASSROOM BEHAVIORS- 1 2 3
_____ CAN IMPROVE MERIT SKILLS BY:

ADULT RELATIONS- 1 2 3
PEER RELATIONS- 1 2 3
SCHOOL RULES- 1 2 3
CLASSROOM BEHAVIORS- 1 2 3
_____ CAN IMPROVE MERIT SKILLS BY:

ADULT RELATIONS- 1 2 3
PEER RELATIONS- 1 2 3
SCHOOL RULES- 1 2 3
CLASSROOM BEHAVIORS- 1 2 3
_____ CAN IMPROVE MERIT SKILLS BY:

ADULT RELATIONS- 1 2 3
PEER RELATIONS- 1 2 3
SCHOOL RULES- 1 2 3
CLASSROOM BEHAVIORS- 1 2 3
_____ CAN IMPROVE MERIT SKILLS BY:

ADULT RELATIONS- 1 2 3
PEER RELATIONS- 1 2 3
SCHOOL RULES- 1 2 3
CLASSROOM BEHAVIORS- 1 2 3
_____ CAN IMPROVE MERIT SKILLS BY:

## GOALS

T.I. _____    S.I. _____

Along with giving written feedback, each teacher should share his or her comments with the student through brief discussion. This helps clarify ambiguous or vague notations and allows students the opportunity to clearly understand the feedback. Students need this level of understanding so they can then relate specifics and conceptual areas to their homeroom teachers. During the off-card Merit student's conference time, he or she shares information from the Weekly Review Card with the homeroom teacher. Failure to obtain a written statement from one or more of his teachers would constitute an irresponsible behavior, and the student probably should compensate in some manner. During the card review and discussion, the student and teacher develop a goal statement for the next week.

For example, during the conference between Terence and his homeroom teacher, they find that Terence earned "3s" from all his teachers in "Adult Relations" and "School Rules." He earned "2s" and "3s" in "Peer Relations," and had some difficulties in the area of "Classroom Behaviors" as he earned a "1" and two "2s" in addition to his other "3s." Teachers' notes indicated strengths in the areas of following instructions, completing assignments, and being on time to each class. Various teachers noted weaknesses with ignoring inappropriate peer behaviors, and controlling noise and rowdiness. After some discussion, Terence and his teacher develop a goal statement such as, "I will work on controlling noise in class and make sure I ignore other kids when they are misbehaving." Once agreed upon, Terence and his teacher initial the card next to the goal statement.

For the student just beginning Merit Weekly Review, the teacher should provide a brief praise statement regarding the student's strengths. Then the teacher and the student should focus on skill-learning and problem-solving. To prepare the student for "real life" in the regular education program, however, this aspect of the conference should be faded fairly quickly. Students typically will not receive a great deal of positive input from their teachers when behaving in an expected manner, but will be held accountable for deviations from expected standards. In fact, students being "mainstreamed" from specialized settings may be held more accountable for misbehavior, as teachers sometimes unknowingly set different and more stringent standards for these students. As such, you'll need to focus considerable attention on the implications of the student's negative or inappropriate behaviors during your conference time to help prepare him or her for the regular education program. Students must be able to maintain appropriate behavior even in the face of little or no recognition of positive efforts. Unless students are prepared for this "shift," they may be unsuccessful. The goal of the conferencing process, then, is to teach students strategies for monitoring their own behavior and reinforcing themselves.

Once the student-teacher conference is completed, the card is filed rather than taken home by the student. Generally, the homeroom teacher will make a telephone call or write a brief note to the parent or other designated adult summarizing the student's progress.

# ▶ Special considerations

By the time students achieve Merit status, they have developed fluency with many skills and have shown the ability to make responsible decisions about their own behavior. At this point, students should be in a refinement or mastery stage of learning. As such, the nature and frequency of your teaching changes.

One change is that teaching and praise interactions may be shortened to include only essential and descriptive steps. For example, Anne has been on Merit for six days. She is doing well on the Merit System, but in class today she's been off task for the last few minutes even though you gave her a brief prompt about getting back to work. Anne is quite familiar with the skill of "How to Be On Task," so you may choose to say something like, "Anne, I know you're a little tired, but you need to keep working on your assignment. Otherwise, you could fall behind in class and end up with more homework or a lower grade."

Another difference is that the teaching becomes much more interactive, requiring the student to provide considerable input. In the previous example, you may ask Anne to give rationales for being on task or to evaluate her behavior over the last few minutes, instead of giving all the information yourself.

These alterations are very appropriate when the skill is familiar to the student or the emphasis is on problem-solving. If, however, you are teaching an entirely new skill, your instruction should be explicit and complete, more closely resembling Preventive Teaching or Teaching Interaction sequences.

Merit students are expected to maintain a high level of acceptable behavior. Given this expectation, the consequences for serious or frequent inappropriate behaviors escalate more quickly than for students on Daily Points or Progress. When inappropriate behaviors are observed, the teacher should discuss the situation with the student, helping to determine options and the possible consequences associated with each. Similarly, Merit students should be aware that misbehavior (depending on the frequency and severity) could result in an office referral.

A likely sequence for addressing minor misbehavior that occurs within a fairly short time period may be:

1. First occurrence: Teaching and concern statement

2. Second occurrence: Teaching and office warning

3. Third occurrence: Teaching and office referral

For example, Rocky has been an off-card Merit student for two weeks when he begins to have problems being on time to your third-period class. The first time Rocky is late, you teach in response to the problem, discuss options and possible contributing factors, and provide a concern statement. The next day, Rocky arrives late again. You discuss the problem with him, have him make up the time with you after school, and inform him that he'll be referred to the office if he is late again that week. Rocky makes it to your class on time the next day, but is late again on the fourth day. You talk to him about the problem once more, then refer him to the office for further teaching and consequences.

The office referral helps Rocky understand the significance of his behavior in light of his Merit status, provides him with clear expectations associated with this level, and prepares him to be more successful in the regular education program. The consequences and teaching may result in extended time on the Merit Card, which could be used to help Rocky develop better self-management and/or problem-solving skills.

As previously outlined, office referrals generally result in the student being placed on a more restrictive system. Depending on the nature of the behavior, an off-card Merit student who is referred to the office may be put back on card for a designated period of time. However, a student who is on the Merit Card probably will go back to Progress or even Daily Points, depending on the severity of the behavior, under the terms of the Merit Contract. Although these consequences may seem somewhat harsh, Merit is designed for the student who demonstrates consistent skills in a variety of environments and situations. Engaging in serious or frequent misbehaviors indicates the need for additional skill learning, refinement, and self-motivated change. This learning is best taken care of on a more restrictive system such as Progress or Daily Points.

## Summary

Merit is the highest of the three-level Motivation Systems. It is earned through refinement of social skill use and the purchase of bonds. Behavioral expectations for Merit students are quite high and must be maintained in the absence of frequent positive reinforcement. This requires Merit students to develop an internalized set of rules and rationales to guide their behavior, as well as a means to reinforce themselves.

Merit students continue to receive points, but these come in the form of noncontingent "allowances." Additional privileges, available only to Merit students, help motivate students to move up to and maintain Merit status.

Teachers help Merit students gain more control and ownership of their behavior by changing the frequency and nature of the feedback they provide. Teaching Interactions and Effective Praise interventions are shortened to contain only the essential information, and students are much more involved in evaluating, managing, and reinforcing themselves for their own behavior. Considerably more negative prompting is used to reflect the "real life" atmosphere of a regular education classroom. Nearly all consequences are natural or logical instead of card-based.

Through carefully planned teaching and shaping, teachers help Merit students achieve the goal of the Motivation Systems — full inclusion in the regular education program without the artificial constraints of the system.

## ▶ Mainstreaming

In 1975, Public Law 94-142, The Education for All Handicapped Children Act (EHA), mandated that all children, regardless of handicapping condition, are entitled to a free and appropriate education. That goal was to be accomplished by placing children in the least restrictive environment to best meet their educational needs. The law states that children would only be removed from the "regular educational environment...when the nature or severity of the handicap is such that education in regular classes...cannot be achieved satisfactorily" (EHA, 1975). Often, that meant mainstreaming "handicapped" students into the regular school program alongside their "nonhandicapped" peers. Unfortunately, in trying to fulfill the letter of the law, some students' needs were not best served; although students were mainstreamed in an attempt to provide the least restrictive environment, such placement was not always the most appropriate. Today, with the Regular Education Initiative and movement toward full inclusion for all students, many "handicapped" children and their parents continue to face the challenges of succeeding in a "regular classroom" environment without first having been adequately prepared.

In his 1982 paper entitled, *Misguided Mainstreaming: The Case for Social Skills Training with Handicapped Children*, Frank Gresham challenged the notion that automatic inclusion of handicapped students in regular classrooms is always best. He reviewed a considerable body of research related to the assumptions and success of the mainstream process, and found that mainstreaming handicapped students itself does not result in increased social interactions with or acceptance by their nonhandicapped peers. Instead, his findings suggested an increase in rejection and isolation of these students. Additionally, although mainstreaming was intended to provide an environment which would allow special-needs students to learn and model behaviors of their "normal" peers, merely placing these two groups side by side fell far short of the intended goal.

These findings indicate that more is required to successfully prepare students for mainstreaming. Regardless of etiology, behaviorally disordered students lack the ability to initiate behavior changes just by being around a "good" model. They may be unable to "read" social cues and act on them in ways that come automatically to persons who are socially skilled. Consideration must be given, then, to a student's interest in and ability to imitate prosocial behaviors, as well as to the reinforcement that has occurred in the past to sustain maladaptive behaviors or encourage "positive" behaviors.

The persistence of maladaptive behavioral patterns and continued association of behaviorally disordered students with one another may be partially explained by processes described by Dishion, Patterson, Stoolmiller, and Skinner (1991). Antisocial and maladaptive behavior patterns, which interfere with academic progress and the development of relationships, lead to limited social reinforcement of these children in the school setting. These "rejected" students, who seem to be more tolerant or even encouraging of maladaptive patterns, seek out one another. As a peer group, these students receive the maximum amount of social reinforcement from each other for the least amount of energy. They select peers who don't cause them to use behaviors that are "nonexistent or weak in [their] behavioral repertoire[s]" (Dishion et al., 1991).

The difficulties of reintegration are apparent. Data from the United States Department of Education (1989) and Walker, Singer, Palfrey, Orza, Wenger, and Butler (1988) indicate that once a student is placed in a special education program for behavioral difficulties, the chances of that student being fully reintegrated into the regular education program are less than 10 percent. Given peer association dynamics and these data, we must conclude that our efforts toward mainstreaming will be futile unless we systematically and thoroughly prepare students for successful reintegration. We concur with Gresham (1982) that direct social skills instruction must precede mainstreaming to increase the likelihood of student success. Proper implementation and fading of the Motivation Systems, coupled with consistent social skills teaching, provide students with replacement skills that will increase their chances of success in school and life.

## ▶ ■nclusion in the "regular" education setting from the Merit System

Since most of our students have been excluded from the mainstream of education because of their behavioral difficulties, attaining Merit status is a good, objective indicator of readiness for the integration. Merit students have demonstrated considerable skill proficiency and have been faded from most of the artificial constraints of the system. Their success in the program indicates a need to move on to a less-restrictive setting.

Ideally, preparation for the reintegration process begins when the student first reaches the Merit System. While on the Merit Card, the student begins to learn many strategies necessary for the change. Target skills reflect a shift toward self-management and the use of previously mastered skills in new situations (i.e. generalization training). In addition, you're helping the student get ready by familiarizing him or her with various aspects of the regular program. You can explain class procedures and expectations, respond to concerns, and have the student observe classes. It's helpful to schedule many opportunities for the student to role-play his or her responses to potential situations.

Whenever possible, identify a teacher or class that will encourage the student's success. Consider variables such as the teacher's receptivity to students of varying needs, the class size and dynamics, student interest, academic "workload," and student or parent concerns.

A good time for students to begin attending mainstream classes is after their 10 days on the Merit Card. To facilitate communication between you and the new teacher(s) and to assist in a student's transition, the student uses a Classroom Goal Card (Figure 5 and 5a) and a Classroom Pass and Goal Card (Figure 6). These tools take very little time to complete and allow the student to receive feedback at the end of each new class. The

## Figure 5

Front of Classroom Goal Card

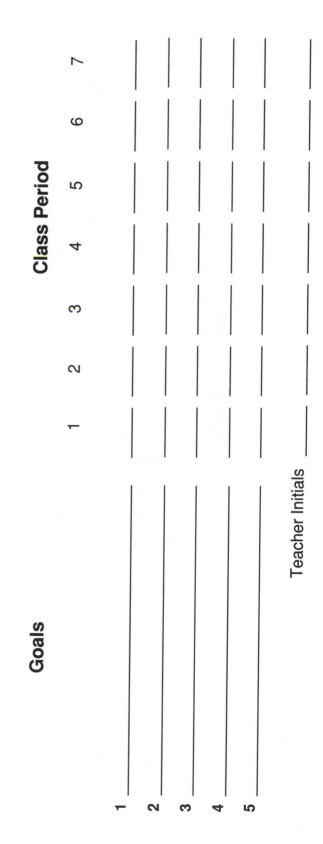

# Classroom Goal Card

_____ is working on the goals listed below. Please indicate if they were achieved [ + ] or not [ O ], initial below, and return it to the student. Thank you.

_____
date

**Goals**

**Class Period**

|  | 1 | 2 | 3 | 4 | 5 | 6 | 7 |
|---|---|---|---|---|---|---|---|

1 _____

2 _____

3 _____

4 _____

5 _____

Teacher Initials

**Figure 5a**

Back of Classroom Goal Card

| Period | Homework Assignment | T.I. |
|--------|---------------------|------|
| 1 | | |
| 2 | | |
| 3 | | |
| 4 | | |
| 5 | | |
| 6 | | |
| 7 | | |

Comments

© 1991 FFBH

**Figure 6**

# Classroom Pass and Goal Card

TO: _____

DATE: _____

FROM: _____

PERIOD/TIME: _____

_____ is working on the goals listed below. Please indicate if they were achieved [ + ] or not [ O ], sign below, and return it to the students. Thank you.

1 _____

2 _____

3 _____

4 _____

5 _____

_____
Teacher Signature

teacher simply indicates the presence or absence of the behaviors you targeted with the student that week. For example, in Figure 7, Shanice followed her teacher's instructions and completed her work, but didn't participate frequently in class. As Shanice's teacher, you would address her participation through teaching, and reinforce positive behaviors. The length of time you use the Goal cards will depend on the student and his or her degree of success in the new classes.

Although he or she is no longer earning points, the newly mainstreamed student still needs access to reinforcers while in your classroom. This access should be structured so that it is similar to that in a regular classroom. For example, if Shanice finishes an assignment 10 minutes before the end of the period and asks if she can play a game on the computer, she may be given that privilege. While a Daily, Progress, or Merit student would have to purchase that reinforcer, the mainstreamed student has open access to it, with the teacher's permission. By this time, mainstreamed students should also be fairly proficient at reinforcing themselves. They should be able to reflect on what they have accomplished, determine whether it is praiseworthy or noteworthy, and "pat themselves on the back" for what they've done. This self-reinforcement may even include a tangible reward, activity, or privilege, depending on a student's perceived level of achievement. The process is much like that used by adults when they reward themselves as needed for their accomplishments. Also, consider developing individual privileges that are tailored more to the mainstreamed students' tastes and interests.

If a student has difficulty meeting his or her goals in a new class, view it as a learning opportunity. Help the student generate options to solve any problems he or she may be experiencing. Although you want to provide adequate support and guidance, you don't want to "rescue" the student or solve all his or her problems. If you perceive the problem as "teacher-driven," meet with that teacher, while continuing to help the student make good behavioral choices.

Repeated difficulties over time or an office referral **may** result in a student's removal from a mainstream class. However, a student can be removed from a mainstream class only if the behavior problems are occurring **in that class**. For example, if a student gets referred to the office from your class, and as a result is put back on the Merit Card, the student still can remain in the mainstream class. The student probably won't be able to add other mainstream classes until he or she is off of the Merit Card, but again, the mainstream class is not lost.

If the mainstreamed student has been put back on the Merit Card because of an office referral, you may consider these measures. The student must stay on the card for a minimum of five school days, depending on the severity of the behavior. Five days is a guideline; you'll need to decide if the student has demonstrated "mainstream" behaviors and compensated for the inappropriate behavior that led to the referral. While the student is on the card, your efforts should be focused on teaching about the referral behavior and providing plenty of opportunities to practice alternative behaviors. During that time, the student receives

**Figure 7**

# Classroom Pass and Goal Card

TO: _Ms. Bock-Taylor_          DATE: _1/28/93_

FROM: _Mr. Waller_          PERIOD/TIME: _3rd_

_Shanice_ is working on the goals listed below. Please indicate if they were achieved [ + ] or not [ O ], sign below, and return it to the students. Thank you.

+  1  _Following instructions_

+  2  _Completes assignments_

O  3  _Participates in class_

___  4  _____

___  5  _____

_I.J. Waller_
Teacher Signature

notations on the card, has conferences with you at the end of every school day, and negotiates for privileges based on demonstrated behaviors. Compared to a mainstreamed student, he or she now receives a greater amount of supervision, structure, and feedback. This should motivate the student to try to regain status as an off-card student.

## ▶ Other considerations

Your attempts to mainstream your students will probably never mirror these ideal conditions. Curricular needs, parent requests, and scheduling demands probably will overshadow the conditions you would ideally set for each student's reintegration process. Additionally, you may be adopting the Motivation Systems program at a time when many of your students are already mainstreamed to some extent. You won't be able to (or probably won't want to) remove students from these classes until they've achieved Merit status, but you may consider the following guidelines before adding further mainstream classes.

— All students will start on Daily Points, regardless of their length of stay in the program or other factors. Refer to Chapters 6 and 15 for additional discussion and rationales for this procedure. Students who currently leave your classroom for other subjects will maintain their placements in other classes unless they are experiencing considerable difficulties there. Evaluate each student's level of success in each of his or her mainstream classes. Students who will continue attending their "outside" classes carry a Goal Card to facilitate communication about their program

goals or targets. Use the Goal Card that matches the student's program needs; if the student has more than one mainstream class, the Goal Card must reflect the multiple-class format.

— Additional classes shouldn't be added until the student achieves off-card Merit status. This guideline is suggested to increase the student's chances of success and to give you the opportunity to help students gain skills while working toward the goal of attending regular classes. Your goal should be to help students be productive members of their mainstream classes, rather than students who attend classes merely "by right."

— Students' privileges should match their system levels. Daily Points students earn points and purchase bonds and reinforcers; Progress students negotiate points and purchase bonds and reinforcers; and on-card Merit students receive point allowances that they can use to purchase their reinforcers. "Open access" to reinforcers is available only to off-card mainstream students. Attending mainstream classes does not determine the level of access; the Motivation Systems level the student has earned determines status in the program and eligibility for reinforcers.

## ▶ Summary

The mainstreaming process should systematically prepare students for successful reintegration into the regular education program. Continued emphasis on self-management, self-reflection, and self-reinforcement increases the likelihood of a student's success.

Without adequate social skills preparation, a student's academic success and ability to be accepted and included by other students will be hindered or completely thwarted. Given the personal histories of the students in our classes, additional failed attempts in school can only serve to further damage their chances for positive outcomes. Therefore, limiting their inclusion in mainstream classes until they show they are ready is done only to best serve the needs of the students.

# End-of-day conference

At the end of the school day, teachers meet individually with each student to discuss the day's events that were recorded on the student's Motivation Systems card. This one-to-one daily interaction enhances the teacher-student relationship and conveys the importance of learning social skills. Together, the teacher and student review, summarize, and document the information on the card. The student also decides what to buy with the points he or she has earned.

## ▶ Purpose

The end-of-day conference is a focused discussion about a student's day. You give uninterrupted, personal attention to students about their social behavior and communicate to each student his or her importance.

This process also helps the students understand the primary benefit of the system — that you will help them learn self-management skills.

Students are able to objectively reflect on their daily progress by drawing conclusions from the data on their cards. This process gives students opportunities to set goals for social behavior and move toward achieving them. Students are active participants in determining their individual social skills development as well as their individual academic programs.

By meeting with students, you can help them conceptualize their day instead of seeing it as a collection of individual behaviors. When the isolated events are consolidated into a "behavioral whole," students can begin to focus on their patterns and analyze their progress toward targets or goals.

Finally, this process allows for continuity of the system by helping the student set the next day's goals. Providing closure to the day, the conference emphasizes the "clean slate" aspect of the system, especially for the Daily Points student. Each student begins the next day with a fresh card.

## ► Process

When you meet with a student to summarize his or her day, you should engage in a discussion — not a lecture — and provide many opportunities for the student's involvement. Reviewing target areas, discussing where improvements have been made, and noting progress toward goals are essential components of this discussion.

The nature of your feedback should reflect the student's needs, determined by his or her level of the Motivation System. For example, a Daily Points student requires considerable reinforcement regarding improvements and progress toward goals. The focus of your feedback with "advanced" Progress or Merit students, on the other hand, should be on areas of concern or improvement. These students also will take much of the responsibility for directing the conference by reflecting on their own behavior and formulating goal statements.

### Example 1

Juan is a seventh-grade Daily Points student in your class. His target areas are "Following Instructions," "Accepting Criticism," and "Staying On Task." Juan earned a net total of 29,500 points today. He had four point fines, three of which were for accepting criticism inappropriately. Many of the positive entries on his card were in the areas of staying on task and following instructions.

When beginning the conference with Juan, you should point out the successes noted on his card: "Juan, nice job! Look at all those points you earned for staying on task and following instructions today. Way to go! Tell me about these negatives under 'Accepting Criticism.' What happened in Mr. Jensen's class?" Juan responds with an explanation. You say, "Sounds like you had lots of opportunities to practice accepting criticism with Mr. Jensen and some of your other teachers. What do you think about continuing to work on accepting criticism tomorrow?" Juan responds favorably.

### Example 2

Olivia recently moved to Merit. Her current goals are "Helping Peers," "Completing Assignments on Time," and "Greeting Adults." These skills will help Olivia enter in the regular education program. Olivia's card showed a problem with remembering an assignment in one class. She earned one positive entry each for greeting an adult, helping a classmate with an assignment, and working well in a cooperative group.

You could begin the conference with Olivia by saying, "Tell me about your day." Olivia reviews the card entries as well as the positive interactions not noted on the card. You say, "What happened with your assignment in science class?" Olivia explains the negative entry, to which you respond,

"What do you plan to do about it?" Olivia should be able to explain how she plans to compensate for her mistake.

After you and the student finish discussing the card, the student can purchase items from the menu, provided there are enough points in the account book, including that day's total. Remember that the student decides what to purchase; you only provide guidance if necessary. (See Chapter 19, "Purchasing and Menus.")

After recording all card data in the student's Motivation System Account Book (Figure 1), you close the card by initialing the total, and entering the student's bonds-to-date and account balance. The student is to take the card home to show parents (or guardians) and to obtain their signature before returning it to you. Next, you should help the student prepare a card for the next day. The student writes in his or her name, and the next day's date. Daily Points students number their classes; Progress and Merit students write the names of their classes next to the corresponding class periods. You and the student also determine target behaviors for the next day.

## ► The account book

The Motivation System Account Book is a centralized record of each student's accumulated points (Figure 1). It provides at-a-glance information about a student's spending habits, purchases, point and bond balances, and other card data.

Before entering the data in the student's account book, verify a Daily Points student's calculations by quickly checking his or her addition and subtraction. A Progress student will complete the negotiation process to determine his or her point total. Merit students receive their daily "allowance" of 30,000 points.

The following descriptions define each column of the student's account book. Figure 1 and Figure 2 are sample account book pages.

**Date** — the date an entry is being made.

**Total Points Today** — the net total points for Daily Points students, meaning that the point fines have already been subtracted; negotiated points for Progress students; the daily allowance for Merit.

**Points Lost Today** — the total negative points a Daily Points student accumulated that day.

**Amount Withdrawn** — the amount the student uses to make purchases.

**Withdrawn For** — items the student purchases.

**# Bonds Purchased** — the number of bonds the student purchases.

**# Bonds To Date** — the total number of bonds the student has purchased, including any bought that day.

**System** — the student's current system level (D= Daily Points; P = Progress; M = Merit).

**Balance** — the total number of points the student has in his or her account (Previous Day's Balance + Total Points Today - Amount Withdrawn = Balance).

## Figure 1

**Motivation System Account Book**

D - DAILY POINTS
P - PROGRESS
M - MERIT

NAME _____

| DATE | TOTAL POINTS TODAY* | POINTS LOST TODAY | AMOUNT WITHDRAWN | WITHDRAWN FOR | # BONDS PUR. | # BONDS TO DATE | SYSTEM | BALANCE | OFFICE REFERRAL | SUSPENSION PENALTY PAY. | SUSPENSION PENALTY BAL. | T.I. |
|------|---------------------|-------------------|------------------|---------------|--------------|-----------------|--------|---------|-----------------|-------------------------|-------------------------|------|
|  |  |  |  |  |  |  |  |  |  |  |  |  |
|  |  |  |  |  |  |  |  |  |  |  |  |  |
|  |  |  |  |  |  |  |  |  |  |  |  |  |
|  |  |  |  |  |  |  |  |  |  |  |  |  |
|  |  |  |  |  |  |  |  |  |  |  |  |  |
|  |  |  |  |  |  |  |  |  |  |  |  |  |
|  |  |  |  |  |  |  |  |  |  |  |  |  |
|  |  |  |  |  |  |  |  |  |  |  |  |  |
|  |  |  |  |  |  |  |  |  |  |  |  |  |
|  |  |  |  |  |  |  |  |  |  |  |  |  |
|  |  |  |  |  |  |  |  |  |  |  |  |  |
|  |  |  |  |  |  |  |  |  |  |  |  |  |

* Net total

Revised 6/87      © 1991  FFBH

## Figure 2

## Motivation System Account Book

NAME  Jenna E.

D - DAILY POINTS
P - PROGRESS
M - MERIT

| DATE | TOTAL POINTS TODAY* | POINTS LOST TODAY | AMOUNT WITHDRAWN | WITHDRAWN FOR | # BONDS PUR. | # BONDS TO DATE | SYSTEM | BALANCE | OFFICE REFERRAL | SUSPENSION PENALTY PAY. | SUSPENSION PENALTY BAL. | T.I. |
|------|------|------|------|------|------|------|------|------|------|------|------|------|
| 3/13 | 31,000 | 7,000 | 12,000 | Bonds | 2 | 10 | D | 216,000 | | | | AP |
| 3/14 | 29,500 | 9,000 | 210,000 12,000 | Can of pop Bonds | 2 | 12 | D | 24,000 | | | | MPK |
| 3/17 | 12,000 | 17,000 | — | — | — | 12 | D | 36,000 | * | | | AP |
| 3/18 | 32,000 | 5,000 | 12,000 | Bonds | 2 | 14 | D | 56,000 | | | | AP |
| 3/19 | 30,500 | 6,000 | 6,000 12,000 | Poster Bonds | 2 | 16 | D | 68,500 | | | | MPK |
| | | | | | | | | | | | | |
| | | | | | | | | | | | | |
| | | | | | | | | | | | | |
| | | | | | | | | | | | | |
| | | | | | | | | | | | | |
| | | | | | | | | | | | | |
| | | | | | | | | | | | | |

* Net total

Revised 6/87      © 1991  FFBH

**Office Referral** — checked if the student has an office referral that day.

**Suspension Penalty Pay and Balance** — see Chapter 20, "Systems Level Changes."

## ▶ The Teaching Record

The Teaching Record (Figure 3 and Figure 4) helps you track teaching opportunities that result in point penalties for students. This cumulative record allows you to review problem areas regarding social skills development. It assists you in making data-based decisions about a student's target behaviors: choosing targets, changing targets, and focusing teaching efforts.

Toward the end of the conference, transfer any negative card entries to the Teaching Record by placing "hash marks" in the appropriate columns. To denote an office referral, place an asterisk corresponding to the day and skill deficit.

## ▶ General considerations

To prevent problems while you are having a conference with a student, preteach the class your expectations for the end-of-day conference. At a planned, neutral time, discuss with students how they can spend their time (e.g. reading, visiting quietly with friends, doing homework, using the computer) while other students are in conference. Be sure to reinforce your students for their cooperation through points, positive entries, and social praise.

You occasionally may need to have a conference with some students more often than once a day; for example, with students who need frequent access to reinforcers because of their difficulties maintaining appropriate behavior throughout the school day. Also, when first introducing the Motivation Systems, you may choose to have students total up and allow them to make purchases more than once a day to encourage interest.

## ▶ Summary

The end-of-day conference is an opportunity for you and each of your students to review, summarize, and document a student's day as reflected on his or her card. The nature of the conference changes as students progress from one level to the next, shifting responsibility for card interpretation and reflection to the students as they acquire improved self-management skills. The conference not only provides a chance to reflect on progress and set goals but also is used to complete the bookkeeping tasks of the Motivations Systems in a relatively brief time. The conference's interactive nature enables students to be actively involved in their program, thereby enhancing ownership of the process.

**Figure 3**

# Teaching Record

Name: _____  Month: _____

| ADULT RELATIONS | Week _____ | | | | | _____ | | | | | _____ | | | |
|---|---|---|---|---|---|---|---|---|---|---|---|---|---|---|---|
| | M | T | W | TH | F | M | T | W | TH | F | M | T | W | TH | F |
| Not Following Instructions | | | | | | | | | | | | | | | |
| Not Accepting Criticism | | | | | | | | | | | | | | | |
| Not Accepting "No" | | | | | | | | | | | | | | | |
| Swearing/Disrespectful Language/Voice/Comments | | | | | | | | | | | | | | | |
| Not Greeting | | | | | | | | | | | | | | | |
| Inappropriate Gestures or Facial Expressions | | | | | | | | | | | | | | | |

| PEER RELATIONS | | | | | | | | | | | | | | | |
|---|---|---|---|---|---|---|---|---|---|---|---|---|---|---|---|
| Swearing/Disrespectful Language/Voice/Comments | | | | | | | | | | | | | | | |
| Inappropriate Gestures or Facial Expressions | | | | | | | | | | | | | | | |
| Teasing | | | | | | | | | | | | | | | |
| Arguing or Threatening | | | | | | | | | | | | | | | |
| Hitting or Fighting | | | | | | | | | | | | | | | |

| CLASSROOM BEHAVIORS | | | | | | | | | | | | | | | |
|---|---|---|---|---|---|---|---|---|---|---|---|---|---|---|---|
| Not having proper Permission/Interrupting | | | | | | | | | | | | | | | |
| Not Attending to Homework/Classwork | | | | | | | | | | | | | | | |
| Noise or Rowdiness | | | | | | | | | | | | | | | |
| Carelessness (Materials & Furniture) | | | | | | | | | | | | | | | |

| SCHOOL RULES | | | | | | | | | | | | | | | |
|---|---|---|---|---|---|---|---|---|---|---|---|---|---|---|---|
| Late for School or Class | | | | | | | | | | | | | | | |
| Chewing, Smoking, Candy, Gum etc. | | | | | | | | | | | | | | | |
| Cheating, Lying, or Stealing | | | | | | | | | | | | | | | |
| Not Returning Card | | | | | | | | | | | | | | | |
| Loss of Point Sheet | | | | | | | | | | | | | | | |

**Figure 4**

# Teaching Record

Name: ___Jenna E.___  Month: ___March___

Week ___3/10-3/14___  ___3/17-3/21___  _____

### ADULT RELATIONS

| | M | T | W | TH | F | M | T | W | TH | F | M | T | W | TH | F |
|---|---|---|---|---|---|---|---|---|---|---|---|---|---|---|---|
| Not Following Instructions | I | II | I | | | III | I | I | | | | | | | |
| Not Accepting Criticism | I | I | II* | I | II | I* | I | I | | | | | | | |
| Not Accepting "No" | | | | | | | | | | | | | | | |
| Swearing/Disrespectful Language/Voice/Comments | | | | | | | | | | | | | | | |
| Not Greeting | | | | | | | | | | | | | | | |
| Inappropriate Gestures or Facial Expressions | | | | | | | | | | | | | | | |

### PEER RELATIONS

| | M | T | W | TH | F | M | T | W | TH | F | M | T | W | TH | F |
|---|---|---|---|---|---|---|---|---|---|---|---|---|---|---|---|
| Swearing/Disrespectful Language/Voice/Comments | | | I *(Comment)* | | I | | | | | | | | | | |
| Inappropriate Gestures or Facial Expressions | | | | | | | | | | | | | | | |
| Teasing | | | | | | I | I | | | | | | | | |
| Arguing or Threatening | | | | | | | | | | | | | | | |
| Hitting or Fighting | | | | | | | | | | | | | | | |

### CLASSROOM BEHAVIORS

| | M | T | W | TH | F | M | T | W | TH | F | M | T | W | TH | F |
|---|---|---|---|---|---|---|---|---|---|---|---|---|---|---|---|
| Not having proper Permission/Interrupting | | | I | | | I | II | | | | | | | | |
| Not Attending to Homework/Classwork | HW I | HW I | | OT I | | | | HW I | | | | | | | |
| Noise or Rowdiness | | | I | | I | | | | | | | | | | |
| Carelessness (Materials & Furniture) | I | | | I | | | | | | | | | | | |

### SCHOOL RULES

| | M | T | W | TH | F | M | T | W | TH | F | M | T | W | TH | F |
|---|---|---|---|---|---|---|---|---|---|---|---|---|---|---|---|
| Late for School or Class | I | | | | | | | I | | | | | | | |
| Chewing, Smoking, Candy, Gum etc. | | | | I | | | | | | | | | | | |
| Cheating, Lying, or Stealing | | | | | | | | | | | | | | | |
| Not Returning Card | | | | I | | | | | | | | | | | |
| Loss of Point Sheet | | | | | | | | | | | | | | | |

*Indicates Referral to Office

# CHAPTER NINETEEN

# Purchasing and menus

The points awarded for appropriate behaviors are attractive and meaningful to students because of what they represent. In and of themselves, points have no real value; their worth is defined by the privileges and reinforcers they can purchase. Money, for example, is valuable only because it can be used to buy things we value. Points function in much the same way; they serve as the bridge between behavior and outcomes. If privileges are desirable, students will be motivated to choose behaviors that will result in earning more points. Points are generalized, secondary reinforcers, and students must learn their value over time. Once students understand this value, the ability to earn points becomes an effective motivator. Students learn that by controlling their behavior, they control the rewards they can earn as a result of their behavior.

## ▶ Developing a menu

When developing a point exchange menu, you need to consider many factors. Students are not a homogenous group; each student will be reinforced by many different items and activities. You should make sure your menu reflects and includes reinforcers that meet students' needs based on factors such as age, interests, developmental levels, and tastes. Students can provide valuable input about what to include; sometimes the most efficient way to find out what they want to earn is to ask them. You also can conduct "reinforcement surveys" that ask students to state preferences for specified items or activities (e.g. "I would rather read a book than play a board game"), or observe students during free time to see what they choose to do.

To help you develop menu items, consider the following categories: equipment rental, independent time, special events, learning activities, school materials, tangibles, food, and social/activity reinforcers. Remember to include bonds on your menu so that students can "buy up" to the next Motivation System level.

## Setting prices

The point exchange menu must include items at all price levels to meet individual spending needs, habits, and abilities. The prices attached to each item must reflect their actual and perceived values. Items that are highly desirable to students or that are expensive for you to buy should be priced at a high point amount (e.g. "independent" time, snacks, and special events like movies). You also should be sure to include lower-priced items — possibly reflecting lower desirability and cost — for students who buy items frequently or have difficulty saving large amounts of points.

Some students are reinforced by one-to-one time with certain staff members. For example, a student may enjoy purchasing the opportunity to have lunch or play a game with a teacher or administrator. Activities involving staff time usually are priced higher because the staff's time is valuable. To encourage students to buy items with educational value (e.g. extra computer time, independent reading time, viewing a film strip), you may want to price them slightly lower.

The educational items on your menu should reflect activities beyond the standard curriculum. All students have basic educational rights; anything available to all students during a regular school day cannot be restricted. These include, but are not limited to, class attendance, access to necessary materials, help with assignments, inclusion in class activities, eating lunch, participating in recess, and taking restroom breaks. Privileges can include anything beyond the regular school program, such as attending another class, working with a friend, accessing the computer during free time, and using additional/special materials.

Sample menus are shown in Figures 1, 2, and 3. Note the range of items and costs in each menu, as well as any additional restrictions. For example, on the Kennedy School menu, students spend both points and money for soda pop. You also may charge students a set number of points for the privilege of drinking pop or eating snacks in class. Some privileges, such as extra recess, attending other classes, and "rec hall" are reserved for Progress and/or Merit students. Allowing only those students who have achieved the higher levels of the Motivation Systems to purchase these privileges rewards them for "moving up," and encourages others to earn enough points to move to the higher levels. This restriction also helps prevent problems that could arise if Daily Points youth are allowed to engage in activities that require greater self-management.

## Encouraging interest in menu items

To encourage student interest in menu items, either at the beginning of the school year or when adding new items to the menu, allow students to sample items at a

**Figure 1**

# Kennedy Elementary
## Standard Menu

| Item | Cost(Points) |
|---|---|
| Swimming | 180,000 |
| Bowling (70 cents) | 180,000 |
| Bingo | 150,000 |
| Atari (15 min.) | 80,000 |
| Free Time with Staff (15 min.) | 60,000 |
| each additional minute | 2,000 |
| Learning Center (15 min. Progress or Merit Level) | 60,000 |
| School Supplies | |
| Pencil or Eraser | 30,000 |
| Paper or Notebook | 100,000 |
| Apple Computer (15 min.) | 80,000 |
| Extra Recess (Progress or Merit Level) | 50,000 |
| Extra Recess with Friend (P or M Levels) | 60,000 |
| Lunch with Staff (off school grounds) | 250,000 |
| Free Time (each minute) | 1,000 |
| Free Time with a Friend (each minute) | 2,000 |
| Grab Box | 150,000 |
| Spirit Master & 10 Copies | 40,000 |
| Class Party (per student) | 50,000 |
| Extra Restroom Break | 5,000 |
| Snack | 50,000 |
| Early Lunch with a Friend (Merit Level only) | 50,000 |
| Pop   (35 cents) | 30,000 |
| Art Materials & Time (20 min.) | 30,000 |
| Polaroid Camera (each picture) | 100,000 |
| Day in the Regular Classroom (Merit Level) | 250,000 |
| Lamination | 150,000 |

**Figure 2**

# Standard Point Menu

| Activity | Cost |
|---|---|
| Bond | 6,000 Points |
| Rec Hall (Progress or Merit **only**) | 3,000 Points/Minute |
| | 120,000 Points/Period |
| Play pool with staff of your choice | 150,000 Points/Period |
| Extra Recess (Progress or Merit **only**) | 3,000 Points/Minute |
| | 120,000 Points/Period |
| "Seconds" for Lunch | 225,000 Points |
| Extra dessert | 210,000 Points |
| One approved item from auction case | 300,000 Points |
| Attend any class of your choice (Merit **only**) | 150,000 Points |
| Lunch off campus with administrator of your choice | 400,000 Points |
| Sit with another class for lunch | 45,000 Points |
| Special class party (per student) | 60,000 Points |
| Grab box | 90,000 Points |
| Serve as Media Aide for 2 periods | 150,000 Points |
| One dozen donuts/cookies | 250,000 Points |

# Media Menu

| Activity | Cost |
|---|---|
| Independent reading time (1 period) | 90,000 Points |
| View film loops (1 period) | 30,000 Points |
| Listen to story on cassette tape (1 period) | 30,000 Points |
| View a sound filmstrip (1 period) | 60,000 Points |
| Computer (1 period) | 200,000 Points |
| Lamination of one small item (less than 12") | 90,000 Points |
| Lamination of one large item | 180,000 Points |
| Book (sale to be announced) | 3,000-6,000 Points |
| Two pictures with Instaprint Camera (15 minutes) | 300,000 Points |

# Special Events Menu

| Activity | Cost |
|---|---|
| Movie | 300,000 Points |
| Swim | 180,000 Points |
| Bingo | 180,000 Points |
| Game Show Contestant | 180,000 Points |
| Game Show Audience | 100,000 Points |

Figure 3

# School Store

| Item | Cost |
| --- | --- |
| Pop | 210,000 Points |
| Candy Bar | 210,000 Points |
| Sugar Daddies (40,000 each) limit 4 per person | 40,000 Points |
| Lifesavers (80,000 each) limit 4 per person | 80,000 Points |
| Assorted candies | 180,000 Points |
| Tootsie Pop (40,000 each) limit 4 per person | 40,000 Points |
| Chips | 150,000 Points |
| Gummi Bears | 80,000 Points |
| Poster | 90,000 Points |
| Comic Book (50,000 each) limit 4 per person | 50,000 Points |
| Magazine | 30,000 Points |
| Folder | 15,000 Points |
| Pencil | 12,000 Points |
| Pen (choice of razor point or ballpoint) | 50,000 Points |
| Metal rulers | 75,000 Points |
| Book cover | 50,000 Points |
| Colored pencils | 210,000 Points |
| Colored markers | 270,000 Points |
| Box of crayons | 210,000 Points |
| Eraser | 15,000 Points |
| Sticker | 9,000 Points |
| T-shirt iron-on (limit 1 per day) | 130,000 Points |

Special miscellaneous items as announced

lower "introductory" price. You may want to offer "sales" or "specials" throughout the school year to increase and maintain a student's motivation or to attract new buyers.

Items that are difficult to keep in supply, or are "one of a kind" or donated, can be sold at auctions. This is a creative way to sustain interest. Students "bid" as many of their saved points as they wish on items offered at the auction. As a special activity, attendance at the auction also must be purchased with points. "Silent" auctions also are fun for students and staff. Rather than bidding aloud at the auction, students submit written point bids. The highest bids win and are announced at the auction. Offering lottery-type games or "grab boxes" are other exciting ways to pique student interest. Teachers put numbered chips in a box; the numbers correspond to items on a grab box menu. Students purchase a chance to draw a chip out of the box, then get a receipt from the teacher for that item. Most items on the list are standard menu items of varying values so that students have relatively equal chances of choosing items of lesser or greater value than what they paid.

## ▶ Monitoring purchasing of privileges

In order to maintain motivation and thereby increase responsible behaviors, students need daily access to their reinforcers. Thus, students should have the opportunity to purchase privileges every school day. Generally, a student makes purchases at the end-of-day conference; purchases are restricted only if the student has had an office referral that day. All purchases are recorded by the teacher in the student's account book (see Chapter 18, "End- of- Day Conference") and the student is given a receipt for each purchase (Figure 4), which is exchanged for the item. Students can spend only the points they have earned; there is no credit.

**Figure 4**

Receipt

_____  _____
Name                Date

Item _____

_____

How to be used _____

_____

_____

_____
Teacher Signature

Generally, purchases are final and points cannot be refunded. For example, if a student purchases a grab box turn and is disappointed with the item he gets, he may not return the item for another chance at a better "prize." Likewise, a student who purchases a ticket to a campus movie and then loses it cannot attend the movie unless she buys another ticket. The goal here is to instill responsibility and hold students accountable through logical consequences. Some students may have difficulty keeping track of receipts over a period of time. In these cases, teachers should problem-solve with the students in order to avoid such situations.

Once points are earned, the student decides how to spend them. This gives students opportunities to make their own choices and decisions and to live with the consequences. Sometimes, however, you might have to guide their purchasing decisions. For example, if a student has been on Daily Points for a number of weeks, but hasn't bought any bonds, you may suggest that he or she consider doing so. On rare occasions, you may need to veto student purchases, such as when a diabetic student wants to buy only candy. A veto generally is for situations related to student safety.

When a student makes a purchase, teachers give him or her a receipt to use to buy the item. Receipts allow teachers, parents, and other school personnel to know what students are buying and serve as a legitimate purchase record. Because students take the receipts home with them, parents can see what motivates their child at school. This may even help parents deal with their child's behavior at home by "tuning in" to their child's motivators. (See Figure 5.)

**Figure 5**

```
┌─────────────────────────────────────┐
│          Receipt                     │
│                                      │
│    Jason V.           3/17           │
│     Name              Date           │
│                                      │
│  Item      One (1) can of pop        │
│                                      │
│  210,000 points                      │
│                                      │
│  How to be used    go to front office for │
│  pop – must drink outside of the building │
│                                      │
│           Aaron E. Page              │
│         Teacher Signature            │
└─────────────────────────────────────┘
```

A receipt should include the following information: the student's name, the date of purchase, the item name, the cost, how the item is to be used (when the activity will occur, where it will take place, where the item will be picked up), and the teacher's signature.

▶ ## Common problems with point exchange menus

Teachers sometimes offer a very limited menu, which usually does not include enough selections to meet a wide range of student needs and interests. As a result, students quickly get tired of the existing menu items. Menus must reflect student preferences and include many creative selections so that students stay motivated to change behavior.

Restricting purchase opportunities also can create problems with the system. All students must be able to buy menu items daily or they may lose interest in the menu. Students who have difficulty waiting until the end of the day to make purchases may need to "total up" at least twice daily and have more frequent access to their reinforcers.

If students are allowed to have reinforcers without having to purchase them, they will lose their motivation to work for points. Students need to spend points to obtain privileges. If they have access to their reinforcers outside of class, teachers need to develop options for the menu that maintain interest. For example, if students can obtain candy from school vending machines, allow them the option to buy the privilege of eating their snack in class.

▶ **Summary**

The points students receive or negotiate serve as the medium of exchange for privileges and other reinforcers. Reinforcement menus must be varied to meet students' changing needs, preferences, and spending patterns. Purchasing privileges generally occurs during the end-of-day conference, where students make their own decisions about what to buy. By requiring students to buy their reinforcers, rather than giving them open access, the earning of points through appropriate social skills is very motivating.

# CHAPTER TWENTY

# Systems level changes

Students who are referred from the classroom because of behavioral difficulties work with an administrator to resolve the issues that lead to the office referral. Although the office intervention has a **teaching** focus and is respectful of students' rights and feelings, consequences are used to encourage students to make better choices about their behavior in the classroom and to avoid future office referrals. The size of office consequences reflects the severity of a student's behavior, thereby teaching students that outcomes match the magnitude of their behavior. The large size also allows for greater positive correction opportunities; a behavior severe enough to warrant a student's removal from regular class activities needs to be addressed through many corrective skill practices soon after it has occurred.

System reductions occur only as a result of behavior that leads to an office referral or removal from the class for intervention. Which of these is used is determined by who takes care of "office" interventions. Ideally, an administrator or behavior management specialist is available and trained to work with students who have been referred from the classroom. In many settings, however, the special education teacher handles nearly all behavioral interventions and must be prepared to give the associated consequences as well. The process and end results are essentially the same, but the teacher who takes care of "crisis" situations in addition to classroom management must plan carefully, communicate specific expectations to students about "referral" procedures, and demonstrate considerable finesse and skill to be successful in each area.

The purpose of this chapter is to provide guidelines for establishing office consequences and to familiarize you with processes of moving a student down and back up within the Motivation Systems. Figure 1 shows how office consequences are used and how they progress over time.

# ▶ Intervention consequences

As discussed in previous chapters, there are standard consequences associated with each office referral. Daily Points students receive a 10,000-point fine. Because these students generally engage in the most "acting out" behaviors, the large fine gives interventionists a large pool of points (up to 5,000) to teach prosocial alternatives. Progress students earn a major negative for any office referral. Since the "half-back" rule doesn't apply to Progress, interventionists have unlimited opportunities to teach and reinforce replacement skills. Merit students who are referred from the classroom are reduced to the Progress level as stipulated in the Merit contract. In addition to these standard consequences, students and interventionists develop contracts outlining potential consequences of future referrals.

## Incident report

The first time a Progress or Daily Points student is referred to the office during the school year, the interventionist writes an Incident Report. This document is written only once per student per year, and serves to teach students the referral process and to indicate future consequences (Figure 2). Each Incident Report includes the student's name, date referred, system level, and name of the referring teacher. The interventionist writes

out a behaviorally specific description of the problem that resulted in the referral (as in Figure 3). Both the interventionist and the student sign the referral, and copies are filed and distributed to designated people. These people may vary from one school to the next; we suggest they include the homeroom teacher, referring teacher, and parents.

Incident Reports also include a "difficulty rating" which reflects the severity of the student's behavior once he or she was referred to the office. The interventionist bases the rating on a four-point rating system:

1. Student reports promptly to the intervention and follows all instructions.

2. Student reports promptly, but extended teaching time is required in the intervention.

3. Student refuses to report or leaves during the intervention.

4. Parents/police need to be contacted to help deescalate the behavior or find the student; student damages school property; student harms self or others.

Each of the student's referrals is numbered sequentially to assist in bookkeeping and treatment planning. Most importantly, the Incident Report establishes consequences for the next office referral, should one occur. By having a set process, interventionists help make consequences predictable for students.

## Student contracts

For a student's second office referral, the interventionist writes a

**Figure 1**

# Increasing Office Consequences

| Office Visit | Consequences | Escape/Termination Clause | Home Contact |
|---|---|---|---|
| 1 | Incident Report filed | Incident Report stands for entire school year | Note on Point Card |
| 2 | Contract written for:<br><br>a. In-school suspension (Daily Points students)<br>b. System Reduction (Progress students) | Contract expires when student moves to next level of system.<br>Contract expires after designated date not to exceed 20 school days based upon student office referral pattern. | Phone call to parent(s)<br><br>Copy of contract sent home |
| 3 | Contract enacted:<br>a. In-school suspension (Daily Points students)<br>b. System Reduction (Progress students) | a. Completion of assigned task(s)<br>b. Purchase 25 bonds to return to level; current assets frozen and student may purchase no more than 2 bonds per day. | Phone call to parent(s)<br><br>Copy of suspension report or reduction report sent home |
| 4 | Contract written for:<br><br>a. In-school suspension plus 250,000-point suspension penalty. (Daily Points students)<br>b. Return to Step #2. (Progress students) | Contract expires when student moves to next level of system.<br>Contract expires after designated date not to exceed 20 school days based upon student office referral pattern. | Phone call to parent(s)<br><br>Copy of contract sent home |
| 5 | Contract enacted:<br><br>a. In-school suspension plus 250,000-point suspension penalty. (Daily Points students) | Completion of assigned task(s).<br>Use 2/3 of daily earnings to pay suspension penalty.<br>Earn bonus points from administrator for improved behavior to pay suspension penalty (up to +20,000 daily). | Phone call to parent(s)<br><br>Copy of suspension report sent home |

**Figure 2**

# Incident Report

Date: _____ _____
(Present System)

Referred by: _____

_____ was sent to the office today for the following behavior:

_____

_____

_____

_____

_____

_____

_____

_____

_____

_____

_____

_____

_____

     If I am sent to the office again for this or similar behavior, considerations should be given to entering into a behavior contract.

_____        _____
Administrator/Counselor                                Student

cc: File
     Homeroom Teacher

                           _____        _____
                           Referral #                         Difficulty

**Figure 3**

# Incident Report

Date: _____ *April 7* _____          _____ *DPS* _____
(Present System)

Referred by: _____ *M.Dolan* _____

_____ *Cathy* _____ was sent to the office today for the following behavior: _____ *not accepting criticism from her teacher. When her teacher began to speak with Cathy about being off task, Cathy rolled her eyes, sighed, folded her arms and mumbled something like, "You're such a bitch!" When referred, Cathy left the room immediately, but slammed the door on her way out. She then reported to the office immediately.* _____

_____

_____

_____

_____

_____

_____

_____

   If I am sent to the office again for this or similar behavior, considerations should be given to entering into a behavior contract.


_____ *Emma Furst* _____          _____ *Cathy S.* _____
Administrator/Counselor                    Student


cc: File
    Homeroom Teacher

_____ *1* _____          _____ *2* _____
Referral #              Difficulty

behavioral contract. A form of negative rein-forcement, the contract outlines what the student needs to do to avoid the future consequence. Each contract contains an "escape clause." This means that if a student fulfills the contract, as specified, he or she avoids the stated consequence. If not, the contract and its consequences are enacted. Again, consequences are predictable for students and help them make better choices about their behavior.

Contracts contain the same "identifying" information as the Incident Report, including the student's name, system level, referring teacher, and current date. Following an intervention, the student writes the description of his referral behavior to promote ownership of the behavior. If the student is unable to write the description, the interventionist uses the "first person" when writing the contract. See Figures 4, 5, and 6 for examples of contracts. As with the Incident Report, both the interventionist and student sign the contract. The interventionist also numbers and rates the referral, as described earlier.

The negative consequence is system-related. For Progress students, the contract is written for reduction to Daily Points (See Figure 5). Daily Points students, since they cannot be reduced further in the system, have contracts written for In-School Suspension (ISS). This is illustrated in Figure 6. Note that to escape her contract, Lisa (Figure 5) must go 20 school days without an office referral, whereas Bevan's is only written for 10 days. The contract "escape clause" is determined by the student's past referral behavior, difficulty ratings, and current System Standing. Interventionists should

choose a time frame that they think the student can be successful in. Because Daily Points students are in the acquisition stage of social skills learning, their escape clauses are typically shorter than those of Progress students. This allows the focus to be on skill development instead of punishment. The goal is to increase the length of time a student stays in class without an office referral. Another way to escape the contract is by moving up to the next system level. Each contract form states this escape mechanism explicitly.

The third time a student is referred to the office, his or her contract is enacted. If the student has escaped that contract's consequence, a new contract is written using the same principles stated earlier. A student who is referred before the earlier contract expires, however, receives the consequences of that contract. The Progress student would be reduced to Daily Points, while the Daily Points student would serve an In-School Suspension.

## System reduction

The interventionist completes a System Reduction Form for the Progress student (Figure 7) who does not escape his or her contract. In addition to the standard identifying information, the form includes the student's previous system level, the level to which he or she is returning, and a description of the referral behavior. To regain Progress status, the student must begin buying bonds toward that goal. This time, instead of 100 bonds, only 25 bonds are needed. The student may buy only two bonds

**Figure 4**

# Student Contract

Date: _____    System: _____

Student: _____    Referred by: _____

_____

_____

_____

_____

_____

_____

_____

_____

_____

_____

_____

_____

This contract will be void when I move up a system or if I go ___ school days without an office referral.

Upon Dismissal _____
                              Date

_____        _____
Administrator/Counselor                    Student

cc: File
    Homeroom Teacher
    Parent
                                 _____    _____
                                 Referral #        Difficulty

**Figure 5**

# Student Contract

Date: _____4-15-93_____    System: ____*Progress*_____

Student: _____*Lisa T.*_____    Referred by: _____*A. Pape*_____

___*I was referred to the office today for not accepting criticism from my teacher.___ When she was talking to me about my incomplete homework, I pushed my books off my desk, and I laughed at her and turned my back on her.*_____

___*I understand that if I am referred to the office again within the next 20 school_days,_ I will be returned to the Daily Points System.*_____

_____

_____

_____

_____

_____

_____

This contract will be void when I move up a system or if I go  **20**  school days without an office referral.

Upon Dismissal ____*5-13-93*_____
                                   Date

_____*M. Carmichael*_____          _____*Lisa T.*_____
Administrator/Counselor                    Student

cc: File
    Homeroom Teacher
    Parent              _____2_____     _____1_____
                          Referral #            Difficulty

**Figure 6**

# Student Contract

Date: ___1-22-93___          System: ___DPS___

Student: ___Bevan H.___          Referred by: ___Mrs. King___

___I was referred to the office today for not accepting criticism from Mrs King.___

___While she was talking, I argued and continued talking.___

___I understand that if I am referred to the office again within the next 10 school___

___days, I will have to serve an in-school suspension.___

_____

_____

_____

_____

_____

_____

_____

_____

This contract will be void when I move up a system or if I go **10** school days without an office referral.

Upon Dismissal ___2-5-93___
                              Date

___Emma Furst___          ___Bevan H.___
Administrator/Counselor          Student

cc: File
    Homeroom Teacher
    Parent          ___4___          ___2___
                    Referral #          Difficulty

**Figure 7**

# System Reduction

Date: _____

Referred by: _____

**_____ , previously on the _____ system, has been returned to the _____system because of the following behavior(s):**

_____

_____

_____

_____

_____

_____

_____

_____

_____

This student must purchase _____ bonds before returning to the _____system and may purchase no more than _____bonds each day. If on the Progress System, a rating of "Good" or "Excellent" is required to purchase bonds.

_____          _____
Administrator/Counselor                          Student

cc: File
　　Homeroom Teacher
　　Parent

_____  _____
Referral #            Difficulty

a day to ensure adequate time for skill development. Any previous bonds bought toward system advancement are "frozen," as is the student's current point balance. He or she may not use either of these balances toward regaining Progress status; these balances are returned to the student , however, once he or she moves back up.

A Merit student who is referred (Figure 8) is automatically reduced to Progress or Daily Points, depending on the severity of the behavior. Again, all assets are frozen and he or she is only allowed to buy back up at a rate of two bonds per day. In order to buy bonds, the student must attain a "Good" or "Excellent" rating on his or her Progress card. In either case, the student is free to spend accumulated points on anything he or she chooses. No points have to be spent on bonds.

## In-school suspension

When a Daily Points student's contract is enacted, he or she serves an In-School Suspension. ISS is given near the end of the intervention, at the "Consequences" stage of the Teaching Interaction. In-School Suspension is behavior-based; once a student completes the assigned task and demonstrates classroom behaviors, ISS is over. Since suspension time is determined by the student's behavior, the student has control over the situation.

For ISS to work effectively, the assigned task should relate to the student's referral behavior. We suggest that students complete something similar to a "mediation essay" (Figures 9, 10, and 11). This gives the student one more opportunity to think about his or her behavior and its outcomes. It also allows the student a chance to develop alternative responses to similar situations. Since the student was referred to intervention for an error in social behavior, he or she should complete a task related to that behavior.

We suggest that students not be allowed to complete homework or class assignments during In-School Suspension. Some students would much rather "do their work" in situations like ISS to avoid being in class. These students are reinforced by being left alone, and In-School Suspensions can provide just this type of environment. By allowing students to complete class work while in ISS, this cycle of behavior is reinforced (i.e. being referred from class to be "left alone"), and opportunities to learn prosocial alternative behaviors in the classroom environment are removed.

While the student is in ISS, the interventionist completes a Suspension Notice to serve as the referral documentation (Figure 12). The student needs to complete the assigned task to end ISS and return to intervention to prepare his or her apology. (See Chapter 14, "Overview of Administrative Intervention.") The interventionist periodically observes the student to note his or her progress toward task completion and redirects when necessary.

## Additional office referrals

For subsequent referrals, Progress students continue the process of escaping or enacting contracts. But for Daily Points students who are having difficulty escaping their

**Figure 8**

# System Reduction

Date: _____*5-1-93*_____

Referred by: _____*Mrs. Hix*_____

_____*Shanice J.*_____ , **previously on the** _____*Merit*_____**system, has been returned to the** __*Progress*___ **system because of the following behavior(s):**

_____

_____*When approached by Mrs. Hix regarding her incomplete Math assignment, she__ argued, interrupted Mrs. Hix, and swore.*_____

_____

_____

_____

_____

_____

_____

_____

This student must purchase ___*25*___ bonds before returning to the __*Merit*___ system and may purchase no more than ___*2*___ bonds each day. If on the Progress System, a rating of "Good" or "Excellent" is required to purchase bonds.

_____*M. Carmichael*_____       _____*Shanice J.*_____
     Administrator/Counselor                      Student

cc: File
     Homeroom Teacher
     Parent                 _____ ____   _____ ____
                                      Referral #          Difficulty

Figure 9

# Behavior Essay
## Leaving the Room Without Permission

## What Did I Do Wrong?

*I got into trouble for leaving the room without permission. Now I have to write this essay. I know something has to happen to me for leaving the room without permission. I broke one of my class rules.*

## Why is That Wrong?

*It is wrong to leave class without permission. It is disruptive and shows I don't have respect for rules. Someone has to spend time correcting my behavior. My parents may find out I don't follow the rules of my class. They won't like that. When they know I am not responsible in following the rules at school, they may not let me do the things I want at home.*

## What Should I Do?

*What I should do from now on is ask permission to leave the room. If I am not given permission, I should accept "no" and wait until an appropriate time to ask permission again. I will talk to myself and say, "I can follow the rules. When I want to leave the room I will wait to get permission first before I leave. I may be tempted to leave without permission, but I will stop myself and I won't do it."*

## What Good Things Could Happen To Me?

*When I follow the rules at school, other persons see me as responsible and mature. I won't get into trouble. I will set a good example. Other kids won't see me as a troublemaker. I will get to leave the room without a "hassle." My parents may hear that I can follow the rules. They may think that I am growing up and give me more privileges at home.*

*Before I leave the classroom, I'll get permission.*

Essay by _____ Date _____

Figure 10

# Student Essay Questions

## 1. What did I do wrong?

## 2. *Why* is that wrong?

## 3. What *should* I do instead?

## 4. What good things could happen to me if I do it this way?

_____          _____

**Student Signature**                                         **Date**

**Figure 11**

# Mediation Essays

**Goals:**  1. To help a student think about (mediate) his/her inappropriate behavior.
2. To serve as an aversive consequence.

**Methods:** 1. Provide an example for the student to copy.
2. Take dictation from the student.
3. Take dictation from the student and have the student copy what he/she dictated.
4. Have the student develop his/her own essay following a prescribed format.

**Criteria:**  1. Completion of a essay.
2. Completion of an essay to _____% accuracy (spelling and mechanics).
3. Completion to _____words/page (length).
4. Completion to the satisfaction of the crisis interventionist.

**Format:**  1. Describe the inappropriate behavior — What I did wrong:
2. Describe the appropriate behavior — What I should do:
3. Giving a rationale
   a. Why I shouldn't do this:
   b. What will happen if I don't engage in this inappropriate behavior:
4. Apology
   a. Statement of remorse (include appropriate behavior):
   b. Assurance that the behavior will not be repeated:
   c. Indication of the desire to return to the classroom:

**Figure 12**

# In-school Suspension Notice

Date: _____4-15-93_____     Number _____

To: File
    Referring Teacher
    Parent

_____*Bevan H.*_____was in in-school suspension today from _____*10:00 a. m.*_____
    (student)                                                                                      (time entered)

to _____*10:30 a.m.*_____. The reason for this in-school suspension was:

*__Bevan was referred to the office for repeated problems in Science class. He worked with chemicals without permission, he talked out of turn repeatedly, he teased another peer, and he failed to follow teacher instructions. Bevan is under a contract dated 1-22-93 which specified I.S.S. as a consequence for any office referral through 2-5-93.*

_____

_____

_____

Please use the space below to comment on the student's behavior during in-school suspension and the conditions and circumstances or returning to class.

*10:00 Began serving I.S.S.*     *Bevan needs to complete his essays,*

*10:10 working on essay*     *complete the office intervention, and*

*10:15 continued on task*     *apologize to his teacher to return to class.*

*10:30 completed essay*

_____*T. Connolly*_____          _____*Bevan H.*_____
Administrator/Counselor                              Student

contracts (even when the interventionist "shortens" the escape clause to help increase chances for success), additional contingencies are used. Generally, the consequence of serving an In-School Suspension is sufficient to help Daily Points students be successful in class. But sometimes a Suspension Point Penalty is used to serve as additional motivation. After examining the referral data, the interventionist may decide to write a contract for ISS plus a point penalty.

The interventionist can use up to 250,000 points for the penalty. If the Daily Points student is referred again before his or her contract for ISS/Suspension Point Penalty "expires", the student serves an ISS and earns the point penalty. The point penalty is recorded in the student's account book (Figure 13), and her assets and bonds are temporarily frozen, as in the system reduction process. Then, of the points she earns daily, she must spend at least two-thirds to "pay off" that penalty, using the remaining points however she chooses. She also has the opportunity to earn a 20,000-point daily bonus for staying out of the office. This bonus is applied toward the point penalty (Figure 14). While paying off the penalty, this student cannot "buy up"to the Progress level. It's important that she stay on Daily Points; if she's having such difficulty avoiding office referrals, she needs the structure this level provides.

## Office intervention log

The Office Intervention Log helps interventionists and teachers track a student's referral behavior (Figure 15). The log provides information essential for interventionists to know when they've issued consequences.

A log is created for each student who has been referred. The following information is recorded for each referral: referral number, date, system level, a brief description of the referral behavior, the consequences issued, the escape clause, if applicable (usually just the date the contract expires), difficulty rating, and the interventionist's initials (if more that one person does interventions with students).

This log helps you keep track of essential information. You can see the following information at a glance: the student's current system level; behavior(s) for which a student is being referred (to assist in your Preventive Teaching efforts); if a student has gotten out of a contract or if one needs to be enacted; and if the student's difficulty ratings are improving, staying the same or getting worse.

## Summary

When students are referred to the office, the administration uses teaching and consequences to help the students learn that an outcome will match the degree of their behavior. Typical consequences include an Incident Report, point penalties, contracts, and In-School Suspensions. Students can avoid increasing consequences by maintaining appropriate classroom behaviors, thereby avoiding further office referrals. The goal is for students to understand that the benefits of using social skills across various school settings are better than the consequences for office referral. This helps students develop internalization of behavioral control and self-management.

## Figure 13

## Motivation System Account Book

NAME ___ Jenna E. ___

D - DAILY POINTS
P - PROGRESS
M - MERIT

| DATE | TOTAL POINTS TODAY* | POINTS LOST TODAY | AMOUNT WITHDRAWN | WITHDRAWN FOR | # BONDS PUR. | # BONDS TO DATE | SYSTEM | BALANCE | OFFICE REFERRAL | SUSPENSION PENALTY PAY. | SUSPENSION PENALTY BAL. | T.I. |
|------|------|------|------|------|------|------|------|------|------|------|------|------|
| 3/13 | 31,000 | 7,000 | 12,000 | Bonds | 2 | 10 | D | 216,000 | | | | AP |
| 3/14 | 29,500 | 9,000 | 210,000 / 12,000 | Can of pop Bonds | 2 | 12 | D | 24,000 | | | | MPK |
| 3/17 | 12,000 | 17,000 | — | — | — | 12 | D | 36,000 | * | | | AP |
| 3/18 | 32,000 | 5,000 | 12,000 | Bonds | 2 | 14 | D | 56,000 | | | | AP |
| 3/19 | 30,500 | 6,000 | 6,000 / 12,000 | Poster Bonds | 2 | 16 | D | 68,500 | Frozen | 3/20  SG | | MPK |
| 3/20 | — | — | — | — | — | — | D | — | * | | 200,000 | SG |
| 3/20 | 12,000 | 22,500 | 8,000 | Susp. Penalty | — | — | D | 4,000 | | 8,000 | 192,000 | SG |
| | | | | | | | | | | | | |
| | | | | | | | | | | | | |
| | | | | | | | | | | | | |
| | | | | | | | | | | | | |
| | | | | | | | | | | | | |
| | | | | | | | | | | | | |

* Net total

Revised 6/87 © 1991 FFFBH

## Figure 14

# Motivation System Account Book

**NAME** _Jenna E._

D - DAILY POINTS
P - PROGRESS
M - MERIT

| DATE | TOTAL POINTS TODAY* | POINTS LOST TODAY | AMOUNT WITHDRAWN | WITHDRAWN FOR | # BONDS PUR. | # BONDS TO DATE | SYSTEM | BALANCE | OFFICE REFERRAL | SUSPENSION PENALTY PAY. | SUSPENSION PENALTY BAL. | T.I. |
|------|------|------|------|------|------|------|------|------|------|------|------|------|
| 3/13 | 31,000 | 7,000 | 12,000 | Bonds | 2 | 10 | D | 216,000 | | | | AP |
| 3/14 | 29,500 | 9,000 | 210,000<br>12,000 | Can of pop<br>Bonds | 2 | 12 | D | 24,000 | | | | MPK |
| 3/17 | 12,000 | 17,000 | — | — | — | 12 | D | 36,000 | * | | | AP |
| 3/18 | 32,000 | 5,000 | 12,000 | Bonds | 2 | 14 | D | 56,000 | | | | AP |
| 3/19 | 30,500 | 6,000 | 6,000<br>12,000 | Poster<br>Bonds | 2 | 16 | D | 68,500 | Frozen | 3/20 SG | | MPK |
| 3/20 | — | 22,500 | — | — | — | — | D | — | * | | 200,000 | SG |
| 3/20 | 12,000 | 22,500 | 8,000 | Susp. Penalty | — | — | D | 4,000 | | 8,000 | 192,000 | SG |
| 3/21 | 30,500 | 6,000 | 6,000<br>12,000 | Bonds<br>Susp. Penalty | 1 | 1 | D | 8,000 | | 40,000 | 152,000 | SG |
| | | | | | | | | | | | | |
| | | | | | | | | | | | | |
| | | | | | | | | | | | | |
| | | | | | | | | | | | | |
| | | | | | | | | | | | | |

\* Net total

Revised 6/87    © 1991 FFFBH

## Figure 15

# Office Intervention Log

STUDENT NAME _____

PARENTS _____

ADDRESS _____

PHONE _____

| # | DATE | LEVEL* | BEHAVIOR | CONSEQUENCE(S) | ESCAPE CLAUSE | DIFFICULTY** | A.I. |
|---|------|--------|----------|----------------|---------------|--------------|------|
|   |      |        |          |                |               |              |      |
|   |      |        |          |                |               |              |      |
|   |      |        |          |                |               |              |      |
|   |      |        |          |                |               |              |      |
|   |      |        |          |                |               |              |      |
|   |      |        |          |                |               |              |      |
|   |      |        |          |                |               |              |      |
|   |      |        |          |                |               |              |      |
|   |      |        |          |                |               |              |      |
|   |      |        |          |                |               |              |      |
|   |      |        |          |                |               |              |      |
|   |      |        |          |                |               |              |      |
|   |      |        |          |                |               |              |      |
|   |      |        |          |                |               |              |      |

**DIFFICULTY RATING:**
1 - Reported promptly/followed all instructions
2 - Reported, but extended time/effort required
3 - Refused to report or left office
4 - Parent contact/police contact; property damage, disruptive behavior, harm to self or others

*DP - DAILY POINTS
P - PROGRESS
M - MERIT

# References

Alberto, P.A., & Troutmann, A.C. (1990). **Applied behavior analysis for teachers,** (3rd Edition). Columbus, OH: Merrill Publishing Company.

Anderson, L., Evertson, C., & Emmer, E. (1980). Dimensions in classroom management derived from recent research. **Journal of Curriculum Studies, 12,** 343-356.

Aspy, D., & Roebuck, R. (1977). **Kids don't learn from people they don't like.** Amherst, MA: Human Resource Development Press.

Bandura, A. (1969). **Principles of behavior modification**. New York: Holt, Rinehart & Winston.

Bandura, A. (1977). **Social learning theory.** Englewood Cliffs, NJ: Prentice-Hall.

Baron, R.L., Cunningham, P.J., Palma, L.P., & Phillips, E.L. (1984). **Family and community living skills curriculum** (rev. ed.). Boys Town, NE: Father Flanagan's Boys' Home.

Becker, W., Engelmann, S., & Thomas, D., (1975). **Teaching 1: Classroom management.** Chicago: Research Press.

Bluestein, J. (1988). **21st century discipline: Teaching students responsibility and self-control.** Jefferson City, MO: Scholastic Inc.

Borich, G.D. (1971). Accountability in the affective domain. **Journal of Research and Development in Education, 5,** 87-96.

Braukmann, P.D., Ramp, K.K., Braukmann, C.J., Willner, A.G., & Wolf, M.M. (1983). The analysis and training of rationales for child care workers, **Children and Youth Services Review, 5**, 177-194.

Bronfenbrenner, U. (1970). **Two worlds of childhood: U.S. and U.S.S.R**. New York: Russell Sage.

Brophy, J. (1983). Research on the self-fulfilling prophecy and teacher expectations. **Journal of Educational Psychology, 75**, 631-661.

Brown, L.J., Black, D.D., & Downs, J.C. (1984). **School social skills rating scale and manual**. East Aurora, NY: Slosson Educational Publications.

Bush, R. (1957). **The teacher-pupil relationship**. Englewood Cliffs, NJ: Prentice-Hall.

Cartledge, G., & Milburn, J.F. (1978). The case of teaching social skills in the classroom: A review. **Review of Educational Research, 1**, 133-156.

Charles, C. (1989). **Building classroom discipline: From models to practice,** 3rd ed. New York: Longman.

Clark, H.B., Wood, R., & Northrop, J. (1980). The family and education: New directions for promoting healthy social interactions. In J.B. Gordon, D.A. Sabatino, R.C. Sarri (Eds.), **Disruptive youth in school** (pp. 151-172). Reston, VA: Council for Exceptional Children.

Combs, M.L., & Slaby, D.A. (1977). Social skills training with children. In B.B. Lahey and A.E. Kazdin (Eds.), **Advances in clinical child psychology** (pp. 161-201). New York: Plenum Press.

Cooper, J.O., Heron, T.E., & Heward, W.L. (1987). **Applied behavior analysis**. Columbus, OH: Merrill Publishing Company.

Cormany, R. (1975). **Guidance and counseling in Pennsylvania: Status and needs**. Lemoyne, PA: ESEA Title II Project, West Shore School District.

Coughlin, D.D., Maloney, D.M., Baron, R.L., Dahir, J., Daly, D.L., Daly, P.B., Fixsen, D.L., Phillips, E.L., & Thomas, D.L. (1983). Implementing the community-based Teaching-Family Model at Boys Town. In W.P. Christian, G.T. Hanna, & T.J. Glahon (Eds.), **Programming effective human services: Strategies for institutional change and client transition**. New York: Plenum Press.

Coughlin, D.D., & Shanahan, D. (1991). **Boys Town Family Home Program Training Manual,** Third Edition. Father Flanagan's Boys' Home.

Czerwionka, J. (1987). **Influences of structured learning on the prosocial behavior of behaviorally disordered adolescents**. Unpublished doctoral dissertation. Dekalb, IL: Northern Illinois University.

Dishion, T.J., Patterson, G.R., Stoolmiller, M., & Skinner, M.L. (1991). Family, school, and behavioral antecedents to early adolescent involvement with antisocial peers. **Developmental Psychology, 27(1),** 172-180.

Dowd, T., & Tierney, J. (1992). **Teaching social skills to youth: A curriculum for child-care providers**. Boys Town, NE: Boys Town Press.

Downing, J.A., Simpson, R.L., & Myles, B.S. (1990). Regular and special educator perceptions of nonacademic skills needed by mainstreamed students with behavioral disorders and learning disabilities. **Behavioral Disorders, 15(4)**, 217-226.

Downs, J.C., Bastien, J., Brown, L.J., & Wells, P.L. (1987). **Motivation systems workshop manual** (rev. ed.). Boys Town, NE: Father Flanagan's Boys' Home.

Downs, J., Kutsick, K., & Black, D., (1985). The teaching interaction: A systematic approach to developing social skills in disruptive and non-disruptive students. **Techniques: A Journal for Remedial Education and Counseling, 1**, 304-310.

Doyle, W. (1986). Classroom organization and management. In M.C. Wittrock (Ed.), **Handbook of research on teaching**, 3rd ed. New York: MacMillan.

Duke, D., & Meckel, A. (1984). **Teacher's guide to classroom management**. New York: Random House.

D'Zurilla, T.J., & Goldfried, M.R. (1971). Problem solving and behavior modification. **Journal of Abnormal Psychology, 78**, 107-126.

Eitzen, D.S. (1974). Impact of behavior modification techniques on locus of control of delinquent boys. **Psychological Reports, 35(3)**, 1,317-1,318.

Elder, G.H., Jr. (1963). Parental power legitimation and its effect on adolescents. **Sociometry, 26**, 50-65.

Evertson, C., & Emmer, E. (1982). Effective management at the beginning of the school year in junior high classes. **Journal of Educational Psychology, 74**, 485-498.

Goldstein, A.P. (1988). **The prepare curriculum: Teaching prosocial competencies**. Champaign, IL: Research Press.

Goldstein, A.P., Sprafkin, R.P., Gershaw, N.J., & Klein, P. (1980). The adolescent: Social skills training through structured learning. In G. Cartledge and J.F. Milburn (Eds.), **Teaching social skills to children**. New York: Pergamon Press.

Greenspan, S. (1979). Social intelligence in the retarded. In N.R. Ellis (Ed.), **Handbook of mental deficiency, psychological theory, and research** (2nd edition). Hillsdale, NJ: Lawrence Erlbaum Associates.

Gresham, F.M. (1981). Assessment of children's social skills. **Journal of School Psychology, 19(2)**, 120-133.

Gresham, F.M. (1982). Misguided mainstreaming: The case for social skills training with handicapped children. **Exceptional Children, 48(5)**, 422-433.

Grosenick, J.K., & Huntze, S.L. (Eds.) (1984). **National needs analysis in behavior disorders: Positive alternatives to disciplinary exclusion**. Columbia, MO: University of Missouri, Department of Special Education.

Hansen, D., St. Lawrence, J., & Christoff, K. (1980). Conversational skills of inpatient conduct disordered youth. **Behavior Modification, 12(3),** 424-444.

Hope, H., & Cobb, J.A. (1973). Survival behaviors in the educational setting: Their implications for research and intervention. In L.A. Hammerlynk, L.C. Hanay, & E.J. Mash (Eds.), **Behavior Change** (pp. 193-208). Champaign, IL: Research Press.

Jones, M., & Offord, D. (1989). Reduction of antisocial behavior in poor children by nonschool skill-development. **Journal of Child Psychology and Psychiatry, 30(5),** 737-750.

Jones, V.F., & Jones, L.S., (1981). **Responsible classroom discipline: Creating positive learning environments and solving problems.** Boston: Allyn and Bacon, Inc.

Jones, V.F., & Jones, L.S. (1990). **Comprehensive classroom management: Motivating and managing students,** 3rd Ed. Boston: Allyn and Bacon.

Kaplan, J. (1991). **Beyond behavior modification.** Austin, TX: Pro-Ed.

Kaplan, J.S. (1991). **Beyond behavior modification** (2nd Edition). Austin, TX: ProEd.

Kendall, P., & Braswell, L. (1982). Cognitive-behavioral self-control therapy for children: A components analysis. **Journal of Consulting & Clinical Psychology, 50,** 672-689.

Kounin, J. (1970). **Discipline and group management in classrooms.** New York: Holt, Rinehart, and Winston.

Larson, K. (1989). Task-related and interpersonal problem-solving training for increasing school success in high-risk young adolescents. **Remedial and Special Education, 20,** 244-253.

Mager, R.F. (1992). No skill-efficacy, no performance. **Training, (4),** 32-36.

Meadows, N., Neel, R.S., Parker, G., & Timo, K. (1991). A validation of social skills for students with behavioral disorders. **Behavioral Disorders, 16(3),** 200-210.

Miller, C.S. (1984). Building self-control. **Young Children,** 15-19.

Montague, M. (1988). Job-related social skills training for adolescents with handicaps. **Career Development for Exceptional Individuals, 11(1),** 26-41.

Morse, W. (1964). Self-concept in the school setting. **Childhood Education, 41,** 195-198.

Mortimore, P., & Sammons, P. (1987). New evidence on effective elementary schools. **Educational Leadership, 45,** 4-8.

Nichols, P. (1992). The curriculum of control: twelve reasons for it, some arguments against it. **Beyond Behavior, Winter,** 5-11.

Norman, J., & Harris, M. (1981). **The private life of the American teenager.** New York: Rawson, Wade.

Northwest Regional Education Laboratory (1990). Effective schooling practices: A research synthesis. In **Onward to Excellence.** Portland, OR: Author.

O'Leary, K.D., & Drabman, R. (1971). Token reinforcement programs in the classroom: A review. **Psychological Bulletin, 75,** 379-398.

Peter, V.J. (1986). **What makes Boys Town so special?** Boys Town, NE: Father Flanagan's Boys' Home.

Phillips, E.L. (1968). Achievement place: Token reinforcement procedures in a home-style rehabilitation setting for "predelinquent" boys. **Journal of Applied Behavior Analysis, 1,** 213-223.

Phillips, E.L., Phillips, E.A., Fixsen, D.L., & Wolf, M.M. (1974). **The Teaching-Family handbook** (rev. ed.). Lawrence, KS: University of Kansas Printing Service.

Pikas, A. (1961). Children's attitudes toward rational versus inhibiting parental authority. **Journal of Abnormal Social Psychology, 62,** 313-321.

Porter, A., & Brophy, J. (1988). Synthesis of research on good teaching. **Educational Leadership, 45,** 74-85.

Purkey, W., & Novak, J. (1984). **Inviting school success: A self-concept approach to teaching and learning,** 2nd ed. Belmont, CA: Wadsworth.

Roosa, J.B. (1973). **SOCS: Situations, options, consequences, simulations: A technique for teaching social interactions.** Unpublished paper presented to the American Psychological Association, Montreal.

Rosenshine, B. (1970). Enthusiastic teaching: A research review. **School Review, 72,** 449-514.

Sarason, I.G. (1968). Verbal learning, modeling, and juvenile delinquency. **American Psychologist, 23,** 254-266.

Schneider, B.H., & Byrne, B.M. (1984). Predictors of successful transition from self-contained special education to regular class settings. **Psychology in the Schools, 21,** 375-380.

Schumaker, J.B., Hazel, J.S., Sherman, J.S., & Sheldon, J. (1982). Social skill performance of learning disabled, non-learning disabled, and delinquent adolescents. **Learning Disabilities Quarterly, 5,** 388-397.

Serow, R.C., & Soloman, D. (1979). Classroom climates and students' intergroup behavior. **Journal of Educational Psychology, 71,** 669-676.

Shah, S.A. (1966). **A behavioral conceptualization of the development of criminal behavior, therapeutic principles, and applications.** A Report to the President's Commission on Law Enforcement and the Administration of Justice. Washington, DC: U.S. Government Printing Office.

Shah, S.A. (1968). Preparation for release and community follow-up. In H.L. Cohen, A.L. Cohen, I. Goldiamond, J. Filipczak, & R. Pooley (Eds.), **Training professionals in procedures for the establishment of educational environments,** Silver Springs, MD: Institute for Behavioral Research, Educational Facility Press.

Shores, R.E., Gunter, P.L., & Jack, S.L. (1993). Classroom management strategies: Are they setting event for coercion? **Behavior Disorders, 18,** 92-102.

Spivack, G., & Schure, M.B. (1974). **Social adjustment of young children.** San Francisco: Jossey-Bass.

Steinberg, Z. (1992). Pandora's children. **Beyond Behavior, Spring,** 5-13.

Steinberg, Z., & Knitzer, J. (1992). Classrooms for emotionally and behaviorally disturbed students: Facing the challenge. **Behavioral Disorders, 17(2),** 145-156.

Stephens, T.M. (1978). **Social skills in the classroom.** Columbus, OH: Cedar Press, Inc.

United States Department of Education (1989). **Eleventh annual report to Congress on the implementation of the Education of the Handicapped Act.** Washington, DC: Author.

Venziano, C., & Venziano, L. (1988). Knowledge of social skills among institutionalized juvenile delinquents. **Criminal Justice and Behavior, 15(2),** 152-171.

Walker, D.K., Singer, J.D., Palfrey, J.S., Orza, M., Wenger, M., & Butler, J.A. (1988). Who leaves and who stays in special education: A 2-year follow-up study. **Exceptional Children, 54,** 393-402.

White, O.R., & Haring, N.G. (1980). **Exceptional teaching** (2nd Edition). Columbus, OH: Merrill Publishing Company.

Willner, A.G., Braukman, C.J., Kirigin, K.A., Fixsen, D.L., Phillips, E.L., & Wolf, M.M. (1977). The training and validation of youth-preferred social behaviors of child care personnel. **Journal of Applied Behavior Analysis, 10 (2),** 219-230.

Wolf, M.M., Phillips, E.L., & Fixsen, D.L. (1972). The Teaching-Family: A new model for the treatment of deviant child behavior in the community. In S.W. Bijou & E.L. ribes-Inesta (Eds.), **Behavior modification: Issues and extensions** (pp. 51-62). New York: Academic Press.

Wolfgang, C., & Glickman, C. (1986). **Solving discipline problems: Strategies for classroom teachers,** (2nd Ed.). Boston: Allyn & Bacon.